Mista Wilkins

'an ordinary man who made
an extraordinary difference'

The memoirs of
Darvall Wilkins

Mista Wilkins
'an ordinary man who made an extraordinary difference'

First published in Australia by Simon Wilkins 2021
www.www.wilkinsfamilyfoundation.com.au

Copyright © Simon Wilkins 2021
All Rights Reserved

 A catalogue record for this book is available from the National Library of Australia

ISBN: 978-0-646-83679-9 (pbk)

Typesetting and design by Publicious Book Publishing
Published in collaboration with Publicious Book Publishing
www.publicious.com.au

No part of this book may be reproduced in any form, by photocopying or by any electronic or mechanical means, including information storage or retrieval systems, without permission in writing from both the copyright owner and the publisher of this book.

Table of Contents

Foreword - Jerry Marston i
Foreword – Former First Head of State, Republic of Vanuatu,
His Excellency Ati George Sokomanu. OV, MBE iii
Mista Wilkin i Kam - An introduction by Stan Combs v

1922 Early Life 1
A Beginning 1
Dulla Dulla 3
The Depression 7
Country Life 7
Swimming 9
Boarding School 12
Gap Year 14
University, War Looming 15

1941 My War 18
Enlisting 18
New Guinea 20
The Royal Navy 24
The Duke of York 26
The Surrender 28

1946 Into the Colonial Service 33
Preparation 33
Cambridge 34

Vignette - Death of King George 37

1953 Africa 39
Sumbawanga, Tanganyika, Africa 39
Safaris 40
Ida 42
Wildlife 44
Marriage 47
Karen 48

Vignette - Dar es Salaam 1957- Article for the Australian Women's Weekly by Ida M. Wilkins 49

1957 South Pacific 55
Vila, New Hebrides 55
Arriving 56
Vila Life 56

1958 Tanna 60
The Agency 65
The Southern District 67
Administration 68
Touring 69
Sir John Rennie Visit 71
Joint Touring 71

Vignette – Tanna 73
Healing and Witchcraft 73
Nangalat 73
Air Services 75
Emergencies 77
Simon and Sallie 77
Health 78
Daily Life 79
Dr Beaglehole 80
Queen's Birthday 81
Isangel Storm 81
Tidal Waves and Earthquakes 83

Vignette – Pirates and Poachers 85
Jon Frum 90
Kava and Copra 92
The 'Duc' 93
Madame 'Duc' 95
Local Characters 95
Tanna Summary 97

1962 Santo 98
CD2 (Central District Number 2) 99
French Colleagues 102
Easter Cyclone 105
Ambrym Volcano Eruption 106
Santo Life 107
Events 109
High Commissioner for the Western Pacific Visit 110
Move to Malekula 111
Keneri 115

1964 Lakatoro 117
Lakatoro Base 117
Move to Lakatoro 120
1964 High Commissioner's Visit 121
Lakatoro Home 122

1965 Settling into Lakatoro 124
Earthquake 1965 128
A Wedding 130
French High Commissioner's Visit 132
District Summary 133
Peter 133
Schooling 134
Lakatoro Life 134

1967 Lakatoro 138
Routine Administration 138
Local Councils 141

1968 Lakatoro 142
Metemet Club 143

Vignette – Notable Maritime Visits 149
HMAS Supply 1965 149
HMS Dampier 1967 150
Craigstar 1969 150
HMS Decoy 1969 150

1970 Lakatoro 152
Barry Weightman 152
Public Works 154

Vignette –The Duke of Edinburgh Visit 155
Lakatoro Life Continues 166

1972 Lakatoro 168

Vignette - South Pacific Festival in Fiji 1973 174

1974 Lakatoro 177
Queen's Proposed Visit 177
Station Life 178
Practical Jokes 180
Station Life 181
David Attenborough 182

Vignette - The Royal Visit	**185**
1975 Lakatoro	**196**
1976 Lakatoro	**201**
Resident Commissioner's Visit	*201*
OBE & Silver Jubilee Medals	*202*
Santo Break	*203*
Janet and Horrie's Wedding	*204*
Vignette - General District Life in CD2	**205**
Ida	*205*
Lakatoro – A Garden of Eden	*205*
Queen's Birthday Celebrations	*207*
My French Colleagues	*208*
Volunteers	*209*
The Big Nambas	*211*
Pigs	*219*
Travel and Toilet Facilities	*219*
Food	*220*
Marine Services	*221*
Newsletter and Clubs	*223*
The Metemet Club Updated	*224*
Apprentices	*225*
Tautu Land	*226*
Masing Lauru	*227*
Graham Talo	*227*
Vignette - Letters from Lakatoro	**228**
Henry	*228*
Kilman	*228*
Chinchoo, Avok and Spooky	*229*
Cyclone Elsa 1976	*229*
Chief Elections	*230*
Political Situation in 1976	*230*
Jimmy Stephens Nagriamel	*231*
House Inspections	*232*
Staff Meetings	*232*
Entertaining the French	*233*
1977 Leaving Lakatoro	**234**
The Final Farewell	*235*

1977 Retirement 236
Vignette - Ida Mary Wilkins Obituary 239
1999 Tweed Heads 243
2017 Return to Vanuatu 245
Vignette – Dad (by Simon Wilkins) 246
    The Last Journey 246
The Wilkins Family Foundation is Formed 251
    Our Purpose 251
    Our Core Values 252
Conclusions - A Life Well Lived 253
    Closing Thoughts 253

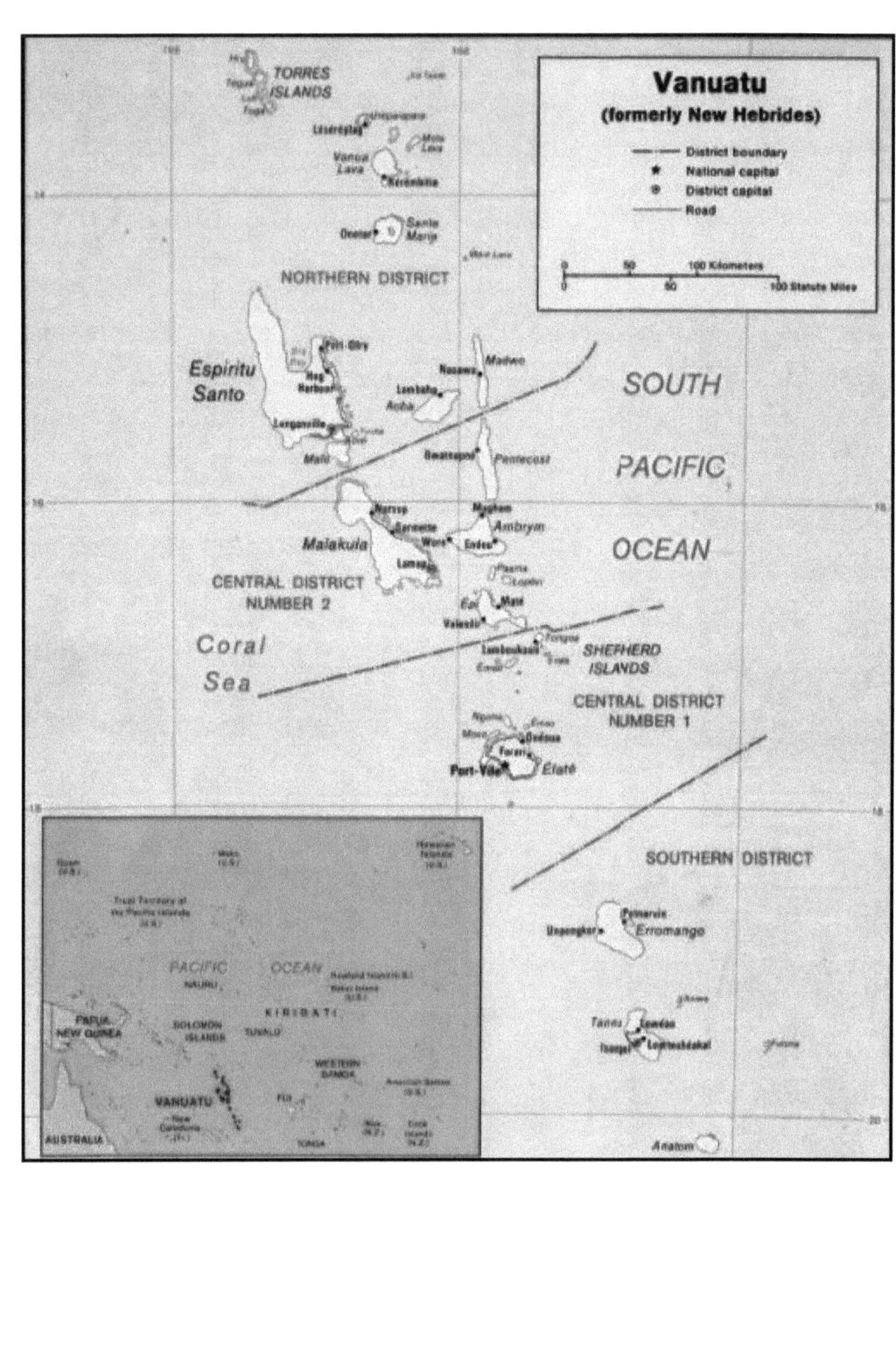

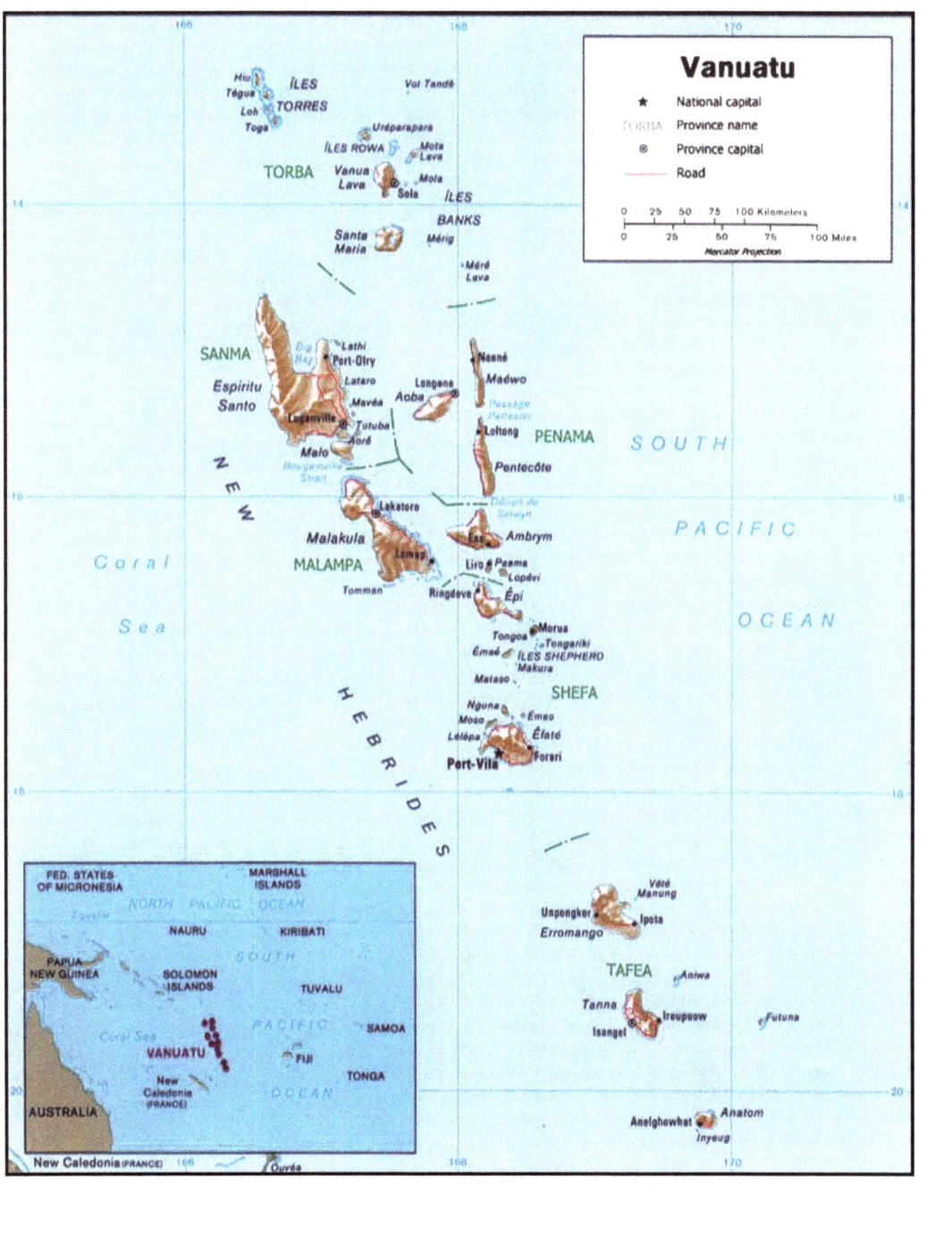

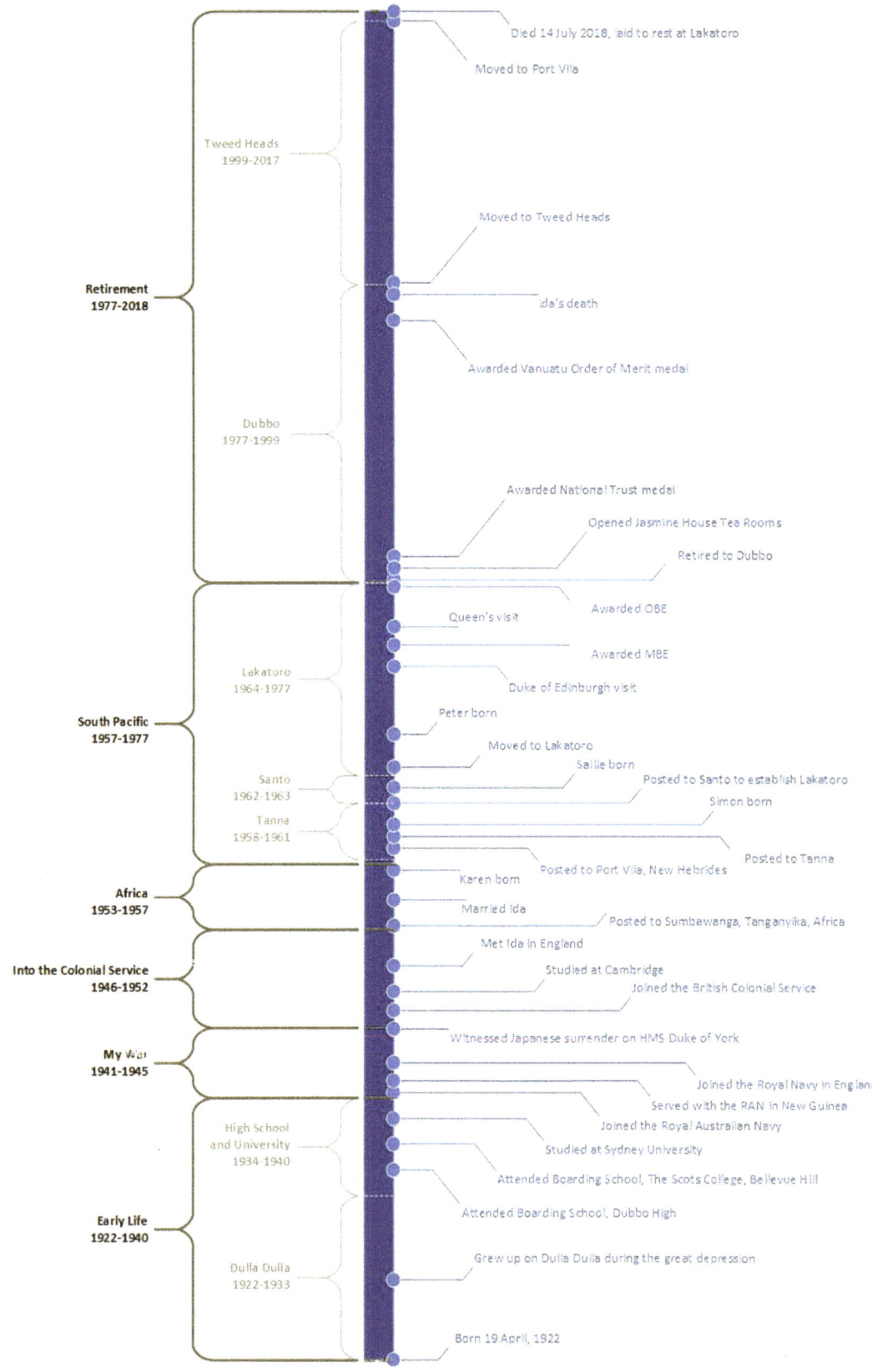

Timeline

Foreword - Jerry Marston

Darvall Keppel Wilkins was born on April 19th, 1922 in Dubbo, Australia. He passed away peacefully on July 14th, 2018 in Port Vila, Vanuatu at the age of 96. He had returned to the islands and was living with his youngest daughter.

Following his wartime service in the Navy, Darvall trained for and joined the British Colonial Service and was posted in 1952 to Tanganyika as a cadet District Officer where he served for five years. He was then posted to the New Hebrides where he worked for 20 years as a British District Agent, retiring to Australia in 1977.

In his last year, in collaboration with particularly his youngest daughter, Sallie, and her husband, John, Darvall 'wrote' his memoirs, covering his war service and time in Africa, but mostly concentrating on his 20 years in the islands of the New Hebrides (now Vanuatu), where he served in all four districts.

The content of his memoirs derives mainly from a mountain of letters written over his adult life (both Darvall and his wife, Ida, were prolific and enthusiastic letter writers) refreshed and fleshed out in reflective conversation with family members and close friends. The result is a fascinating read, written in a style which both reflects the character of the man and captures and brings to life his singular experience and distinctive perspectives on the times he lived and worked through. They reveal a man endowed with the self-confidence, single-mindedness, and resolve to achieve as much as he possibly could in support of the people he had been entrusted to serve. At the same time, there are regular moments of humour and self-deprecation which illustrate the humility and empathy that literally made him a legend in his own working lifetime. I had the privilege of five years' working with Darvall, and a further 40 years of his close friendship and that of his family. Asked to say a few words at his 90th birthday celebrations, I described him as 'simply the finest man I've known'.

Following a state funeral in Vila to commemorate his passing and the contribution he made to the country, he was laid to rest after a funeral service at Lakatoro, the regional government station he established on Malekula.

Both services were attended by the Head of State President Obed Tallis, who spoke at length of the contribution Darvall made to the country, and his crucial work in helping build and nurture the nation's emerging leaders. He described Darvall as "A living testimony of the good shepherd. A statesman with dignity and compassion for the well-being of the people of our country, whose spirit reflected him as man of Vanuatu".

At his memorial service in Vila, Godwin Ligo, a long-serving and respected communications and media professional and one-time staff member in Darvall's team, offered this testament:

"The voice of Darvall Wilkins still echoes through the mountains and valleys of these islands, and wherever he walked, he left footprints which remain forever".

I hope and expect the publication will prove a positive contribution to the social and political history of this period, which effectively was the final chapter in the British Colonial story.

Enormous thanks should go to John and Sallie Latella (née Wilkins) for their enthusiasm and long hours of patient commitment to transcribing Darvall's letters into the initial draft manuscript; to Simon Wilkins for reviewing and assembling the structure of the manuscript; to the proof-readers and fact checkers who include his children, Stan Combs, Anna Bishop, Mary Bishop and myself; to the Wilkins and Marston families for assisting and working through endless photographs to ensure the correct ones made it into the final draft, and to the publishers.

All proceeds from the sale of the book will go to the Wilkins Family Foundation, established in Darvall and Ida's memory, to support education for the many outer island girls who otherwise would not get the opportunity to achieve their full potential.

Foreword – Former First Head of State, Republic of Vanuatu, His Excellency Ati George Sokomanu. OV, MBE

It was in 1966, my family accompanied me to Lakatoro Malekula, the headquarters of the British district administration, Central District No.2 of the Anglo-French condominium of the New Hebrides (Vanuatu). The archipelago was divided into four administrative districts.

Having served in the other three administrative districts, the experience gained apart from district administrative duties from my immediate superiors gave me an understanding of the task ahead of them, especially in a territory jointly administered. With passion and perhaps patient courage and determination they toiled on for the advancement of the people whom they served and their land. Resources be it human or fiscal, for a district administration especially in the colonial era was always found wanting, and extras to keep the pot boiling rested on the shoulders of the administrators.

Darvall Keppel Wilkins was the British District Agent in Malekula when my family and I arrived to work at Lakatoro as his assistant administration officer. His family and mine had a wonderful friendly relationship that still exists to date.

Darvall to me was an outstanding administrator, I say this with deep respect to other British District Agents who served in our territory during the colonial era. The advent of Lakatoro station as it was known in those gone-by days, was a dream come true. It shows his wisdom and dedication to his duties.

In the early days of the missionaries, they had to face many challenges, before settling down knowing that a foundation had been laid, not only to Christianise but also to build a haven and to educate the people for a better life. Darvall was no exception to the early missionaries.

From a plantation and uncultivated land, Lakatoro was established, with bush materials offices and staff houses were built. His family lived in a plantation house. Slowly but surely other permanent facilities came into being including; roads, sports fields, and wharf.

Today Lakatoro is a new and vibrant provincial headquarters, with a sports stadium named after Darvall, schools, trade and market centres flourish. People busy as bees tending to their chores and livelihoods. All due to an extraordinary man of vision and dedication.

I had the privilege to visit and speak to Darvall in his bed. I left with a heavy heart, a few days later he departed to the other world.

It was his wish to be buried in Lakatoro and his family honoured that. This also showed his love and dedication to a place and its people.

Darvall left a legacy that generations in Malampa province will share at nakamals, churches and homes and Vanuatu as a whole is very fortunate and thankful to have had such a wonderful and dedicated man. I salute you Darvall and may God richly bless your family.

Ati George Sokomanu.

Mista Wilkin i Kam - An introduction by Stan Combs

Lakatoro, Malekula Island Local Government Area, Vanuatu July 1987. Canadian volunteer Stan Combs is mildly miffed that the ride he had arranged to pick him up at the Norsup airport upon his arrival from a work trip to another island hasn't shown up. He finds a lift to Lakatoro and soon learns why his ride has dropped down the list of government station priorities.

"Mista Wilkin i kam!" a female office worker sings out in Bislama, the national pidgin lingua franca. "Mister Wilkins has come!" Darvall Wilkins, the former British District Agent, built the Lakatoro government station and headed the UK colonial administration of Malekula and nearby islands from 1965 to 1977.

No wonder the station has been a-buzz for weeks with lawns mown, weeds removed, bushes trimmed, buildings cleaned, and vehicles washed—this is a Big Deal. Stan has read the bronze plaque in front of Mr Wilkins' former residence, which declares him to be a 'Man Ples', or 'Man of this Place'. A rare honour in a culture where each person's spiritual identity is intimately tied to the very soil of their ancestral terrain.

During Stan's absence, his boss, Local Government Council Secretary Keith Mala, has been taking Darvall Wilkins to one welcoming ceremony after another in villages all over Malekula Island. Soon after Stan's arrival, Keith brings Darvall up the hill to see the building that formerly housed the Wilkins' house girl and truck. This, after the garage and clothes washing area were walled in, is where Stan, his wife Holly, and their two small children are living. Indeed, oil stains from the truck mark the master bedroom floor.

Recognizing an opportunity to learn more about Malekula, Stan invites Darvall Wilkins inside for a chat. At close quarters he is a man of average height, red hair and blue eyes, and appears to be kindly. He shakes their hands and sits down in his ex-laundry area (now Stan's living room) to chat for a while. Darvall emphasises the importance of visiting all of the villages in the Local Government Area; Stan soon realises that although he has been to most of them, he hasn't toured a fraction of the amount Darvall did during his residence here. Stan and Holly fall under his spell and are drawn into friendship. Darvall offers details about himself when asked; however, he is more interested in them, their hopes, dreams, and plans. With seemingly little effort, he draws information, encourages, and inspires them, showing confidence in them. They both now understand why there was so much excitement when "Mista Wilkin i kam" was proclaimed around the station. Others have sat where they now sit.

Stan and Holly move onto another life after their term in Vanuatu; however, they remain special friends with Darvall Wilkins and his family. Perhaps the most telling outcome from this visit is their home on Hornby Island in British Columbia is also now called Lakatoro. They join a large group of lifelong friends of Mista Wilkin.

One

1922 Early Life

A Beginning

A well-known Australian dictionary refers to Dubbo as meaning "red earth" (purportedly from a local Aboriginal dialect) or a colloquialism for an idiot. In any case this was where I was born, a small town in the middle of New South Wales, Australia, in the Henry James private hospital with one Dr Flower attending. I am not sure if this was somewhat prophetic given my later talents in horticulture, nevertheless he was my first doctor.

I arrived with a shock of red hair which apparently caused my father, Stanley James, some alarm. He had conveniently forgotten my great-grandfather, William Wilkins, had red hair, and as it subsequently turned out, so would my future children—Simon, Sallie, and Peter. I was named Darvall Keppel by my mother, Lila, who for some unknown reason admired the name. It may have been as the name was well-known in Dubbo and the Narromine district, being also attached to Darvall Harricks, a local member of the landed aristocracy. I doubt whether my father (who idolised my mother) had much of a say. He did contribute Keppel after his eldest brother, Keppel Nelson Wilkins. There may have been a link to the Royal Navy somewhere since there was an Admiral Keppel who served with Lord Nelson, however I was never really sure about its genesis.

I was taken home to 'Dulla Dulla' (the family property) which was some distance by horse and sulky. Given my father's family owned the Wilkins Kennedy and Spence factory in Talbragar Street (which burnt down in 1927), he had a pretty flash sulky and, of course, handsome horses. My parents had moved into Dulla Dulla homestead after their marriage in Melbourne. As was common in those days, other family shared the house. In our case, this was Aunty Hilda and Uncle Bill Martin along with my wonderful grandfather, Charles Albert Wright, who had provided the property for his four sons (one other son, Bert, was killed in France in 1917). Dad owned land on the northern side of the Dulla property which bordered on the Burraway Road. I recall going up to the back paddock with my mother who had already chosen a site for their home which never eventuated. Poor Mum. Dad was a bit of a nomad who tended to be overly generous towards his friends and their children. He was a cattle man and a good one at that. He had quite an extraordinary ability to correctly estimate the weight of a beast dressed and hanging in a butcher's shop and used this skill to win quite a few competitions at local shows. His life was spent travelling the region buying and selling cattle and making a comfortable living. Mum was finally able to have her own home in 1949 when Dad responded to her nagging, possibly because she delivered an ultimatum: either you buy or I go. In any case, he purchased the lovely old but neglected 'Baringa' in Tamworth Street Dubbo for the princely price of three thousand pounds.

My very early memories are pretty vague, however I do remember my cot being at the end of my parents' bed at Dulla. Other than that, I don't recall much about my early childhood, but I assume it must have been a happy one. I remember trailing along behind my grandfather as he pottered around in his garden, hoe in hand, calling my aunt Hilda 'two mum' (rather original I thought); telling my mother I loved her to the moon and back, and loving Bert our part Aboriginal cook who would periodically go walkabout. Bert had a deformed hand as a result of being burnt as a baby. His hands were soft and if we were sick, he would stroke our foreheads ever so gently and oh-so soothingly. He worked at Dulla for many years then went walkabout and never returned.

The memories become clearer as the years slipped by but above all I knew I was loved by so many people; my parents, my aunt and uncle, my 'big brothers' cousins, Kel and Buv, and housemaid Barbara who stayed with us for a long time. Above all there was Dulla, my home which as the years went by became increasingly more important in my life.

I nearly lost my life when I was five when I contracted diphtheria, a much-feared disease in the days before modern drugs. I had an awful rasping cough followed by breathless whooping as I struggled to get air into my lungs. The cough and the whoop grew worse and my aunt Hilda kept saying, "Stan, I think you should take that boy into the doctor." But Dad with his typical optimism felt I'd be okay. Finally, Dad rang Dr Flower who said in no uncertain terms to bring me in or he would wash his hands of the whole affair. Dad took me in that night, and it was now a diphtheritic croup.

I can remember Dad carrying me from the horse yards where he had been feeding the large draft horses with hay drenched in molasses (a smell I will never forget), me whooping away and then later him carrying me up the steps of Dubbo Base Hospital. I was put in a cot covered with a sort of tent, into which steam was pumped. The foot of the bed was raised with six bricks I proudly told people later.

It was obviously touch and go for a day or two. My mother was in Melbourne and I don't know if Dad kept her informed. Eventually the cot foot was slowly lowered, and the tent removed. The nurses were wonderful and my first memory after I began to take notice was Dad calling to me from the outside of the gauzed ward, as I was an isolation case. I fretted for Dad and home. To lift my spirits, Dad appeared one day in a nurse's cap and gown which he had persuaded a nurse to lend him. That was my dad! I was soon well and my idyllic life at Dulla resumed.

Dulla Dulla

Dulla was situated on the Macquarie River about 16 miles west of Dubbo. As I got older, I slept in the same room as my cousins. We had narrow beds with horsehair mattresses all lined up along the verandah. It was warm as toast on a frosty night and you could hear farm noises clearly: lambs crying until their mothers found them after being in the sheep yard all day, frogs croaking down in the swamp, and the occasional bark of a fox. Our pet pig, with the original name of Piglet, would come trotting down, tap-tap-tapping on the wooden boards and grunting quietly, until he found a blanket hanging low enough from someone's bed. Tugging gently, he would pull off enough blanket to wrap himself in it and then settle down to sleep.

But it was the Macquarie River we loved the most. Through long hot summer months, we would spend every free moment we could immersed in its unpolluted waters, playing hide and seek under the submerged logs or in the thick green algae; and later, training for competitive swimming, lap after lap across and back in the deep pools. Or we would play on the slippery dip: a channel from the highest sloping bank to the waters' edge. We took it in turns to lug a kerosene tin bucket to the top, sit carefully on a folded, well-soaked wheat bag, tip the water down the channel, and away we would go.

In the winter months after school, Kel carved out dirt roads for his cast iron Vauxhall, and Buv and I were allowed to have a go sitting on it with all our body weight on the tough little car, as we would shunt it through the dusty tracks accompanied by suitable engine sounds.

Later it was tennis that came into our lives. Tennis played an important part in the social life of the district, and once a month the district team would meet a neighbouring team and do battle—in between partaking of delicious morning and afternoon teas and lunches. My mother was one of the champions and I was very proud of her. Dad used to amuse everyone by taking a running serve, starting from the back of the fence and finishing on the serving line. More often than not he'd serve a double fault.

Later when Kel and Buv went to Huntingtower Christian Science School in Melbourne, they were professionally coached and became expert players. On one occasion during the NSW Western District Championships, they played against Jack Crawford and Adrian Quist (the famous Davis Cup players for Australia at the time). Dulla had its own clay surface court and Buv and I would work meticulously to have the court in perfect order before Kel started coming home for Christmas school holidays. We used two planks to ensure the lime lines were not only dead straight, but not spreading beyond the designated two-inch width.

Aunty Hilda was a devoted Christian Scientist and every Sunday she would gather her family in the 'big room' (ballroom was too grand a name). It had thick pisé walls and a lovely Wunderlich pressed iron ceiling and was designed and used as the party room in my mother's youth. I would potter about outside wondering what they were doing inside. My parents were not particularly religious, though both were baptised Church of England, and periodically I would be dragged along to Sunday school after an adult's service in the Rawsonville District HQ church, a modest little weatherboard church.

The services would be taken by my uncle Claude Leavers (married to Dad's sister Lily). I was rather afraid of him, but not as afraid as I was of the big neighbouring children who no doubt were also dragged along. We would stand and stare at one another from a distance of about 20 metres until we were called inside. It was always a relief to hitch up the sulky again and head home to Dulla.

At the age of seven I was enrolled with the Blackfriars Correspondence School and joined Buv and Kel in the 'school room', a spare bedroom. I think my mother and my aunt used to take it in turn to give what little supervision was necessary. They also took it week-about to cook and clean.

I can always remember my mother during her cleaning duties. She was a meticulous housekeeper and worked like a Trojan. Aunt Hilda's brother-in-law Fred, who would visit from Melbourne occasionally, called Mum the "old Dutch Cleaner", referring to some cleaning agent favoured at that time. Mum used to whistle as she worked, usually the popular tunes of the day. She was good too I recall.

Because my aunt did not enjoy optimal health, and she rather enjoyed the highlights of Sydney where she had old school friends (so I suspected), my mother seemed to run the house and the two families most of the time. Incidentally my father and Uncle Bill took it in turns to cook breakfast every day and substantial breakfast it was: fried chops, liver, sheep's brains, bacon and egg, with the inevitable Uncle Tobys rolled oats. I do not think that either my mother or Aunt Hilda enjoyed getting up too early.

Music played a big part in our lives. There was a Rönisch crown piano in the big room and an upright record player with Dame Nellie Melba and Paul Robeson records. My mother used to buy sheet music with the popular tunes from time to time. Mum was a well-qualified pianist and I loved to hear her practise. I'd often ask her to play *Weber's Last Waltz* because sometimes she would tell me the little story that went with it. We would often have a sing-song around the piano after the evening meal—there was no radio at that time. My mother played while Aunt Hilda and Uncle Bill sang, with the kids trying our best to join in. We always enjoyed it.

I remember very little of my early school days except that I looked forward to mail day, possibly because once a week the mail man also brought us luscious fresh bread from Narromine. Also, my school papers would be returned from Blackfriars Sydney with a little note from my teacher who had marked my work. She always had something nice to say about what I had done and said when we came to Sydney, we must visit her at the school. This my mother and I did one time and I thought my teacher was very nice. I do recall sitting at a table drawing a map of Australia, pouring over the atlas and the map of the world, and thinking how nice it would be if the red colouring indicating the membership of the British Empire, could be extended in Africa all the way from north to south.

The three of us, Kel, Buv, and I, usually all worked in the school room together. It was convenient for my mother or Aunt Hilda to pop in occasionally to check on us. Buv was always up to some mischief, and one morning popped a pen nib into his pop gun and suggested to the unsuspecting Kel that he put his finger over the barrel to feel the pressure. The nib must have hurt because Kel, normally a very placid soul, let out a yell and shouted, "I'll kill you," and pursued Buv out through the house. Their mother, sweeping the verandah, heard the threats, and saw them racing through the garden and down towards the swamp. Fearing she was about to lose her second son, she set off in hot pursuit brandishing her broom. I watched fascinated from the verandah but Buv was a speedy runner and Kel and his mother abandoned the chase.

In due time more Martin children arrived: Ronnie, who was three years younger than I, Meg five years younger, Billy a born wag, and David the youngest. We all adored Meg with her flaxen hair and if I woke with a nightmare, which I often did, my mother would say, "Now turn over and dream about Meg." When Bill was due (he was seven years younger than I) we were sent down to the river to play and usually took a picnic lunch of sandwiches. I remember Dad appearing over the crown of the bank with a mob of dogs with handkerchiefs tied around their necks to celebrate the new arrival.

Of my younger cousins—they were really more like my brothers and sister—Ronnie was the most unusual, almost bizarre. He had a practically square face, with a wide mouth and brown hair. As a baby, he seemed to cry incessantly for no apparent reason and my father nicknamed him 'Mis' (short for Misery)—a name with which my father addressed him all his life. Once mobile, he took a liking to the good soil, and to stop him eating large quantities of it, his mother would wrap a piece of mosquito netting over his head so that he always had a large brown patch over his mouth giving him an Al Jolson-like appearance. He and I seemed to have every childhood ailment together at a time when castor oil was the home remedy for most illnesses. When my mother would appear with the castor oil bottle, a large spoon and a glass of orange juice (to alleviate the taste) to deal with mumps or measles or whatever, Ronnie would scream, "Gid to Darby" which was me. To this day I sometimes taste the aftertaste of castor oil when I have an orange juice.

Ronnie used to spend what seemed like years crying under the dinner table, stopping to occasionally beat the cedar tabletop with his spoon and shouting, "Don't want dead fox." He owed this turn of phrase to my humorous father who had trained him to refer to meat as dead fox. One day, when my big city Aunt Ess and Uncle Charles were visiting, Ronnie shouted, "I won't eat dead fox" and she turned quite pale.

He was a spoilt child, but of course he left us all for dust becoming an accomplished pianist and agricultural scientist, winning the William Farrer medal (for breeding some of the most widely grown wheats in Australia, such as Eagle, Kite etc.) and the Order of Australia. Sadly, as a devout Christian Scientist, he died of a debilitating disease, untreated by doctors.

On reflection, it was an unusual household at Dulla. Parents and children got on well together with little bickering. And there was the constant presence of a benign grandfather whom we all loved. He was a handsome old man, grey hair still around the temples and a full white moustache; he would sit in his armchair in front of the fire at night and smile at our antics. He was very deaf and it was my job to call him to tea, which was our evening meal. I would bellow into his ear, "Tea's ready, Grandfather."

Finally, he accepted professional advice and got some sort of trumpet. I used to get the giggles talking into it, and I really don't think it was any help. He watched the weather with a farmer's eye; he would stand out on the verandah looking out to a cloudless sky and a wind in the wrong direction and say, "Eeee, no good, no good."

His third son, Jack, lived on an adjoining property, 'Waikerie' (originally Grandfather's first holding and passed onto him by his father). They were certainly bred tough as he followed his own father's example of settling all four sons onto their own properties. This was all from a man who started out with nothing but made a living building dams with a team of horses and scoops at Wilcannia. Jack would come over regularly and argue, which he loved doing with his father. He was rather eccentric but no fool. He played the violin, was a health fanatic, took on unusual diets, cleaned his teeth with fire ashes, and would walk stark naked out in the frosty morning to catch the winter sun. His family seemed to adopt his eccentricity, with his son being the best tap dancer in the district (often demonstrated in front of us all by a squirming boy), and his wife the best driver (women drivers were something of a novelty in those days).

My cheeky father decided he would one day intervene in one of the regular arguments over the weather. Grandfather maintained that we would get a storm coming up from the south-west, Uncle Jack pooh-poohing the idea. While they were standing arguing on the west verandah at dusk, Dad slipped out with a torch and, well out of sight, began flashing it intermittently. "There you are, Jack. I told you so," Grandfather said, "storm coming up fast." Uncle Jack evidently decided to get home before the deluge.

The Depression

The 1930s depression seemed to have passed over our heads. No doubt the adults had heeded Grandfather's warning to "pull our horns in", but unlike many others, we always had plenty to eat, most of it from the farm of course: milk, butter, meat and vegetables, and the mailman continued to deliver the bread in his sulky.

Occasionally we would get a visitor with his swag on his back asking for food, and my mother or aunt always made up some sandwiches of cold meat and gave him a cup of tea before he headed off down the dusty road again. Grandfather had handed over management of the property to my uncle Bill and spent a lot of time reading, but his interest was the vegetable garden. Each morning and evening he would head down to the vegetable garden, hoe in hand, and I would traipse after him, probably more hindrance than help but I believe I inherited my love of gardening from my grandfather.

Country Life

Not long after this idyllic time, there were big changes in our education. The older boys went off to boarding school in Melbourne and the state government had agreed to the establishment of the Dulla Dulla Subsidised School. When it opened at the beginning of 1935, there was an enrolment of 13, and of course we were all related. The first official teacher was a 17-year-old high-school graduate, Miss Bald, who would board for some months at a time in each of the children's homes.

She was a born teacher even at that tender age and we all thought she was lovely. She coped with all 13 of us of different ages and different classes, all in the one room. The school was built by the parents and was made of galvanised iron and had two tiny glassless windows. I suppose glass was expensive, but without any lining the galvanised iron roof and walls radiated the heat, and in summer it was very, very hot. However, that did not seem to bother us or Miss Bald. At playtime, and over lunch, we would sit under the surrounding spindly gums and have great fun.

It was my job as the eldest to take Ronnie, Meg, and Billy to school in the sulky. I had to catch and harness the pony and unharness her when we arrived, when she would be put in a small yard nearby, then harness her up again to head home and unharness her on arrival home. I became pretty adept at harnessing, and I think even to this day some 80 years later I could still harness a pony into a sulky blindfolded.

A highlight in our school day was when my father would join us for lunch. We would sit around him fascinated by his stories. He had a wonderful imagination, and at Dulla for many years at bedtime we would gather around one of our beds on the long verandah and listen spellbound to stories of his adventures with his favourite dogs, Nettle and Bluey. We would be dying to hear the next episode. Looking back, I realise what a great love of children my father had. He would go out of his way when on one of his innumerable cattle and sheep buying travels, to stop over to eat with 13 kids. Sometimes at lunch he would pass around his hat and say, "Don't forget poor old WotWot hasn't had anything to eat today, so put your crusts into my hat for me." WotWot was his nickname, which I suspect was derived from Mum's exasperated "what, what" responses to him. It apparently happened so often he thought it was his name. Believing him, we would duly do so and whether he actually ate the crusts I do not remember, but we thought we had done a kindly deed.

My father always seemed to have a supply of sweets in his utility, and the children in the neighbourhood always looked forward to his visiting. He would often stay overnight, strike a deal over a mob of sheep or cattle and move on. Dad said that Tommy Williams at Rawsonville used to keep his stud ram in the guest bedroom and if it was good enough for the ram, then that was good enough for Dad. He was a gentle man who could not bear to see animals suffer. He always carried a pair of shears in the ute, and would stop at once if he saw a flyblown sheep in a nearby paddock, catch the sheep, and dress the flyblown area to alleviate its suffering before continuing his journey.

The halcyon days of the subsidised school, with long holidays spent mostly in the Macquarie River, and visits from Aunt and Uncle with their five children from Melbourne soon came to an end, and I was packed off to Dubbo High School, boarding during the week at the Church of England Boys hostel.

Despite the fact that the hostel was under the control of the rector, my Uncle Claude, with Matron Jones as the hostel supervisor, I hated it and longed for the weekend when usually my father would appear to pick me up in the ute to take me home. The weekend would always go too quickly, and I would be taken back to the hostel by my father or would get a lift in with a neighbour. I was always so desperate to get home that on one occasion when there was no one to collect me, I walked the 16 miles home. Later I would ride my bicycle, slower of course than a car, but at least I was sure to get home. The ride back on Mondays always seemed so much longer and the corrugations on the road much worse. I usually learnt my homework poetry as I peddled along and *The Bells* comes vividly to mind—'Hear the tolling of the bells … bells, bells, bells …'

I was horribly shy as a young boy and I found it very difficult to make friends either at the hostel or at the school. At the hostel, the big boys smoked and bullied although they tended to leave me alone, most likely as I was the rector's nephew. It's funny how little things remain in your memory. I hated having to wear shoes and the little ration of butter at meals was never enough. My mother had arranged for me to slip over to the rectory after school for a glass of milk to help sustain me. Cousin Mary, who had had rickets as a child and was a short little thing whom I hardly knew, ran the rectory house for her father after Aunty Lily died suddenly of a cerebral haemorrhage.

Although I found it terribly difficult to settle down, I did enjoy classes. I was made class captain and wrote a note to my parents to tell them, signing it "your class captain son". Heaven knows why I was chosen, possibly it was the teacher's selection, but I remained class captain for my final three years at Dubbo High School.

I loved English and History, and adored my English teacher, Miss Thornton, who had lovely brown eyes and encouraged my reading. After the half-yearly and yearly examinations, Miss Thornton would finally arrive with a great stack of papers which were handed out starting with the lowest marked paper and progressing to the highest. I must have always had a tortured look on my face because she would say to me, "It is alright, Darvall. Your paper is at the bottom." I did well in English and History over the three years, but I found maths very difficult and was rather afraid of Fred Everett, a good teacher who expected me to do better than I did. He was a football fanatic and was disgusted when I chose to play tennis in the winter instead of football which I knew absolutely nothing about. However, I excelled at swimming.

Swimming

Buv and Kel, coming home from Melbourne, were both proving to be excellent swimmers and we all joined or were press-ganged into joining the Dubbo Swimming Club. Kel had swum once or twice in competitions in the river at Dubbo, but in 1936 the Olympic swimming pool was opened, and school carnivals and club competitions were held there.

That summer the English swimming team, in Sydney for the British Empire Games, were invited to attend the annual swimming carnival in Dubbo and give an exhibition of swimming and diving. Much to our delight, the team came out to Dulla to visit a stud sheep farm. Dulla was then specialising in breeding stud Corriedales. Buv and I, too shy to make verbal contact, idolised them from afar.

My father had written to Boy Charlton, an Olympic world champion, to ask advice on training. A letter came back from him recommending a good diet of meat and salads, plenty of sleep, and above all to swim and swim. We were bursting with enthusiasm and during the summer months we spent hours in the river swimming and training.

Buv and I took part in swimming carnivals all over the western districts (by this time Kel had gone to Sydney to start an engineering course). I remember once at Mudgee swimming and winning a junior 50 metres in the Cudgegong River, clambering out onto the weir wall exhausted, and thinking I was going to fall over the edge. Only recently I went back to Mudgee to look for the "pool". It was unchanged with the water still as murky as ever but the drop from the wall not as high as I remembered.

The inter-town relay teams were the most exciting, Buv swimming for the seniors, and I for the juniors. During my last year at Dubbo High School, I also swam for the seniors and was very proud of myself. Competitive swimming gave me a lot of satisfaction and it stood me in good stead both at Scots College and at university. My opposition at Scots was Forbes Carlyle who was later to rise to dizzy heights as coach for many of Australia's great swimmers, including Shane Gould. Forbes was too good for me at all the school championships I have to admit.

I usually went to Melbourne in the hot months after Christmas with my mother and grandfather, where we would stay at Brighton with my aunt Top (my maternal aunt, born Ellen Anna) and uncle Arthur. Uncle Arthur insisted on having me coached by Guy Froehlich, one of Melbourne's leading coaches, and paying the fees.

With the war, poor Guy was interned in 1940 given his German heritage. My swimming career came to an end as a result. Although I competed for St Andrew's College for the three years (I was there after the war). I used to train at the Domain Baths sometimes with Margaret Dovey—later Mrs Gough Whitlam—who was, I think, the NSW breaststroke champion. In my last year at college we won, for the third successive year, the Rawson Inter College Cup and as captain I had to respond to the toast to the team. Before replying, however, I had to finish off what was left in the cup, which by tradition passed round all the members of the team. There was a strike in the breweries at the time and no beer available, and apparently there wasn't much else available in the way of alcoholic beverages because the cup was filled with Sauternes. I finished it with considerable effort and began my speech. I had three points. The first was training as a team was helped by one of the crew member's enormous old Rolls Royce into which we would all clamber each morning to go to the baths; my second point, my second … my second, and I collapsed. I don't think that I have ever been so sick; two of the medicos put me under the showers and one sat by me all night, but it took days to recover.

It was in 1937 that our grandfather died. It was during the school holidays and I remember that day very vividly. As the hearse drove up the dusty road to the Rawsonville cemetery, the phone rang incessantly. I ran out the front door along the path and under the road trellis to where Aunty Top was standing watching the hearse and cars disappear into the dust. I said, "Aunty Top, the phone is ringing." She turned with tears in her eyes and said abruptly, "Let it ring." It was the only time in my life that she spoke tersely to me. Grandfather was such a kind, wise, tolerant man; it was cruel that the last two years of his life were indeed a misery. I suspect he had prostate cancer, and to my own dying day I will see and hear him under the peppercorn trees, unaware of me, and saying over and over, "Oh, God, let me die. Let me die."

Only once do I recall him being really angry with us kids who inevitably were always up to mischief. One day when he was dozing on the verandah in his favourite squatters' chair, Buv quietly got the hose and filled his pockets with water. Another day while he was resting on the verandah, Buv directing me from the lounge room door, I crept under Grandfather's bed and gave a little push up. He did not stir. Buv signalled again to push harder. I did so and he stirred. On the third push he got up, to return a few moments later. I pushed again and he lent over with a peppercorn switch and let me have it hard. Buv almost had apoplexy. This was minor mischief which he took in his stride, but when we cut down one of his treasured and long-nurtured kurrajong trees to make shanghais, he was really angry and told us he was calling the police. We lived in terror for the rest of the day.

Grandfather was buried at Rawsonville, no cremations in those days, though I know he would have preferred a cremation. There are plans to have a plaque erected there to commemorate the early pioneers who were buried there—the Roberts, Harveys, Uncle Bill Martin, Tommy Williams, the Cornish family, and others.

There was a little weatherboard church, St James Anglican Church, at Rawsonville. Inevitably it was Anglican as there were only two Roman Catholic families in the Rawsonville district—Harold Harvey at Oakbank and Mr Cecil and Mrs Mary Harvey (she was known as the only local to have attended university). There was scepticism of Catholics in my youth, but in later years Mrs Claire Harvey lived next door to us in Tamworth Street Dubbo, and she became a close friend of my mother's. She played the piano beautifully and it was a joy on hot summer afternoons to hear her practising through our kitchen window. She also used to play at Rawsonville dances.

Rawsonville was, in the early days, a vital cultural centre for the local community. It was originally known by the lovely name of Bilarbegil, but was sadly renamed Rawsonville to honour the visit of the Governor General Sir Harry Rawson, who came to lay the foundation stone to the new hall which was to commemorate servicemen from the First World War (and later the second war).

The annual Rawsonville carnival was a big day predominantly for horse events but there were competitions like driving the nail, hoopla, guessing the number of peas in a jar etc. I never really enjoyed going as I was so terribly shy and it meant getting dressed up in shoes.

The little cemetery, neglected and overgrown like most rural cemeteries, contained some of the earliest pioneers like Mary Bootle who when widowed, brought a buggy with goods and chattels across the Blue Mountains. She roped logs behind the wagon to act as a brake descending the Great Dividing Range onto the Bathurst Plains. She took up land on the junction of the Coolbaggie Creek and the Macquarie River and Grandfather later bought her holding to have a frontage to the river. He then built the present homestead Dulla Dulla within half a mile of Mary's old house, of which there were only ruins when we were children, but I remember the well, a few bricks, and broken china. It was to disappear completely under the plough.

Boarding School

1938 was my last year at high school, and despite hating living in the hostel, I did well in the Intermediate Certificate and with Grandfather's generosity was enrolled at the Scots College at Bellevue Hill Sydney for the following year. Grandfather had left sufficient funds for this because he told my mother, "Garvel (he never could get my name straight) must have a good education." My mother had scorned the great public schools and decided that Scots, a Protestant school, had the best open site with its fine oval and boarding houses overlooking Rose Bay and golf links, and decided that I would be happy there. It was, I think, a good choice, and when I had settled in I enjoyed it.

My first introduction to Scots was when Mum deposited me and my luggage by taxi at the steps of Kirkland House, where I was met by the matron—a very large and forbidding lady in a white uniform. She turned out to be a kindly motherly soul and the senior boys teased the life out of her. It took me many weeks to settle in and at night I would curl up in my bed and dream of being home again at Dulla. In my first year, I did reasonably well at classes and won several English and History prizes at the end of the year. I rowed in the first four at the regatta, and was runner-up swimming champion to my arch enemy, Forbes Carlyle.

Christmas 1938 went all too quickly and Mum moved into the Wallaringa Mansions, an enormous boarding house at Cremorne not that long ago demolished. All my uniform was purchased at David Jones and Mum was kept busy sewing my name tag on every item. I still have a handkerchief labelled with Darvall Wilkins.

Piano lessons, which I'd had during my three years at the Dubbo hostel, were to continue under Miss Edson who lived at Dee Why. She had studied under a German professor at Leipzig before the first war and taught the Haller method where tone and touch came from the muscles in the back. I loved my lessons with Miss Edson, going out by tram from Rose Bay to Dee Why after school and getting back in time for prep at eight. Miss Edson would give me a light tea after the lesson which I also enjoyed. I continued lessons there for three years until I joined the navy. Cousin Ron was to also study under Miss Edson.

On the 9th of September whilst I was home on holidays, war was declared. The war clouds had been gathering throughout the year as Hitler's power overtook Europe. And from time to time in assembly, the headmaster, A.K. Anderson, 'AKA', would talk about the war which was to engulf our lives, but I at any rate took little notice and life went on as usual. But that September evening as we sat around in the 'little sitting room' as it was called, and where grandfather had installed the enormous radio with its rows of knobs and big His Master's Voice trumpet speaker, we listened quietly whilst we heard Prime Minister Menzies announce that we were again at war. I could see the tears in my mother's and aunt's eyes; they doubtless were thinking back to the First

World War when Bert had been killed in France and many of their young friends had either not returned or returned physically and mentally changed. No doubt they were thinking of us too: Kel 20, Buv 19, and me 17, inevitably to be swept up in an agonisingly long and terrible war.

It was not until 1940 came that we began to hear of ex-school students enlisting mostly in the air force which seemed to carry all the glamour, and in the streets of Sydney we began to see more and more service uniforms. For myself, I did not think much of the war and what I was going to do about it. The Leaving Certificate was my big objective. I took honours in History and English and was successful in both at the end of the year. I was made a prefect, giving me freedom and more influence. Joe Robilliard was school captain and seemed to enjoy being able to cane the recalcitrant. Looking back, I think he may have taken his job too seriously.

I returned early and reluctantly in first term because I was selected to row with the first eights for the Head of the River on the Nepean River. This involved a lot of hard training. We camped in the Scots boat shed on the waters near Drummoyne. We were up each day at dawn to row, with the coaches following in a speedboat screaming at us for miles and miles. Then back to the shed to shower and change into school uniforms before travelling by taxi through the city and on to Rose Bay just in time for first classes—only to repeat the routine in the reverse order in the afternoon. Tired and early to bed after the afternoon row, we had little time to study.

I seemed to be a thorn in the coach's flesh. I was moved in position several times, the assistant coach would join in discussions about me and I was extremely worried and wondered if I would be dropped from the crew, with great loss of face. In the event I stayed put. The climax was the GPS Regatta. The last night we stayed at the Nepean Hotel, all jittery and nervous. All our various parents came to Sydney for the event, full of hope for us to win. In fact out of nine of the beautiful shells that lined up on the oily Nepean, we came an ignominious last. To give us our due, a post-mortem confirmed what we had experienced: we were placed on the outside, eastern side of the river, and because there was a drought and the river was very low, for the first five or six hundred yards we had to row through thick and heavy water weeds. By the time we were able to get to clear water, we were well behind.

Rowing did not give me very much time for my first love, swimming, though I tried to train whenever opportunity offered. The school championships were held in the Rose Bay pool and in all the freestyle events I had to battle it out with Forbes Carlyle. Our photo appeared in *The Sydney Morning Herald*—we had just finished the one hundred yards. Forbes went on to study physiology at Sydney University and played an important role in the development and training of our Olympic swimmers.

My mother rented Miss Edson's small two-bedroom cottage after she vacated. In my last year at Scots, my mother and sometimes my father came down from time to time and I was able to join them on free weekends. It was that year that my mother took me to see the Ballet Russe and I quickly became a balletomane. I loved the music, the stage settings, and above all, the dancing. Serge Lifar was the choreographer and had been trained under the great Diaghiler in Paris. From Scots I was sometimes permitted to go to the ballet on a Friday night and after the performance I would wait at the stage door and see the dancers leaving for their hotel. They always looked exhausted, so pale but so slim and dainty and, of course, beautiful. Later on with the occupation of Paris by the Nazis, the company found themselves without a home to go to and some settled in Australia and played a part in the creation of Australian ballet.

With rowing and swimming behind me, I settled into study with the Leaving Certificate. I continued my piano lessons with Miss Edson. There were vacant beachfront blocks of land quite close to Miss Edson's; I enquired about cost, about 40 pounds, and I did my best to talk Dad into buying one. I suppose he just did not have the money or had better things to buy, but I was very disappointed.

In October of that year, Aunty Top came over from Melbourne to see Peter off on HMAS Sydney. Cousin Bill was already a prisoner of war having been shot down in his fighter plane on the North African front. Bill spent the remainder of the war in a Stalag in Germany, escaping as the Russian army approached Berlin. He finally met up with American troops. He said that a stout pair of boots that Aunty Top had sent him saved his life, protecting his feet from frostbite.

Peter came over to dinner one night, very glamorous in his rig, his sailor's uniform, and HMAS Sydney on his cap. The ship sailed shortly afterwards. Then it was announced that the ship had been lost, no detail was given, none known at that time. Until months after the war, Aunty Top firmly believed that Peter would turn up, after having been held as a prisoner by the Japanese. He never did and the mystery was finally solved when the wreck was discovered off the West Australian coast in the 2000s.

Gap Year

With the dreaded Leaving Certificate, which I sat for in the Paddington Town Hall out of the way, I looked forward to a long holiday before starting university. One of my school mates Nev Newman had agreed to come with me on a boating expedition down the Murray River, but at the last moment withdrew and I was bitterly disappointed. Then I talked Buv into a biking expedition down the Princes Highway to Melbourne. With our Hartley shorts (precursors of the boxer shorts but possibly a bit skimpier), sleeves cut out of our shirts, a blanket, a change of 'uniform', and ablution necessities, we set off, Uncle Bill giving us a good start by dropping us off at Orange. We peddled on to Bathurst and camped our first night in a paddock near a dam. That night the weather changed from a ferocious midsummer 40-degrees-plus to an icy blast that is typical of the Orange/ Bathurst area and we froze. The next morning, we cycled into Bathurst to buy something warm to dress in and then headed off.

Heaven knows why but we neither had a road map nor checked our route at home to work out the best options on getting to the coast. However, we reckoned the logical thing was to go east via the Jenolan Caves. We started an everlasting descent into the valley counting on at least eating well once we reached Jenolan Caves House. We finally arrived at dusk and were greeted by the doorman who took one look at us and said, "You can't come in like that." And that was that.

For the life of me, I don't know why we didn't at least beg for something to eat at the back entrance—but we turned around and started to head up that valley again. Our bicycles had no gears and standard brakes, so more often than not we walked, pushing our bikes alongside us. About midnight we got to the top and crashed hungrily by the roadside.

Refuelled at Bathurst, we somehow got the right road. Crossing the Abercrombie River stands out vividly. Again, we were toiling uphill on the rough gravelled and dusty road. A large vehicle—the first we had seen that day—shot past, hands waving from all the windows and showered us with more dust. At the top there was our car waiting for us. "Have a beer," they said, "before we leave you to it." I think it was the first beer I had ever drunk and how terribly bitter it was, cold and wet.

We travelled slowly down the coast via Eden, and then to Sale. We were each day getting closer to Melbourne. At Sale I think it was, we decided to peddle on into the night, until about midnight when we'd had enough. The night was pitch-dark, and we chose a spot to camp about a few hundred yards into the bush and bedded down. We were woken by shouts and drunken curses; we had set up at the edge of a local camp and they were returning home after a night out. We packed in a hurry and moved on to a quieter site. On the 14th day of our travels, we were met by Helen Newman and my mother, bundled the bikes into the boot of the big Buick, and were soon at the esplanade where after hot baths Aunty Top served up the best meal we had ever eaten.

University, War Looming

So began 1941 with the usual wonderful holiday at 'Seamarch' in Middle Brighton, the Newman's lovely old home. You could walk across the esplanade to the beach, but I still went into the city baths at the top of Flinders Street to train. Uncle Arthur was always generous when invaded by so many relatives. He used to let me, at 17, take one of his cars to coaching in Melbourne city each week.

After returning to Dulla, I began preparing for Sydney University where

I had been accepted for an arts degree. We still had Mrs Kidman's flat at 491 Alfred Street, North Sydney (more accurately a sitting room, bedroom, and shared kitchen/ bathroom). Mrs Kidman was an elderly lady with an equally large smile. When she went into town, she always wore what I called tea cosy hats. Her son, Eric, was badly incapacitated with polio I think, because he had difficulty in walking and was excusably very crotchety and would call, "Mother, Mother" in imperious tones. How Mrs Kidman remained cool and calm I will never know. Periodically he would take me aside when Mrs K was out of hearing range and ask me to get him a bottle of whisky, which I would do. How I was able to buy whisky I cannot recall, not being familiar with pubs, but after all I was 19, so I suppose there was no problem. The Kidman's had a collie dog called Joker who was a bit of a pest.

Going to lectures each day meant an hour's tram trip, changing at Wynyard, and the trams always seemed to be packed. The cars were fitted with the seats running at right angles to the tracks and you clambered in from steps running the full length of the tram. I said "in" but more often than not you had to cling onto the steps because each section was crammed with those sitting and standing and getting on with a bag of books in one hand and clinging on for dear life with the other became a major problem.

I was, at this stage of my life, a budding writer, and the tram journeys gave vent to a short story. *The Tram Conductor* was about the conductor who, because of his persistence with collecting fares—"fares please!"—at awkward times, is rather unkindly shoved under passing traffic as we rocket across the Harbour Bridge. Needless to say, the story was rejected by *The Bulletin*.

Although I knew a few people from Scots, there were none of my close friends, and it was a fairly lonely year. I struggled with Philosophy under Professor Anderson, enjoyed Modern History and English, and did not like Psychology, always embarrassed when the lecturer would discuss sexual matters, Freud etc. In the last term, it came something of a bombshell when the university board wrote to me and told me that I had not matriculated in Latin, only getting a *B* in the Leaving Certificate, and informing me that I would have to do so (which meant obtaining a higher pass) before proceeding to second year. So this meant taking coaching lessons in that subject in some dreary little office high up in a building near Central Station twice a week.

I had by this time decided to join the Navy. For a landlubber this was probably an odd decision but I had vivid memories of my mother's brother, Uncle Charles, talking about the war and the misery of the trenches. And of course I had read many books about the war, most memorable being *All Quiet on the Western Front*. At least, I thought, in the Navy I would have a clean dry bed (not always the case as it happened) and so the plan was to finish the academic year, get a pass in Latin, have Christmas at home, and then sign on. I don't think I ever discussed my plans with my parents who no doubt realised the inevitability of my joining up. For me it was not a decision made in a burst of patriotism, but an inevitable step as everyone would sooner or later become involved. The naval recruiting office was in Loftus Street and the day I went down to enlist, there was a crowd of young men queued up. My details were taken by a man behind a desk in uniform and I was told that in due course I would be contacted. On further enquiry I was informed that it would be in a month or so.

491 Alfred Street, North Sydney was a home away from home over the period 1940 to 1943. It was later demolished along with many other old houses when the Cahill and Bradford Freeways leading onto Sydney Harbour Bridge were constructed during and after the war. The house was not more than 200 yards south-east of the enormous brick sewer vent which still stands today on the corner of North Sydney Park. The park where I would save a penny on my tram fare from Wynyard by alighting at Miller Street and walking across to 491. This practice suddenly ceased when one night about dusk, I had almost reached the sewer chimney and home. It was a cold winter's night and I was wearing my overcoat, when I was accosted by two youths. "Got a match, mate?" I replied "Sorry I don't smoke", patting my pockets to indicate no matches when I was hit on the mouth with a solid punch. I fell back tasting blood and broken teeth. When they began to kick, I realised I had to get away—fear gave me impetus and I ran into the street light. Unsurprisingly they did not follow me. Mrs Kidman insisted that the police be rung which Eric did, and we did a tour of the park in a police car, unsuccessfully, which I was quite happy about. After that, I paid my sevenpence fare right to the Alfred Street stop.

Two

1941 My War

Enlisting

By the end of 1941, the second year of the war was closing in on me. I had completed my year's lectures and sat again to get my matriculation in Latin (after so many months of boring Latin coaching) which I passed. My enlistment in the Navy was still pending so I waited for call up.

Meantime however, the Sydney University Regiment, which involved all eligible young men at the university, had been directed by the government to ensure full-time training during the vacations. In November, we were assembled at Randwick Racecourse (taken over by the military) and kitted with khaki army uniforms, slouch hats, and rifles. We were also provided with paillasses (straw mattresses) to sleep on which smelt strongly of the stables. For days, a bad-tempered sergeant marched us up and down and taught us how to march in step. It was amazing to see that some had difficulty in mastering this feat.

After a week we were told that we were being moved to an army camp at Liverpool where for some unknown reason I was made signalman. Each day between eternal route marches, we would pile into trucks, drive into the bush, and I would lay out a wire cable between patrols, and with a portable telephone keep open-contact. It was an unusually hot summer, something like 35 degrees most days. The nights were breathless and almost as hot, and my most vivid memory of Liverpool is laying in the hot dry grass for hours, waving away persistent flies, my little phone by my side. I don't remember using it much but I suppose I did. At dusk, we would return to camp. I had to roll up all the cable, shower, and sometimes I got permission to go into town for a milkshake or two. A few went to the pub but for me it was milkshakes. It all seemed a futile existence. We also did guard duties, physical training, and peeled potatoes. A notorious 'short arm parade' embarrassed most of us. We assembled around the walls of one of the barracks rooms, dropped our pants and underpants, and waited for the medical officer who examined our genitals to check for any signs of sexually transmitted diseases. Why this public display was necessary I do not know, but it seemed to me to be unnecessarily humiliating.

Then on the 8th of December there was literally a panic. We were called outside in the middle of the night, told to pack up our gear and embark in waiting trucks. Sitting on our knapsacks holding our rifles, we were suddenly driven at speed from one position to another. No one seemed to know what was happening. Eventually after a long and sleepless night we were returned to base to learn that the Japanese had bombed Pearl Harbour. Presumably the authorities also expected us to be bombed as well.

The weeks dragged on. The days were hot and dusty and the nights just as bad. We were not allowed to take any leave but relatives could visit us on Sundays. My mother, staying at Alfred Street in the flat, came out each Sunday and it was good to see her. With Christmas over, the panic began to subside, although Japan was very soon to attack Darwin. There followed the Coral Sea battle, the Japanese midget subs attack on Sydney harbour, and the coast was shelled by Japanese submarines.

I returned to Loftus Street and was taken on as an ordinary seaman. Within a day, along with 50 other young men, we shipped off by train to the Flinders Naval Depot east of Melbourne. For the first time in my life I slept, very uneasily, in a hammock. My unease was justified when my neighbour who had slung his hammock close to mine, evidently suffering a nightmare, tried to throttle me. After that experience I made sure our hammocks were slung well apart.

Our training was arduous and I looked forward to occasional weekends at my aunt's in Brighton. Then my training stopped suddenly when during a sporting afternoon, I was hit by a hockey stick, split my upper lip open, and was hospitalised. The surgeon, who turned out to be a friend of my uncle Arthur Newman, did a good job and within ten days I was back on routine training. Then the authorities decided I was sufficiently qualified for officer training.

Seamanship training had been arduous enough, but for the next two months, along with 20 other young men, we lived by the clock starting at dawn and finishing with lights out at ten. By this time we were both physically and mentally exhausted. I was relieved when the course ended and I was pronounced a sub lieutenant. In a double-breasted navy suit, peaked cap, and one gold ring on each sleeve, I went home on leave before later joining a minesweeper based at Newcastle, along with a fellow graduate. As neither of us were drinkers, we would be forced to accept from the captain at the end of the day's sweeping, one of his many gin and tonics. Whenever possible we would tip our drinks onto the several pots of aspidistra which seemed to suffer no damage. We were both relieved when we were transferred to the naval base at Port Stephens for assault training with landing barges. This was an exciting experience where, as coxswains, we had to land our barges, often in rough seas on the sandy beaches.

New Guinea

Then with little warning I was transferred to a large naval base in Milne Bay, New Guinea. I had been given approval to grow a beard but apparently the commander of the base didn't like it, possibly because like my hair, my beard was very red. The second morning he appeared at my breakfast table and in a loud voice, instructed me to remove it. When he said "now", he obviously meant it and I beat a hasty retreat, missing my breakfast. He checked me at lunchtime and I was left to suffer a very sunburnt face.

A few days later, I boarded an American PT boat and we headed north, first to the Woodlark Island and the next day to Kirwina, the largest of the Trobriand Islands, and a primary base for an enormous US Army and Air Force detachment. No one seemed to know what to do with me and for several weeks I shared a tent with three staff sergeants who seemed to spend their lives playing poker. I would pass my days on the beach with literally hundreds of naked soldiers, black and white. I was then moved to a base on the east coast sharing an upper-storey hut with an American signals operator. Again I had nothing to do and enjoyed the US Army breakfasts of hot cakes and broad beans. I was not so happy about the communal latrines which consisted of a long row of pit latrines open to all and sundry.

One evening after we had settled in our bunks, I was awakened by a lantern light held up by my Texan companion; he was sitting up and staring transfixed at the floor. He kept a pet parrot tied by a cord to his bedhead and an enormous python was in the process of devouring it. Its death cries had evidently awoken my neighbour. "I'm a Texan boy. I don't like snakes," he kept mumbling. Being familiar with, but not particularly fond of snakes, I seized the only weapon available, a stick, but my movements evidently alarmed the snake which must have been at least three yards long. He rapidly moved off between the bamboo floorboards and disappeared. With lantern and stick I hurriedly went down the shaky staircase, followed by the Texan, still calling, "I'm a Texan boy. I don't like snakes." But the python had made a rapid exit. We returned to our bunks, the Texan deciding to keep his lantern alight for the night.

After some weeks, I was provided with a tent and told by the US military (evidently now realising I was a commissioned officer) to make myself comfortable by a nearby beach. A few more weeks went by when quite suddenly a small vessel appeared from the south. She had been a privately owned tourist vessel, now commandeered by the Australian Navy to watch out for enemy vessels and aircraft shot down in the surrounding area. I was to take command and base the vessel, named HMAS Resurgam, at the small island of Kitava, about 20 miles to the west of Kiriwina.

Fortunately for me, the coxswain was familiar with the area and we steamed into our anchorage, very slowly, in pitch-dark. As we crawled in, a light flashed from the clifftop. The signalman answered with a flashing light—it was a Morse code message which read 'welcome to Kitava, a good Rexona town'.

Rexona was a name well-known to travellers on the Hume Highway, with a sign bearing that name erected at the entrance to most towns. I think it advertised a soap. The next day I went ashore to the lovely little white sandy beach and climbed the cliff to make myself known to Noel and Tex, the two AIF coastwatchers ensconced in what had been a missionary's base. They had been there for months and were pleased to meet another Australian. In the months that followed, sandwiched between the advent of wild storms and the periodic search for downed aircraft both American and Japanese, I was to see much of them.

Each morning when anchored in our little harbour, I would go ashore to swim and bathe in the fresh water pools quite close to the shoreline. Initially I was besieged by island onlookers but finally managed to persuade them that I liked to enjoy my ablutions alone.

On anchoring the first night of my Kitava sojourn, I saw an outrigger approaching loaded with half a dozen native girls clad in their very scant grass skirts who then began clambering aboard. I was shattered, and found on enquiry that they always came aboard at night when 'Resurgam' came to anchor. This apparently had been the practice with my predecessor, but it was certainly not going to be the practice while I was in charge. What went on ashore was not my business but aboard it was very emphatically mine. I was initially no doubt very unpopular, but the crew had no choice but to obey. I was soon to find that the unmarried girls were very free with their favours and this was well-known throughout the group. Later I was to read the notable anthropologist Bronislaw Malinowski's detailed accounts of accepted native behaviour.

In the months that followed, we seemed to spend a great part of our time seeking shelter from the wild weather, 'Resurgam' living up to its name (I will arise again). On the leeward side of the island, 'Resurgam' would plunge into enormous seas but happily for us shudder and break through to the surface again. One very wild night there was a shout and one of the crew fell overboard. With the Aldis (signal lamp) we were fortunately able to locate a very white face appearing from time to time above the waves and then disappearing again. Between wild gusts of wind we turned the ship about and more by good luck than good seamanship hauled him back on board.

On another occasion, in a very wild storm, the ship began to drag anchor and we were soon washed up onto a sandbank. The wind had reached hurricane force and looking back on that episode, I don't know how with all hands on the anchor cable, with the anchor digging itself into the sand, we were able to haul the little ship, with each wave providing sufficient water under it, to clear the sand bank, get the engine to start, and crawl out to deep water. Heading into heavy seas, the Aldis lamp on the clifftop began to blink; our signalman with difficulty retrieved the message from the coastwatchers—

"Watchman, what of the night?" Needless to say, we didn't reply but for the next 48 hours, as the winds kept changing, we crept from one part of the coast to another seeking shelter. Finally, thankfully the storms abated and we were once more able to creep back to our sheltered little bay, get the ship shipshape again, and enjoy some balmy days.

Inevitably, and always it seemed in bad weather, a cable would come designating a certain position for us to search, and there we would find nothing, or sometimes the wreck of a Japanese aircraft whose crew had gone down to a watery grave. These events were thankfully few and far between as the months went on.

I became very friendly with Noel Moodie, one of the two AIF coastwatchers. He was of average height, had fair hair and a snub nose, and was 27 years old. Noel and Tex had both served in the Middle East. Noel especially had a chequered career caught up in the siege of Tobruk and later the unsuccessful invasion of Greece when the AIF was quickly driven back to the sea by the victorious German army. He managed to escape to Cyprus and thence back to Alexandria. On returning to Australia when the 9th Division was recalled to help resist the oncoming Japanese army, there was no respite and he and Tex found themselves posted to the tiny little island as coastwatchers—not a very enviable or dangerous job.

They had not long established themselves above the only anchorage at Kitava in the old mission base when they were informed by the local native chief that a small group of Japanese were living on a tiny island a few miles to the east. There was widespread concern amongst the native population which had always been on friendly terms with an Australian missionary based on Kitava, who had wisely returned to Australia in the face of the Japanese invasion. The coastwatchers decided on a course of action and, willingly supported by the local people, they chose calm seas and set out armed with their 303s and hand grenades in a large war canoe. They were paddled across in the dead of night, landing on a small sandy beach. They soon located the Japanese camp and creeping up through the surrounding bush, they found six Japanese sitting around a small fire. Within throwing distance, they let fly two hand grenades followed by 303 rifle fire. The unfortunate Japanese barely had time to know what had hit them. There was no need for finishing off action and they returned to their canoe where their crew awaited them and paddled them safely home.

I saw a lot of Noel over the next few months. We had so much leisure time to explore the island—swimming in the sandy beaches, eating bananas, mangoes and paw paw, and sleeping on mats provided by the villagers in the warm afternoon sun. I was quite sorry when I was instructed to return to Kiriwina, the principal island with its airfield and US Army and Navy base, and await onward transport. During that time, I was able to persuade US pilots on several occasions to fly me across to Kitava to enjoy the day with Noel.

I thought that would be the last I saw of him, but extraordinarily, and to our delight, he turned up at Saidor. He was looking for onward transport to set up a coast watching base north of Madang. We had a couple of great days reminiscing about our Kitava days and I then took him by my small launch (which I used for meeting the American ships) as far as Madang which was as far as I dared go with my precious vessel. I left Noel there to go on up the coast by foot with his meagre belongings, feeling that we probably would not meet again.

Then to my regret, I received a new posting, back to Milne Bay. I handed over my little ship at the Trobriands base and again waited. Finally my transfer came through, by a PT boat to Milne Bay and thence by destroyer to an American Army and Airforce base at Saidor, to act as a pilot to the American merchant vessels bringing supplies to the base, usually the well-known Liberty ships.

I was provided with tent, camp bed, and little else but was able to find a pleasant little spot protected by a small, heavily timbered peninsula. With supplies from the American PIX shop I think it was called, rather like a well-stocked Woolworths, I was very comfortable, digging myself a slit trench to take shelter from occasional Japanese air raids. Invariably they came at night, and equally invariably my trench was half full of rainwater, but I always found myself a dry pair of pyjamas on my return to my tent.

Later I was given funds to employ local labour and materials to have a kitchen/dining room and dormitory constructed for the sailors when they arrived. All of these operations I enjoyed, supervising local labour from my tent home, but then a more senior officer arrived, and we became a Port Directorate. With my familiarity of the bay, the lieutenant commander was obviously relieved to leave the piloting duties to me—unqualified of course—and with a flat-bottomed barge I would steam out to meet the Liberty ships. I'd clamber aboard up the rope ladder let over the side for me, and try to coax the reluctant captains to come a little closer. I was always welcomed, pressed to partake of coffee and eggs and bacon, and thankfully left to pilot the ship in nearer to land. I admit I was always rather nervous about this but not nearly as nervous as the captains who would normally never come within miles of uncharted shores. Looking back now, I am astonished at the tasks I performed, untrained, but more by good luck than good management I was never responsible for putting a ship on a reef.

The little Port Directorate became a homely base with its thatched buildings and we began to receive visitors who were liaising with the Yanks or heading farther north as the Japanese army withdrew. We began to receive a variety of VIPs mostly heading north, some more interesting than others but they all seemed grateful for shelter and a meal.

One of the most unusual guests I was to meet up with during my months at Saidor was a hypnotist. He was with a group of five looking for a meal and shelter overnight. He was the only civilian amongst the other high-ranking officials—a big fellow who said little over dinner. As usual, someone produced a bottle of whisky after dinner and, at one stage, someone brought up the subject of hypnotism. The general consensus of opinion was that it was overrated. This evidently stirred the civilian who said it had its uses, whereupon he offered to demonstrate.

He looked around the room and fixed on me; I thought I caught a wink as he caught my eye. "Let me demonstrate," he said, "if you are willing." I assumed the wink was an indicator for me to cooperate in the act, so I stood before him whilst he looked directly into my eyes. "I am going to put you to sleep," he said. "Now close your eyes and listen." Then he began to talk softly, telling me to relax, to do as he said, to sleep. I felt I should play up to him and to make the act seem real. He talked quietly on saying I would do whatever he said. "Stand stiffly, hands by your side, your body stiff now, stiff as a ramrod. You are going to fall back onto my open hands." I did so and he lowered me to the floor. "Remain stiff," he said, "and I'll raise you back." Which he did, saying, "That's good. Do as I say. This time fall forward." And I did, feeling thankful I didn't land flat on my face. He then called for two chairs to be placed apart, seats facing one another, with one of the audience to stand by to help. To me, he said, "Keep stiff and firm. Remember you are asleep and obeying me." With the helper at my heels, I was told to fall back again which I did, feeling quite confident. I was picked up by heels and head and transferred onto the two chairs, heels on one, head on the other. "Remain still and unafraid and I won't hurt you," said my master. "You are strong and relaxed and unafraid." With that, he stepped briskly onto my stomach. "Relax now, but stay stiff and firm. I'm going to jump on you." And this, to my amazement, he proceeded to do. I felt I must remain stiff and strong or I would spoil the show, so I did so whilst he jumped. Then he stepped down and calling for the helper, stood me up again. "Good," he said. "You did what I said. Remain stiff and calm and slowly I will awaken you. Slowly now, awake slowly. Slowly, good, open your eyes." And to much clapping from the audience, I awoke and sat down, feeling that I had done the right thing in playing up to the audience as he had told me.

When I awoke the next morning, I began to wonder whether I had dreamed the whole act. But then when I sat up, I felt a little stiffness in the stomach and realised it had not been a dream!

The Royal Navy

Our next important visitor was the secretary to the Naval Board in Melbourne who we were warned enjoyed a gin and tonic. After dinner, and mellowed with gin, I took my courage into both hands and raised the matter of my naval career. I pointed out that I had joined the navy to go to sea, but to date my sea time had been limited to a 30 foot air-sea rescue vessel and I really wanted to serve on a 'big ship'. On reflection the next day, I thought what an impertinence it was for me, a very junior sub lieutenant, to have dared to approach an admiral. And though the gin had given me courage, I never believed anything would come of it. On departure, however, he said he would see what he could do, and that, I thought, was that.

A few weeks later came a cable instructing me to return to Australia and report to NOIC (Naval Officer in Charge) Melbourne. I found it difficult to believe my eyes but there was the cable in front of me and I wasted no time in cadging a lift with one of the US Air Force planes to Nadzab Airfield. I was on my way. I had to wait several days and decided to make some enquiries about Noel's unit, thinking someone might have news of him. To my astonishment, I found the man himself. His north New Guinea coast watching was no longer required with the rapid withdrawal of the Japanese forces, and he'd had the good fortune to be picked up by a destroyer and then found his way back to base at Nadzab. We could hardly believe our eyes and again I was able to share a tent—this time his.

It was one of those brief but close wartime friendships. Noel evidently stayed on in New Guinea for some months and then made his way to Australia, finally being demobilised and returning to his home in Nathalia, Victoria. I went off to England for service with the Royal Navy, and it was not until 1946 that I was demobilised. In due course I set out on an interstate trip and hitch-hiked my way to Nathalia. It was late afternoon and I decided to look for him at the local pub. Sure enough, there he was having a beer. I crept up behind him and grasped him around the waist. "Hi, Kitava," I said. He turned around. "Bluey, Bluey," he said, and threw his arms around me. That night we drank together, firstly at the pub, and then at his home where I met his young wife. He found me a bed and the next day I went on to Melbourne assuring ourselves that we would meet up again before long. In fact, that was the last time we met—he developed some sort of illness, cancer I think, from which he never recovered.

While short, it was a friendship which I was never to forget. Most of all I remember those balmy warm days when, without any duties or commitments, we would wander about the island, stripping off our clothes to swim from the white sandy beaches, to be welcomed to the villages, fed with tropical fruits, and given mats to sleep in the afternoon sun.

However, I digress, my transfer to the Royal Navy was in full swing. From Nadzab airfield I got a lift on an air force transport direct to Brisbane, and then by train to Sydney and Dubbo where I had a wonderful week at home before training on again to Melbourne. Here I stayed for several weeks with my aunt at Brighton, always a home away from home, and finally embarked on 'MS Tiradentes', a Norwegian freighter heavily loaded with foodstuffs and bound for the UK. There followed eight wonderful weeks of luxury and leisure.

We sailed for Wellington for a brief stopover and then set out on a long voyage to the Panama Canal. The Captain was a large jovial Norwegian and the passenger list made up of 12, mostly Australians, some diplomats, several involved with the armaments programme and a very glamorous Swedish consul. I shared a cabin with another young South Australian RAN sub lieutenant.

The captain had his own idea about dodging the Japanese submarines cruising Pacific waters, and for the first couple of weeks we ploughed through tremendous south Pacific seas before heading north again—firstly to circumnavigate the Galapagos Islands which the captain said he had never seen before, and then on to Panama, and New York where he apparently had one of many girlfriends.

We spent a very enjoyable week in New York despite it being mid-winter and the snow deep underfoot. It was the first time I had experienced snow and loved it. My navy colleague and I stayed in a very comfortable hotel off Central Park. We were warmly welcomed by the New Yorkers, invited to private apartments, taken to historical sites and the like. One night we went to the famous Zanzibar night club and listened to Louis Armstrong. After a week, our Captain decided it was time to move on—this time to Boston, where he planned to meet another girlfriend.

Alas, our visit was a brief one but permitted us to walk the city centre. The next morning, we sailed north again up to Newfoundland where we met up with an enormous flotilla of ships heavily escorted by Royal Navy cruisers and destroyers bound for London. From now on we wore lifebelts most of the time, and we were attacked by German destroyers off Ireland. It was a relief to sail up the Thames and disembark.

I was domiciled at a Naval Club in central London and awaited instructions. I would breakfast at the club and explore on foot as much of London town as I could each day. I found the club rather off-putting—it was difficult to raise even a good morning at breakfast—there's no doubt the English, though an admirable race, are not exactly easy to get to know.

Despite the V-2s which at that time were attacking London and creating sufficient alarm to cause pedestrians to throw themselves prostrate on the pavement as they passed overhead, I visited the famous sites, around the bomb damage, that I had read so much about, and was sorry when instructed to report to NOIC Liverpool. There I reported to a certain wharf thinking I was to find the 'big' ship I'd been promised. I was more than astonished to find that my 'big' ship was indeed big! A 40,000-ton battleship 'Duke of York', the Royal Navy's latest battleship soon to become the flagship of the British Pacific Fleet.

The Duke of York

Inevitably it took me weeks to settle in and familiarise myself with this enormous ship and its complement of 2,000-odd crew. Settling in was made more difficult by the preparations taking place at the end of the ship's refit to receive a visit from the King and Queen. Fortunately at this stage my duties were not onerous and I continued to find my way about and was to learn that I was the only Australian aboard. I was a junior duty officer in the focsle (forecastle, or upper deck) division and we would fall in under the shadow of the enormous 14-inch guns.

On the morning of the royal visit, the officers were falling in on the quarterdeck; the Rolls Royce drew up opposite the gangway and to the sound of piping, their Majesties King George and Queen Elizabeth came aboard. Under Captain Nicholl's guidance, they were taken on an inspection of the ships. We adjourned to the vast wardroom to await the royal couple. On arrival, we tried not to stare whilst the captain and commander did the honours. I was standing well back, intrigued of course, when a steward informed me that I was to report to the commander which of course I did, wondering what I was being called up to do. The next moment I was being presented to the Queen. I remembered enough of the correct procedure to bow and to address her as 'Your Majesty' and then 'Ma'am'. We talked quite easily for a few moments about Australia and then it was clearly time to withdraw. I remembered to bow and then back away, once away to take a deep breath!

The next day, we set sail steaming north and that night I went down with a wallop: a severe attack of malaria. I found myself in the sickbay for the next week and the centre of interest from the medical staff, unaccustomed to malaria and, of course, preparing for it in the Pacific. On deck once again, I found myself surrounded by a fleet of large ships anchored in the Orkney's principal harbour, Scapa Flow.

For the next few weeks we 'worked up' as the naval expression goes, steaming up into the North Sea, taking up action stations, firing the big guns and also, of course, the little ones (my responsibility was a bank of anti-aircraft guns), and drilling. Finally, we set sail for the Pacific war, the European war now drawing rapidly to a close.

After very heavy weather in the Atlantic, the Mediterranean was like the traditional millpond, and on the day of the end to the long European war, we steamed slowly into Valletta Harbour. Captain Nicholls, a short stocky man, stepped onto the canopy over the bridge—a small figure to us assembled on the upper deck—megaphone in hand, and piloted the ship to its anchorage. We had three wonderful days in Valletta in full fete, celebrating the end of the war, and I was able to see some of the terrible destruction wrought by war. A small piece of marble from the enormous pile of rubble which made up the Royal Opera House remains in my china cabinet to this day.

Each day, some of us went swimming in the deep warm Mediterranean and we were sorry when our ship set sail again, slowly through the Suez and onto Colombo. At Colombo, we made ready for an inspection by Admiral Mountbatten Supreme Allied Commander Southeast Asia. This was scheduled for 8 am but typically of the admiral apparently, he arrived 15 minutes ahead of schedule. We got the impression that our captain was familiar with Admiral

Mountbatten's little tricks and we were prepared for early arrival. Several years later, when he was visiting the New Hebrides with the royal family, I had the opportunity to remind him of this visit and he was quite amused.

From there we travelled down through the Indian Ocean and Australia through the Great Australian Bight, finally into Port Jackson to tie up alongside at Woolloomooloo. As the only Australian aboard, I had been asked to talk to the crew on the Tannoy (public address system) about Sydney. I said of Sydney that with its magnificent harbour and bridge, its many pubs and beer stronger than the beer the crew were accustomed to, its friendly people, and no kangaroos or poisonous snakes to meet in the streets, they would enjoy themselves, and they certainly did.

We spent two weeks in Sydney during which, with cocktail party after cocktail party, we entertained Sydney socialites and service dignitaries and I was able to show off the ship to family and friends. We sailed for Manus Island, a wartime naval base on the north New Guinea coast. We only stayed two days in Manus to take on board Admiral Fraser CIC of the British Pacific Fleet. From here on we were escorted by two destroyers, the 'HMS Whelp' and the 'HMS Wager', the first Lieutenant of the latter being Lt Phillip Mountbatten, later to become Prince Phillip and husband of HM the Queen. As a footnote to Manus Island, over three years later, with my university degree behind me, I was to return to there as a cadet patrol officer with the New Guinea field service but this was short-lived because I was then accepted for service with the British Colonial Service.

At the enormous American naval base on Guam, we were warmly welcomed and entertained on board by the CIC USS naval force's Admiral Nimitz. By this time the war was clearly drawing to a close. The terrible battle for Okinawa was over with many thousands dead on both sides and with 'Whelp' and 'Wager' by our sides, we joined the combined British and American fleets to patrol the coast of Japan. Even with binoculars, as far as one could see was this formidable array of battleships, aircraft carriers, cruisers, destroyers—the greatest fleet of warships the world has ever seen.

I had been drafted to work with Admiral Fraser's staff and was able to see the signals flowing between the 'Duke of York' and Whitehall, London, and the US Commander in Chief. Japanese forces were obviously reluctant to surrender and it was not until the Japanese emperor intervened and instructed his forces to do so, that the war was virtually over.

The Surrender

On the 27th of August 1945, we closed up at action stations and prepared to weigh anchor. As we did so, a plane crashed into the sea half a mile away, and a US destroyer quickly closed in to the site. Led by the US flagship

'Missouri' and the 'Iowa' and 'Duke of York' forming the apex of a triangle, we were led into Tokyo Bay by a Japanese destroyer flying the rising sun and accompanied by two allied destroyers, one on either side. Behind us followed an enormous array of warships virtually filling the harbour. Beyond the harbour foreshores were clusters of small houses and factory buildings, some of which were destroyed by aerial bombing; then green hills, and in the distance Mt Fujiyama, its peak snow-clad and lower down a band of cloud; the heavily bombed city of Yokohama a few miles to the north, and of course 50 miles farther north, Tokyo.

The days dragged on whilst negotiations continued over the peace terms. We moved anchorage again, this time passing the Yokosuka Naval base, and, on the foreshores, lying with its bows on the beach, a Japanese battleship badly damaged. That afternoon Admiral Fraser came up to the quarterdeck to welcome two British marines who, seeing the Wrigley chewing gum papers and Lucky Strike cigarette packages washed ashore (flags not being raised until 8 am), realised it was an allied fleet and swam out to the nearest ship, the 'Missouri'. Being British, they were then taken over to us.

That night we listened to Stanley Maxwell broadcasting their story. The marines had been taken prisoners in Hong Kong on Christmas day 1941. After fighting for almost a week without food and little water came the surrender—their bugler trying unsuccessfully to sound off the ceasefire because he was weeping. They were shipped with many others to a prison camp near Yokohama and for the next four years fed on 10 ounces of rice a day. Slapped and beaten from time to time, they were employed on the docks. When finally they saw their guards standing listening to the radio broadcast with their hats off, they guessed they were listening to the emperor. The next day the guards deserted and the two marines made their way to the bay's foreshores to see the allied ships. They were fed steak and eggs, much of which they couldn't eat, and taken to the cinema where they immediately fell asleep.

Anchored in Tokyo Bay we filled in time whilst negotiations continued. Some of us were allowed ashore to see the damage from allied bombing at Yokohama and the few Japanese we saw passed us with heads bowed. Our prisoners were being evacuated by the 'Whelp' onto the hospital ship 'Benevolence' and aircraft carriers were being converted to hospital ships as the numbers of prisoners increased.

On the 3rd of September, at last the war was officially over. The surrender ceremony took place on 'Missouri's' quarterdeck filled with top brass—high-ranking officials from the allied nations of the world. The Japanese in morning dress and top hats had been brought out to the 'Missouri' by an open launch and then conducted up the gangway escorted by armed guards. General Tojo, the Japanese Prime Minister, was the first to sign the surrender followed by other top officials of the Japanese Government. For the allies, General MacArthur signed for the USA, followed by Sir Bruce Fraser for the British Government. On his return aboard, Sir Bruce told us that MacArthur had asked him for the pen he had used to sign the surrender. Whilst the surrender procedure was carried out, a fleet of 1000 B29 bombers passed overhead in formation.

That evening, at the lowering of the colours, massed bands played and all big ship's buglers sounded off "The Last Post". The next few days with signals passing to and fro about arrangements for collecting prisoners of war, we paid formal visits to 'Missouri' and 'Iowa' and less formally to the Australian destroyer 'Waramanga'. My most vivid memory of the visit to the 'Iowa' was the enormous dishes of ice cream served to us at dinner. Finally, on the 9th of September, we sailed for Hong Kong, leaving behind one of the faithful escorts, 'Whelp', but escorted from Japan all the way to Sydney by the 'Wager'. I continued to work below in the communications office. It was unpleasantly hot and sticky but intensely interesting, reading cyphers concerning the release and collection of prisoners of war. We called at Okinawa where we offloaded reporters to report on the battle where a quarter of a million troops had been involved, and the terrible smell of unburied dead still hung over the island. It was a relief to put to sea again, this time for Hong Kong.

At Hong Kong harbour we found barely enough room to anchor. Hong Kong with its peak towering over the island to the south and Kowloon, with its mass of little houses along the foreshores to the north. The surrender had yet to be signed but all was quiet; the Japanese occupation troops having flown north leaving only a nucleus of high-ranking Japanese at their headquarters to sign the surrender. A top-secret cable came through saying agreement had been reached with the Chinese and Admiral Fraser would sign for Britain the next day, the 16th of September.

That day some of us were allowed ashore at Victoria, the principal town, and found the intrepid Chinese operating their little shops massed with the usual goods. The town itself was filthy but with little damage and we hiked our way up eventually to the peak itself with an impressive but badly damaged mansion at its top. In Victoria itself we had noticed a few Europeans, probably just released from the prisoner-of-war camp, painfully thin, their skin yellowed and drawn, taut over the cheekbones. That night, the ship dragged anchor and we bumped onto a wreck. There appeared to be little damage but it would entail slipping to check for damage when we got to Sydney.

Admiral Fraser had flown to Hong Kong for further discussions with the Chinese Prime Minister, and the next day, on his return we sailed for the Philippines. Here a brief stopover and then off again. A few days later, I came up on deck at daylight after a night watch and to my astonishment found we were sailing through the Admiralty Islands. I sat and watched for an hour and there within sight was Kiriwina to the west and Kitava to the east. With binoculars I was able to pick out our old anchorage with the mission house on the cliff above. There were several outrigger canoes on the beach but no sign of life. My thoughts went back to my friend Noel and the many long yarns up on the verandah of the old mission house. Then I was able to pick out the remnants of the 'Admiral Chase' sitting high and dry on a reef and made a mental note to pursue its history when I got home.

Passing Manus, we rendezvoused with the Australian destroyer 'HMS Quadrant', based at Manus, to collect mail. We passed Long Island on our port side, close enough for me to remember very vividly my cruise in the Beaufort bomber. Thereafter, cruising at about 18 knots, we passed the D'Entrecasteaux Islands and the southernmost tip of New Guinea on our port, and then steamed for Sydney.

Sydney had already celebrated the surrender, so it was an uneventful moment when we entered the heads. We tied up at Woolloomooloo where divers checked for damage from the wreck we scraped whilst in Hong Kong harbour. Within days, my own future was resolved—the 'Duke of York' was to head home to the UK and a cable from NOIC Melbourne told me to report to NOIC Balmoral for further duties. My fascinating days with the 'Duke of York' were over. I said goodbye to my friends, proceeded to the gangway with my kitbag and other personal belongings. I was thrilled to see Admiral Fraser there to say farewell; after my smartest salute, we shook hands goodbye.

Thereafter, I realised I would probably have a long wait until demobilisation and this was so. It was a relief to get away from the naval base HMAS Balmoral and for the next 6 months I was designated to be responsible for two minesweepers tied up alongside one another at Vaucluse. With a crew of six, we kept the little ships at least respectable on the upper decks. Finally came the day they were towed out of the heads and sunk. Back at Balmoral I received my discharge. My four-and-a-half years of naval service was over. I was free.

Darvall, Dubbo

Darvall's homemade canoe, Macquarie River at Dulla Dulla

Darvall in Scots College Cadets uniform

Darvall and Forbes Carlisle swimming competitors

Darvall and Buv riding from Sydney to Melbourne

Darvall at Dulla Dulla

Darvall and his father Stan in Sydney

Darvall, Lila and Stan Wilkins at the family home, Baringa Dubbo

Darvall in the Trobriand Islands with unidentified colleagues

Sub Lt Darvall Wilkins RAN and RN

King George VI and Queen Mary on board the Duke of York

The Duke of York sea trials

Sub Lt Darvall Wilkins Hong Kong 1945

Darvall present at the signing of the Japanese surrender, Tokyo Bay

Darvall in Japan after the surrender

Darvall's Cambridge rowing team

Three

1946 Into the Colonial Service
Preparation

I got out of the navy towards the end of 1946 and went back to Dulla for a few very happy months. During this time, I applied for and was accepted into Sydney University (under a rehabilitation scheme), to do a Bachelor of Arts Degree—something I had begun in 1941 and not got very far with when I'd joined the navy. This meant three years of study and I was based at St Andrew's College—superb years—I enjoyed every minute of it!

Towards the end of the third year, I began to think about what I was going to do for a living, what was going to be my career. About this time, I had a letter from an old shipmate from Royal Navy days on the HMS Duke of York, Ron Neath, who when he wrote was a District Officer with the British Colonial Service in Tanganyika, East Africa (now Tanzania). Ron said, "This is the job for you, Blue—make some enquiries straight away", which I did. Initially it was a pretty frustrating task because no one seemed to have heard of the British Colonial Service.

Most people confused it with the Colonial Sugar Refining Company in Fiji. After a number of dead ends, I found that Professor Steven Roberts, who had the Chair of History at Sydney University, was in fact, the British Colonial Service representative in Australia and, funnily enough, he had lectured me in my first year at Sydney uni. Professor Roberts gave me an extensive interview and a fairly thorough grilling and subsequently I had a letter from him confirming that I should appear before a selection board in Melbourne. The contact there was Professor Wadham, a charming man whom I got to know a little better later. He arranged for me to go to Melbourne, and in due course I turned up at Melbourne University in my best suit and was confronted by a very imposing array of obviously very powerful gentlemen, including Professor Wadham, the Chief Justice of Australia—Chief Justice Herron I think it was, and also I believe the Governor of Victoria.

I was a bundle of nerves but they treated me kindly and I had a very long interview. Several months went by and I had a letter from the Secretary of State in London confirming that I had been accepted into the British Colonial Service and that in due course an appointment would be made.

Another long waiting period, and finally I gave up in despair and applied to the Australian External Territories Department for a job as a cadet patrol officer in New Guinea. I was selected and did a short course at Middle Harbour just up from Mosman, and then ended up in Port Moresby. I had six weeks in Moresby on further training with a group of other young guys and then was appointed as Cadet District Officer to the Admiralty Islands. I got to Rabaul by aircraft and then had to await a ship to the Admiralties—six long weeks waiting for a ship, when I nearly died of boredom. I got to the Admiralties and reported to my District Commissioner and settled in. I was there for about six weeks and just beginning to feel that I knew a little bit about the job, when I had a cable from the British High Commissioner in Canberra. I had been accepted by the British Colonial Service and was to be appointed to Kuala Lumpur in Malaysia and to make my way to Canberra as soon as possible.

This meant flying back to Moresby after I had discussed the matter with the District Commissioner, who was very sympathetic and thought that I would be foolish not to accept. I flew back to Moresby, faced the fray, where I wasn't very popular because I had just settled in and had cost the Government a considerable amount of money on fares, training, and so on, and I was now leaving them in the lurch. Nevertheless, I thought the opportunity in front of me was too good to miss and I returned to Canberra.

I arrived there and reported to the British High Commission, was given a grant of 70 pounds to purchase a uniform, and then told to go home and wait. Fortunately, I did not at this stage spend the money on the equipment, the uniform etc. Because by the time I had made enquiries about where to get everything, another letter came from the High Commissioner. My appointment to Malaysia had been cancelled due to a state of emergency there, and they only wanted experienced people who spoke fluent Malayan. I was to wait for further instructions. Much to my delight, I found I was to proceed to London for an academic year at Cambridge, studying Swahili and law before appointment to Tanganyika.

Cambridge

I travelled to London by first-class passage and my own private cabin plus porthole on the Orient liner, 'Orantes', and was in good company, quickly making friends including the son and daughter of the Australian Governor General, Sir William McKell, who were travelling to the UK on official business.

The six-week voyage in such comfort was easy to take with delicious food, deck sports, a swimming pool, dances, concerts, and so on at night. I was quite sorry to leave the ship.

On arrival in London, I still had almost a month to wait before the beginning of the Cambridge academic year. Such time was not difficult to fill.

I hitchhiked around France and Germany, meeting up at Lubeck with an old friend from Dubbo school days and now a doctor with the British Occupation Services in Germany. In his car we visited Munich and surrounding cities and I returned to the UK to have Christmas with Ron Neath. Still based in Tanganyika as a District Officer, Ron spoke fluent French and had a number of French friends. Over the next month we travelled around southern France before he returned to Tanganyika and I to begin my year's study at Cambridge.

I was placed in Downing College, which was comparatively new having been built at the beginning of the 19th century. I was allocated a wing on the second floor which consisted of two bedrooms, the other being shared by a South African, 'Fuzz' (A.W. Crompton). All the others in my wing were doing postgraduate work. My study, however, was comprised principally of East African language, Swahili, and basic law. We wore academic gowns to dinner and of course to lectures. On my return from the continent, I wore a recently purchased dark green velvet jacket of which I was inordinately proud. To my great embarrassment on appearing at dinner in it, I was 'spooned' loudly until I took my seat. 'Spooning' was a loud beating on the table with the back of a spoon. After that, my disregard for the dress code was accepted. I suppose we all had our idiosyncrasies. The American member of our group always wore a full-length fur coat to our communal bathroom but never dared to wear it to dinner.

My South African room-mate 'Fuzz' was very agreeable, though he had some idiosyncrasies himself. It was not unusual whilst working at my desk, to hear a *ping* and a knife or dagger would be quivering in the wood panelling above my head. I was finally able to persuade Fuzz to desist in this habit, pointing out he might miss his target, and it was not exactly good for the old oak panelling. He was in love with a girl from Bloemfontein who arrived later. Needless to say, during this time I saw little of my room-mate but later, (Fuzz was a keen photographer) very graphic personal negatives would appear drying on the lounge-room curtains. I explained to Fuzz that I thought I was invading his and Mary Anne's privacy but he said, "Oh, she won't mind." A year later, on my way from Tanganyika to Cape Town and Australia, I had dinner with Fuzz and now wife, Mary Anne, in Bloemfontein, but I resisted the temptation to say that in a sense I had already met Mary Anne in Cambridge.

The year in Cambridge passed too quickly with so many distractions: regular visits to London to see the great actors of the day, concerts, and of course sightseeing, leaving little time for studying. But to my surprise, and my tutor's, I did well in Swahili which was, after all, the main purpose of my sojourn.

Mid-year, my mother came to the UK on a visit, taking up a flat at Fen Ditton, a few miles out of Cambridge. With my father's help I bought a little Austin station wagon and we planned a tour of Ireland. I asked Fuzz to join us and my mother suggested that as we could seat three in the back, we also take a couple with whom she had become very friendly on the voyage across from Australia: Ida and her boyfriend, Ian. We had a wonderful tour around Ireland. I had to remove the Australian flag from the bonnet of my car because the locals mistook it for the British flag, not popular in those days. Looking back on that trip, I thought to myself what a pity it was for me that Ida was already committed.

She was teaching at a very exclusive kindergarten in West London, one of her pupils to become the famous musical impresario Andrew Lloyd Webber. I enjoyed her easy relaxed manner, her ready chuckle, and her always attractive appearance. It was not really until my departure for Tanganyika drew near that I wished I had been able to see more of her, especially when I realised that her romance with Ian was over. As it turned out, we started corresponding, but I will get to that a little later.

Four

Vignette - Death of King George VI

During my time at Cambridge, in 1952, I went downtown from college for a haircut when someone put their head in to say there was a rumour spreading like wildfire around the town that the King had died. Later the BBC broadcasted very solemnly to that effect and closed down for the day. When I came out of the barber shop, the street was filled with groups of people standing around discussing the death.

The body of the King lay-in-state in Westminster and the whole town was adorned with red, black, and purple hangings. Lectures were all cancelled. I felt sorry for poor Princess Elizabeth over in Kenya at this time, having to come back and face what, heaven knew. When the proclamation of the Queen's accession to the throne was read out, flags were hoisted and The King's College choir, all in white, sang "God Save the Queen". The Vice Chancellor called for three cheers. Everyone was bedecked in their traditional academic gowns and it was a very impressive ceremony, bitingly cold with an occasional glimpse of sun.

I decided to go down to London for the funeral and had to run all the way from college to the station as I was running late. I went down to Westminster to try and join the queue there but it was miles long and would be a five-hour wait so I gave the idea away. I stayed on awhile in front of the main official gates—there was a huge crowd milling there, and I managed to see some of the celebrities coming in and out. I was fascinated by how the police handled the crowds.

At about 6.30, I went back to Piccadilly, had a snack, and met up with the college gang and friends, among them three Australian nurses, and we went off to a play entitled *Third Person* which was well done. Brian, one of my friends, and I arranged to spend the night on the floor of the nurses' flat in Baker St. There were six nurses sharing a very nice flat and we'd planned to rise at an unearthly hour to see the funeral. So, it seemed like only a few minutes before we were struggling into our clothes again. I had not come prepared for an early morning rise and having to face the cold, so I left my pyjamas on under my suit and was as warm as toast! The girls made sandwiches and armed us with flasks of coffee and off we went.

We were up at Hyde Park just this side of Marble Arch under a battery of television and newsreel cameras by about 6 when it was still dark. But we got into the front row stands, facing the street right on the curb. There were already hundreds of people and as it got lighter and the morning wore on, people flocked in by the thousands and soon there was a solid mass of bodies. Our feet were frozen through. Lord, it was cold! There was no room to move about and we just had to grin and bear it. Still we were lucky to get fine weather later after a bit of snow and sleet.

Then came the horses, perfectly groomed and quiet as lambs, all big fellows too! Cavalry mounted and guards in procession proper and most seemed to be able to keep in step. At 10.30 we heard the first strains of music. The procession had left Westminster Hall at 9.30. I have never seen nor am likely to see again such a magnificent procession. With each accompanying detachment, there would be a brass band of the various famous regiments playing all the different funeral marches; it was very moving, and the crowd so quiet, not a murmur. Every now and then as a new band came and the march passed up Edgware Road towards Paddington Station, there would be a deathly hush except for the slow tread of the detachment and the superb uniforms, plumes, cloaks, swords, armour, and all the rest of the regalia—quite superb! Then came the guns' carriage itself with coffin and imperial crown, with its blaze of jewels, followed by the first of the state carriages and footmen in bright red cloaks. I could see the Queen quite clearly; I was on the same side as she was sitting and I caught a glimpse of the Queen Mother and Elizabeth just as the carriage passed. Princess Margaret leaned forward a moment to wave. They were all wearing veils, poor things. How they had stood all that over the last few days is beyond me. Then came a massive array of famous figures. Despite the fact that they were doing a slow march, they passed too quickly for me but I was able to pick out a few notable people. I was trying to see as much of the Queen as I could but had an excellent view of the royal dukes who were on foot, of course, and only a few yards off. It was inspiring. Next came lots of carriages of the monarchies. Amongst them I saw the Duke of Kent very clearly and Lady Mountbatten, King Haakon of Norway, and other Scandinavian royalty. I missed Montgomery in the rush. The foregoing representatives were arrayed all in coloured uniforms, cocked hats, plumed helmets, swords etc. They were followed by numbers of representatives of Arabia, China, Africa, and India, which made me realise how well-respected England was at that time.

After this we all went our respective ways. I changed out of my pyjama underwear and was glad to do so. It had taken about 10 minutes to get our legs moving again after having to stand motionless in the crowd for so long! I was at Piccadilly Station when a 2-minute silence was observed at 2 o'clock and again it was an awe-inspiring sight. At one moment, a mad, bustling, tearing city and the next, dead quiet, not a sound. You could literally hear a pin drop. The sudden 'hush' I felt was similar to the experience I had during the war when I was coming back from Charing Cross railway station and a V-2 bomb exploded in the sky nearby—everyone paused, seeming to hold their breath. I dashed for the train and just missed it, so was late back to college.

Five

1953 Africa

Sumbawanga, Tanganyika, Africa

After another wonderful year of my postgraduate course at Cambridge, which also gave me the opportunity to do a lot of travelling, both in the UK and on the continent, I was off to Tanganyika in East Africa, by the Union Castle line. There were 14 Cadet District Officers travelling together, and of course we had a whale of a time. Some of us were going to Tanganyika, some to Uganda, and some to Kenya. We were billeted together at the Hotel Dar-es-Salaam and one of our first official engagements was dinner with the governor, Sir Edward Twining.

We sat down at a very impressive table, the governor at one end and Lady Twining at the other, with liveried African servants in long white uniforms with red muslin and tasselled fezzes on their heads. We had a wonderful meal with a lot of interesting talk, particularly with Sir Edward who was a foremost raconteur. However I found myself once again in an embarrassing position. After the main course was served, the big platters of food were passed around again and, being meat hungry after a year in England where there was still food rationing, I helped myself to a second serve of chicken. The platter was carried right around the table and I found myself the only one to have the second helping. I had to gulp down what I had taken with the rest of the 24 people around the table watching me.

I had brought out my little Austin station wagon on the ship with me and this I believe caused a bit of consternation in secretariat circles (possibly due to the cost, or perhaps because I was a colonial). My appointment was to the District Commissioner of Ufipa—bordering on the shores of Lake Tanganyika to the west and the Rukwa Valley to the east—and about 1500 miles inland. The only way to get there was by train, the car was also trucked.

I got to Tabora, where Livingstone based himself at one stage before going down to Lake Tanganyika where he was found by Stanley. I stayed a few days at Tabora reporting to the provincial commissioner, the senior administrator for the whole province (Tanganyika was divided into eight provinces). There was much discussion over my vehicle, but it was finally decided that it could probably make the grade on the rough roads. I think the powers that be were unaware of the fact that I was reasonably experienced on rough roads anyway, and we set out for Ufipa about 150 miles to the south. The provincial commissioner had very kindly located a houseboy for me, Yasini, and he proved to be an invaluable aide, a good Mohammedan like many of the Africans.

At the district headquarters in Sumbawanga, I was domiciled for a week or so with my district commissioner Randall Thornton, a man whom I found fairly difficult to get to know, but who was a very efficient administrator. I was then allocated a little house on the station, built of locally made burnt brick together with lovely red tiles. It was originally built by the Catholic mission—the white fathers in the area. It was a tiny little house with just one bedroom and a separate small kitchen-come houseboy's house about 20 yards away. The house was on the outskirts of the station, and it was not unusual at night to hear a lion roaring up in the hills which edged the Rukwa Valley, hyena scavenging in the yard, and sometimes elephant trumpeting.

Sumbawanga was a fascinating district, full of history. The Germans had established the station in the time Germany was in control of Tanganyika, prior to the First World War. The housing was all well built using local bricks. The jacaranda trees were very well laid out, and the district itself quite beautiful. Lake Tanganyika was on one side forming the westerly border, with the Belgian Congo beyond. To the south, Rhodesia, and to the east the Rukwa valley, which was part of the Great Rift Valley stretching down through the centre of Africa. One of my jobs was sub-accountant for the station, and periodically I used to take Northern Rhodesian currency (which had filtered over the border and circulated in our district) down to the government headquarters in Abercorn Northern Rhodesia, where it could be exchanged for Tanganyika shillings, which of course had filtered in the other direction.

Accountancy had never been my strong point, and I had had no training whatever in that sphere, which surprised me. I think there should have been something included in the initial training courses. About six months after I'd been there, a loss turned up in the books of some 100 shillings; and I was held responsible, although for the life of me I couldn't explain how it had happened. There was a long inquiry and finally the senior auditor from Dar es Salaam appeared and grilled me very severely. Finally, I was surcharged—I've forgotten exactly how much—I think it was the full 100 shillings, which was a big slab out of my meagre salary. Looking back later on that episode, I'm quite certain that it was my clerk, who had diddled the money out of me, but of course I was too slow to catch him.

Safaris

One of the governor's standing orders was that all district administration staff were to spend 14 days out of every month on safari, passing through and living and staying in the villages. Thus, every month I would set off. I would have somewhere near 40 porters carrying all my personal effects—including a kitchen sink. My entourage included Enriko who was there to look after my personal needs, a gun bearer to carry my beautiful 276 rifle, which I had purchased from a retiring provincial commissioner, and an askari (local policeman).

Local government was well established in Tanganyika at this stage, and one of my jobs was to check the council accounts, review the court records, and have discussions with the local council staff in each headquarters. I would go from village to village, staying overnight. I'd be met by the chief on arrival and discuss any problems with him and perhaps hold courts on matters, which were either appealed to my court from the local government court, or more severe crimes which could only be dealt with by myself or the district commissioner.

During my safaris, my practice was to send the porters with Enriko ahead to the village where I intended to camp, and I would diverge to visit neighbouring villages. On one particular occasion, after my porters—with Enriko in charge—had set off, my gun bearer and I on bicycles (which I had borrowed for this particular safari) peddled off in the direction of the next village. It was a beautiful morning, bright and sunny, the temperature just right. I was peddling along with my gun bearer 50 yards ahead with the 276 over his shoulders, me with my camera on my back, and was thinking what a wonderful life it was, when suddenly, without any warning, a buffalo leapt out of the thick undergrowth on my side of the road. He couldn't have been more than three yards away, and I could virtually smell his breath! With his sudden appearance, I jumped off my bicycle, which was probably the silliest thing to do. I later realised I should have just peddled on. I stared horrified at the buffalo which just stared back and I can still see his red bloodshot eyes glaring at me! I looked quickly to the gun bearer, who had also jumped off his bicycle, and signalled frantically to bring the gun back. But quite sensibly, the gun bearer stayed where he was. I thought the best thing to do was to climb a tree, but there wasn't a tree within sight, and in the meantime the buffalo was obviously becoming annoyed at my presence and was beginning to stamp his hoof and lower his head, a sign that he was about to charge. I was just about paralysed with fear by this time, gripping my bicycle which I thought might be some protection when he charged. I suddenly had the inspiration to use the bicycle bell. It was an old-fashioned cling clang bell on the handlebars. I gave the bell a clang and the buffalo suddenly turned, raising his head to look back at me and dashed off into the bush. It was an incredible relief I might say because only a few weeks before a friend of mine had been badly gored by a wounded buffalo. He told me it had been a most horrifying experience. He was in hospital for days with broken ribs and a lacerated chest. The only thing he could remember was seeing the bloodshot eyes, and the stinking breath of the buffalo. This came back to me when I was looking at my friend on the side of the road.

The buffalo episode eventually appeared in the Tanganyikan newspaper—the *Tanganyika Standard*—because the wife of the public works officer there was a correspondent for the paper and was always desperate for news. I remember she enjoyed another of my animal experiences.

When I finally got to the last village of the day, where Enriko with the porters had preceded earlier, I would find my enormous tent erected. It was really a very big tent, I think about 20 foot by 10 foot, the size of a decent room with a verandah front. My canvas bathroom rigged with a canvas shower bucket, separate toilet with a wooden seat on legs (which was all part of the safari equipment in those days), my camp bed made up, a mat on the floor, the safari table and chair set out in the protected hood/verandah affair in front of the actual tent, and the table set of course. Enriko would have heated water over the fire and have filled the shower bucket with the hot water so that I could shower and change for the evening into the regulation long trousers—one had to wear long trousers at night because of the malarial mosquito. I'd sit down to perhaps a roast guinea fowl which I might have shot during the day, or something hot like a stew. After dinner, I'd usually have a meeting with the chief and villagers which would go for a couple of hours before turning in for the night.

Ida

Once settled in Sumbawanga, Tanganyika, I decided to write to Ida, and received welcome replies. The correspondence, so welcome in the outreaches of Tanganyika, developed and it began to dawn on me that she could well be talked into calling in on me en route home to Australia. In hindsight, that idea really could not have been more preposterous but in my next letter I suggested it and to my amazement soon received a reply saying she was looking into the possibility. Within weeks, to my excitement, she had cleared the proposal with her father (much to my astonishment) and arranged to disembark from the P70 liner at Aden. From there she flew to Nairobi, then involved in the Mau Mau uprising, and stayed with friends she'd met on the ship as far as Aden. In Nairobi she was given a small pistol to keep in her bag whilst they did some sightseeing around Nairobi town. Seeing that she had never even handled any sort of gun before I was again astounded that she was unperturbed.

From Nairobi she flew to Dar es Salaam where I had arranged for a friend to meet her and accommodate her until she boarded the train for Tabora, a long overnight journey. In Tabora, I arranged for the District Officer to meet her and provide accommodation overnight when she caught a train to Mpanda; here she was the only European passenger on board. To my shame, I was late meeting the train having driven overnight from Sumbawanga to join her. There she was sitting alone on the deserted platform with not a sign of the anxiety she must have felt after a thousand-mile journey across Tanganyika. She was certainly pleased to see me!

The next month was a very happy one. We had just been allocated a new

Cadet District Officer, Jeffrey Crellin, a tall young Englishman, a very nice fellow, whom I was to get to know very well indeed. Of course, I had to take him along as a chaperone. It would have been frowned upon to have gone off alone in that era—we had our first tour down into the Rukwa valley to see the hippopotami. Later to the shores of Lake Tanganyika by canoe to see the crocodiles and of course more hippo; then inland to the open bush to see lion, giraffe, zebra, wildebeest, buffalo, and herds of smaller game. In between sightseeing, I managed to justify my existence by dealing with the court cases, paying labour, supervising road maintenance, inspecting schools and dispensaries.

When not camping out, accompanied of course by Jeffrey, either in the open bush or in government rest houses, we managed to eat our evening meal alone in my little one-bedroom house, dinner cooked and served by my cook, Enriko. Of course, Ida would stay overnight with my immediate neighbours, Kevin and Beverly, who were very understanding.

On another occasion, I decided to take her out to look for game. So off we went on a safari in my little Austin station wagon. We stayed overnight at one of the rest houses which were strategically placed throughout the district, very comfortable ones too, with essential mod cons.

The next morning, we arose at the crack of dawn which was the time to go and look for game. In the little Austin, we followed a narrow track winding through the scrub. This was a road used by the Arab and Indian traders bringing their merchandise from the railhead to the district. We were driving slowly along when on the right-hand side of the road I noticed a mob of hyena in the process of devouring an animal. We stopped the car and got out—Jeffrey, Ida, and I, together with two game rangers whom I'd picked up that morning to come with us. They both had rifles and I had my own rifle over my shoulder. We walked across and as we did so, the hyena moved back into the bushes. It was just light scrub with a few trees of reasonable size. The dead beast was a kongoni (an African antelope), and the hyena had obviously just come in to finish off what had been the meal of a lion—you could see the lion claw marks on the back of the animal. I was in the process of pointing this out (with all my wide experience of game after a year in Africa) to Ida and Jeffrey when we heard a truck approaching. I said that perhaps we should move on because the truck might disturb the game we were hoping to see. I was suddenly aware that the noise was not coming from the road, in fact it was coming from above us, and we looked up into the small tree that couldn't have been more than 20 feet high. The noise was an angry growling from a lioness that had been sitting in the tree. She leapt down past us, not more than a couple of yards away, and dashed across the road and disappeared into the bush. We were all open-mouthed. I hadn't even thought to unshoulder my rifle, nor had the game wardens.

Obviously, the lioness was in the process of devouring her kill when she saw us approaching in the car, had climbed the tree to be on the safe side so that she wouldn't be seen, and had sat there watching us while we discussed the kill. She then became annoyed, or frightened, or disturbed, and decided to come down, giving a tremendous roar as she did so. This frightened the life out of all of us.

Inevitably we fell in love, and when I took Ida to Abercorn, Rhodesia, our nearest airfield, to catch her flight to Johannesburg and Sydney, we decided to announce our engagement.

Wildlife

On another occasion, I had a third exciting encounter with game, this time an elephant. We were in the same area as I had been with Ida and Jeffrey when we met up with the lioness. It was a fascinating part of the district, flat terrain with lots of the tall acacia umbrella trees that you so often see in African films, and massed with game. To one side of the road, I suppose half a mile in, through fairly thick bush, was a lake. I had never seen so many birds of all descriptions in my life. There were literally hundreds of thousands of them. I decided to turn off the road and follow a little winding sandy track through the bush to the lake, where quite often you would see game drinking, particularly the antelope, and sometimes elephant.

As usual, I was in the little Austin. Enriko was with me and between us we had my rifle which I always carried or a gun bearer carried for me if I was on a foot safari. As we moved slowly along the rough track, I started wondering if we would get stuck. We turned a sharp corner, and there right in front of us was an enormous bull elephant. Without exaggeration, he would have been at least 12 feet at the shoulder because he towered above us. He was not more than five yards away from the front of the car. I stopped immediately as the last thing I wanted to do was to run into him. I left the engine running. Whether the noise or the smell of the engine intrigued him I don't know, but he raised his trunk and peered at us and then very slowly raised his enormous ears, usually a sign of annoyance. I looked across at Enriko, who had turned a rather sickly pale grey. No doubt I had turned completely white. I tried to reverse, thinking that discretion was the better part of valour, but in a panic, I stalled the engine and we got stuck in the sand. It was then that he began to move around us. With his trunk raised sniffing and with ears flapping, the giant of an animal walked slowly around us and then stalked off into the bush. It took us some time to collect our wits and move on, but I must say that we were very lucky not to have been attacked because he was obviously in two minds as to whether we should be trodden on or left alone. Fortunately, he decided on the latter.

Rather shaken, we went on to the lake. There must have been at least 1000 buffalo drinking on the lake that day. They made a black line along the water's edge. The wild game of Africa fascinated me, it had always done so, and I made the most of every opportunity to see all that I could. The Ufipa district was particularly interesting because, although there were no game reserves, there was a tremendous amount of wild game throughout the district: hippo in their hundreds down on the Rukwa Valley, elephant, lion, kongoni and the various antelope, zebra, and giraffe. It was very common to see giraffe, particularly in the early mornings. They were a magnificent sight as they stood and looked at us on the side of the road. When disturbed, they galloped at full speed through the bush, and were seemingly able to dodge every limb with their high necks swaying as they rushed through the timber.

Although I always carried a rifle, I was never keen on shooting. A lot of the government officials used to take out licences which were permitted. One licence a year, for example, to shoot an elephant could be quite a lucrative exercise if you were a good shot. Even in those days the tusks could bring anything from 100 to 200 pounds sterling. This supplemented what was a pretty meagre salary for most of us. But I had no love for shooting game, and the only game I did shoot were antelope, and the superbly edible guinea fowl. They could be seen in the hundreds, and I remember on one occasion having a shot at guinea fowl—there were about 50 or 60 on the road in front of us. I got about five with the one shot, and distributed these later in the village. Enriko was a past master at cooking guinea fowl, and he would do so often with crushed peanuts, making a sort of peanut stew, and it was really delectable.

In normal circumstances game was not that dangerous, however you needed to be sensible, and take avoiding action when you became entangled. For example, if you struck an elephant or a herd of elephants, you would certainly give them right of way, similarly with lions. The only time lions could be dangerous would be when you stumbled upon a female lioness with its young, which I fortunately never did. Several times I ran into a pride of lions on the road, and on one occasion stopped quite close to them, turned off the engine, put up the windows, of course, and waited. They played on the road. One of the male lions came up and examined the car, sniffed the tyres very suspiciously, and then walked back to its family, and slowly they moved off into the bush. This sort of thing was not unusual.

Leopards are very shy, and were seldom seen. The only time I ever saw a leopard was in the early morning, or late evening flashing across the road. We did have one occasion where an African was brought in with an incredibly horrible head wound where a leopard had swiped him. He had apparently been walking through the timbered country when he disturbed a leopard, and she had completely scalped him. He did however recover.

One of the most horrifying experiences was seeing hippo in the Rukwa Valley, during a drought and famine in the district. The river itself and the waterholes had dried up and there was just thick mud. There were literally hundreds of hippo dead and dying in this mud. It was a terrible sight and I'll never forget it. If I recall rightly, the *National Geographic Magazine* did an article on that particular famine.

Famine was, at that time, a terrible problem in parts of Africa, particularly the north, and one of my jobs during the famine was to take out food relief in the form of *muhogo* or cassava—a root crop, very hardy and quite nutritious. I would take truckloads of the *muhogo* and issue it to the village. Although it was nutritious, it looked pretty grim and was always vermin riddled, and I often used to think that it really wasn't suitable for human consumption, but at least it did keep people alive.

The snakes were one of our biggest worries in East Africa. I remember not long after having arrived in Sumbawanga, we had a very tragic accident. Loti Damm was the daughter of a German couple who lived in the district. They had a plantation, or at least a farm not far from the *boma*, the headquarters of the government. She married a very nice young fellow who worked in the Mpanda mine. They hadn't been long married, I think it was only about two months, when he went out early one morning with one of his African workers by foot to bring the cattle in. Apparently, he disturbed a Gaboon viper on the path and it attacked and struck him, and he collapsed within a matter of minutes. The African worker dashed back to the house to call Loti, and she came running and they carried him home where he collapsed. She wasn't an experienced driver, but she got him into the truck to head for the little hospital. It had been raining all through the night and more than half a mile down the road she bogged, and apparently by this time the unfortunate fellow had died. It was a terrible experience, and it cast rather a shadow over the district for a long time.

Probably the most dangerous was the puff adder, a most repulsive-looking thing—short, thick, and fat. I suppose about two or three feet long. They had an unpleasant habit of sleeping curled up at night on the paths—presumably because it was warmer. I always used a torch walking about in the dark. They were as tough as could be.

The Gaboon viper was likely the most feared, because it quite often attacked on sight, and the other very unpleasant snake was the spitting cobra. It was quite amusing, in retrospect, when my parents visited me at Mpanda later on after I'd transferred from Sumbawanga. We had, as elsewhere, an outside toilet, a pit latrine, and on this night my father took a torch to go to the toilet. When he got there, there was a spitting cobra snake curled up on the toilet seat. He very wisely beat a hasty retreat. He asked for a rifle, but I despatched it with a shotgun. The spitting cobra has a very deadly spit and the saliva can cause immediate blindness and sometimes permanent blindness.

I always carried a snakebite kit and in those days it was the Fitzsimmons Complete Snake Bite Outfit prepared in South Africa. It comprised a little vial of Condes crystals which was the treatment then, and a lance fitted into a little capsule and a syringe with an anti-snakebite serum. I had it in a tiny little haversack which I always carried with me. Fortunately, I never had to use it but it was always a comfort to have.

Those two or three years of district work in Tanganyika were quite fascinating, above all because of the game I think. The work was interesting, but I never really felt that I came to grips with the work of a District Officer, as I did later in the New Hebrides. I was known as *Bwana Shauri* which is a master of all business. *Shauri* was a very useful Swahili word which meant 'any particular problem, business, or difficulty' and people would come to the headquarters and want to see the district commissioner or the *Bwana Shauri* District Officer, for any problem or matrimonial dispute, or what have you. Mkuwubwa was the big master—the district commissioner. The Africans always addressed the European officials as *Bwana*. Really the translation would be 'Mr', but *Bwana Shauri* was my title as it was for all the District Officers throughout the territory.

Probably one of the reasons why I never felt that I achieved very much in Tanganyika was that it took some years to become experienced and fluent in Swahili. I had studied it at Cambridge, and had a reasonable working knowledge, but was not articulate enough to feel that I really got to know Africans as I was to know Melanesians in the New Hebrides later on. Looking back, I didn't make any lasting friendships with the Africans. Mind you, I think that the attitude of the European officials of the Colonial Service in those days was perhaps a little different to what it was to become later. They were always, I think, masters, but most certainly very dedicated to the job at hand.

Marriage

When I was able to persuade the authorities to let me take 'local leave' in Australia at Ida's Sydney home, we were married in Mosman on the 30th of April, 1955. With my Peugeot station wagon which I had brought out on leave with me from Africa, we enjoyed a honeymoon on the Gold Coast when it comprised little more than a typical local pub, a couple of restaurants, but with very upmarket blocks of units where, of course, we stayed.

On returning to Africa, we travelled by P&O to Bombay, embarking there and catching an onward vessel, the British India line for Kenya, Zanzibar, and finally Dar es Salaam. En route, poor Ida developed an infected tonsil and the Indian ship's doctor advised us that if it did not improve that night, he would have to "use the knife". To our relief, the next day the infection began to abate and within a few days she had recovered.

Based in Dar Es Salaam (and not up-country again as we had hoped), we settled into a comfortable little cottage (with Yasini, my houseboy from my previous tour to do the basic housework), we continued what became an extended honeymoon. I worked normal office hours under the Chief Secretary, returning home at lunchtime to join Ida or take a picnic lunch to the beach. Within a few weeks of enjoying our beach-time picnics, Ida said one day with panic in her voice, "I can't find my ring." We searched frantically through our clothes, our picnic basket, but no ring. Then we began searching the sand. The tide had turned, coming in fast, and I decided to dash home for a shovel and a piece of gauze. On return, Ida was still frantically searching. I spread out the gauze, took a shovelful of sand, and sifted … and there it was—blue sapphire glinting in the sunlight.

Our most enjoyable weekends were passed camping in the Peugeot station wagon in the middle of the game reserves. At night we often heard animals shuffling around but fortunately probably for us it was too dark to see and we slept on. Thus, a wonderful year passed. Then Ida became pregnant and we celebrated that by spending a local leave climbing Kilimanjaro (some of the way)—training through Nairobi and Entebbe, launching along Lake Victoria, and up the Murchison River to the famous Murchison Falls, which had figured so spectacularly with its crocodiles, hippo, and elephant in the Katherine Hepburn and Humphrey Bogart film, *The African Queen*.

With the imminent arrival of our first child Karen, Ida and I decided we'd like to live closer to Australia. The end of my two year term of employment was approaching and so I applied for a transfer to a country closer to home. When I was appointed to the New Hebrides, we had to look it up on a map!

Karen

On the second of April 1957, after twenty hours of labour, our gorgeous baby daughter Karen was born in the Ocean Road Hospital, Dar Es Salaam, Tanganyika. She was the sweetest little baby with blue eyes and golden hair and a suggestion of a curl. Ida was two weeks overdue and it was an anxious wait for me. I was described as 'looking pale and thin', however that quickly changed to 'relaxed and shining' once Karen had safely arrived. In that first week while Ida and baby were in hospital, I counted the hours and minutes until hospital visiting time which was a measly half an hour daily. In between work I busied myself with final nursery room preparations. Their homecoming was a joyous occasion and thus parenthood began. Looking back, Karen's birth in Tanganyika was certainly Ida's most civilised and safest birthing experience.

When she was six weeks old, we shipped down the African coast to Durban, trained to Johannesburg and Cape Town, and there boarded a merchant ship to Sydney. With only 12 passengers, we were very spoilt, our fellow passengers always ready to look after Karen who was fortunately very easy and happy.

Six

Vignette - Dar es Salaam 1957- Article for the Australian Women's Weekly by Ida M. Wilkins

A hyena shuffling around the house at night and knocking over our garbage tin; a lioness seen by my friends on their way home from the pictures last week; a leopard on the golf course, and a spitting cobra on the back drive of our home are all part of living in Dar es Salaam, Tanganyika's capital.

Life out here for me began in August after becoming the wife of a district officer in the British colonial service, at present stationed in Tanganyika. I had already tasted a little of the life in this territory by spending six weeks in the western corner in 1953, with many exciting safaris and glimpses of wildlife. Presuming that we would be living in a similar spot, somewhere in 'darkest Africa', we sailed from Sydney in July 1955.

To reach Tanganyika, a change over at Bombay was necessary. We docked in a monsoonal downpour! Instead of a leisurely stay over at the luxurious Taj Mahal hotel, we found ourselves transferring to 'The State of Bombay'– a vessel at which we had tossed a disdainful glance from the promenade deck of the majestic 'Himalaya'. Clutching our numerous belongings and battling through hundreds of Indians waving to their friends on board, we were last to clamber up the gangway. We checked our luggage, mopped our brows, and realised we were Africa bound – after a stay of one and a half hours in India.

Out of the passenger list of 900, we found four other Europeans on board. Some of the Indians travelled 'bunk class' (they slept on the hatches, decks and passageways), others in cabins 'with or without food'. We had booked a cabin with food and were very agreeably surprised to find ourselves in a deluxe suite – beds and private bathroom, very pleasant despite the odour of garlic wafting in from the next-door cabin, occupied by a family travelling cabin class without food. We enjoyed getting to know our fellow passengers over biryani, keema curry, samosas and chicken pilau at the dinner table, at deck games and at the ships concert despite the loud and incessant Indian music over the broadcast. After twelve days at sea, we reached the coast of Africa, firstly Mombasa in Kenya and finally Tanganyika.

Dar Es Salaam! Does that sound as intriguing to you as it did to me when I first labelled my luggage with that name which means 'haven of peace?' It is certainly that – a delightful natural harbour, small, with a narrow entrance and fringed with coconut palms. As well as ocean liners, the romantic Arab dhows still sail in from Arabia, India, and Zanzibar laden with Mangalore tiles, camphor wood chests, mangrove poles, carved wood from Kashmir, and Persian carpets.

The town itself is one of contrasting architecture of Arab, Indian, German and European influences. Avenues of Poinciana trees, large, cool homes, and buildings such as Government House and the hospital, show the careful and attractive planning of the Germans when this territory was German East Africa. Today, although progress with the large modern buildings is rapid, there is a decided combined eastern continental look about many – old and new.

The shops are quite fascinating, ranging from very modern up-to-date stores to tiny Indian 'dukkas' with the inevitable sewing machine working overtime, stitching up garments of every kind; made to order at an extremely low cost. A sudden important invitation requiring a new frock need not be a worry – one can always buy a dress length, lovely Indian sari edgings and braids, and have a new creation the next day. A strapless ballerina with stole cost me 50 shillings, - and a cotton day frock 20 shillings; sandals and shoes made to order for 20 or 30 shillings.

Shopping in town is a very hot occupation, even at 8 am, but always full of interest. Early in the morning, along the paths leading around the harbour, streams of Africans always in single file, can be seen hurrying to the open markets with their wares balanced on their heads. Recently I sat in the car and watched them come off the ferry, the men carrying huge baskets of mangoes, oranges, pineapples, bananas and pawpaws; neatly made cages containing three or four cockerels, mats, beds, and baskets; the women with sleeping babies on their backs carrying enormous bundles of coconut fronds; smartly dressed youths with their briefcases tucked under their arms and groups of chattering girls carrying gay bundles to match their attire. I even saw a little girl with a cake of washing soap set firmly on her tightly curled hair. Not only does this method of carrying one's belongings give unrestricted use of both arms but it has given African women a poise which we Europeans seldom attain.

The African loves clothes, especially the men, and the more worn the richer he feels, even if each garment is in threads. So, on the hottest day here in Dar es Salaam or far away in any village, it is not unusual to see an African with two or more pairs of shorts, and similar number of shirts or even an ex– army great coat. The women look very colourful in the gay kangas of red, yellow, orange, and green worn swathed around the body and another draped over the head and shoulders. Muslim women however, wear a black Kanga over the head and held across the face.

The main street is always filled with Europeans shopping like myself and the inevitable tourists from a visiting ship, keenly pricing curios from Kashmir, India, and Zanzibar and bargaining with the Africans on street corners. They sell local ebony carvings of animals, birds and figures, very attractive baskets, mats, wooden stools, and shells. Indian women in the graceful Saris and the men in white with black feathers are to be seen; Arabs in turbans with ceremonial daggers tucked in their belts, and of the African pedestrian, the most striking are the Masai warriors – if one is lucky enough to see them so far away from their own province. One day I saw a group strolling along, holding up traffic at crossroads as they gazed at the busy scene about them. Dressed only in red – brown blankets knotted on the shoulder; orange, mauve, and white armlets, necklets, anklets, and earrings decorating the ochred bodies and hair and carrying spears, they made an intriguing picture.

Our home is only ten minutes from town by car, but I seem to be able to avoid frequent trips for provisions owing to the enterprise of the Indian shopkeepers. There are many to choose from and they all call daily for orders. Our grocer keeps practically everything including bread, fruit, and vegetables, and if I need meat urgently, I can always add it to the grocery list. Mr Megju will obligingly go to the butcher for me, sending everything at midday and just adding the cost of the meat to his account.

The shopping I enjoy most, and I think the African does too, is buying at the door because it always involves a little haggling. A tinkle of a bicycle bell at the back door or the call 'hodi', (meaning may I come in) announces closed baskets of fish, oysters, prawns, lobsters; a huge open basket strapped to a bicycle or balanced on a head and containing oranges, mangos, pineapples, bananas, limes, lemons, corn, tomatoes, a bunch of good garden brooms or Turk's heads at two each a dozen eggs, etc, etc. The amount carried is quite amazing! One gets to know the boys who arrive with a twinkle in the eye ready to ask double the amount they expect to be paid. A one shilling pineapple can usually be bought for fifty cents (100 cents to the shilling); quite often three for a shilling is possible. Limes usually start off at 25 for a shilling but 45 clinches the deal. They make a delicious cool drink. For fish, quite a battle is waged, starting at about four shillings for a medium- sized one and ending up at two shillings with the vendors cycling off quite happily. Yasini called me the other morning before breakfast to do business with an African carrying a forlorn- looking fowl tucked under his arm. He asked for four shillings for it but was quite happy to accept two, and a few minutes later we heard the poor bird utter its last squawk! Yasini had it dressed in no time and was disappointed that I didn't put it on for lunch there and then!

Many interesting and amusing incidents take place every day. The back of our house looks across towards an African village where our house boy lives. On the way through a coconut plantation, he passes a few scattered houses including one owned by an old African woman. He asked if she could have water from us each day – it costs one cent for a debe (a 4 gallon kerosene tin) so each morning she comes twice to have her debe filled. I quite often do it for her as she stands at the door with a toothless grin conversing a little in Swahili.

When filled, it is quite an effort to lift it to her head. Yet she goes off with it balanced easily and gracefully. One morning, I found a bunch of ripe bananas on the kitchen table. Yasini said the 'mama' had sent them to me.

A dark wet day seems to make the usually happy singing African quite miserable. One rainy Saturday morning, I had been playing the piano and not noticed a very quiet house. When I decided to investigate, there was no sign of Yasini and Idi (our garden boy) anywhere, but on leaving the kitchen I heard a faint cough. There they were huddled under the kitchen table, with heads between knees, sound asleep.

Like all house boys, Masini wears a red fez and white kanzu gown. Yesterday, when he came I noticed he looked different but didn't think anything of it until later when he raised his fez with a broad grin. Underneath it, instead of loosely cropped fuzzy hair, was a shining bald head! He said it was much cooler for Dar es Salaam. Speaking of haircuts, Indian barbers visit the houses regularly and if my husband is out when his particular barber comes, no matter as he will call each day until he finds him in!

Here in Dar Es Salaam one has very little contact with Africans compared with life 'up country' where there are a few Europeans and large African villages, but there is still the politeness and unfailing greeting of 'jambo memsahib' or 'jambo bwana' (how do you do lady or mister) by man, woman, or child as they pass by in the street or come to the door. My difficulties with the language is still a daily worry and the Swahili dictionary lives in the kitchen and enables me to cope with the back-door callers. The greater the excitement, the quicker the African speaks, so my chance of recognising one or two words was very slim when the house boy from next door came to tell me something one day. At length, realising that he wanted me to follow him into our neighbour's house, I went, wondering what I was going to find. It was my husband on the telephone, quite a relief after conjuring up a vivid picture of someone lying unconscious on the floor from a snakebite! Before I learned the Swahili words for the various garden tools, our garden boy used to stand at the door and go through the actions of cutting grass, digging, and raking according to whatever tool he required, all done with a broad grin!

The African method of cutting grass by swinging a bent piece of hoop iron brings forth a group of Africans every few weeks to mow the green in front of our house. Laughing, shouting, and singing, they work for a short while then rest for much longer, but never their tongues. Their day is not a hard one but that is typical of a happy people who have always lived from one day to the next, satisfied with enough money for daily food and new clothes.

Some of the enterprising women become work gang followers with a huge pot of food-usually hot beans - dishes and spoons balanced on their heads. They charge 25c a dish, which Yasini says is far too much! When a gang was painting our house, I was quite fascinated by a very large, colourful mama who used to squat on our path each morning with her tremendous pot in front of her, dishing out beans to those who could afford it. The dash of colour, laughter, chatter, and clatter of dishes made a wonderful picture! I noticed it took two people to lift the pot to her head, yet she seemed to carry it without effort.

Although we live on the edge of a suburban area, we often see hyena and snakes. Just picking a banana leaf in our garden to cover some seedlings startled a long green snake which darted at me; a spitting cobra which aims very accurately for one's eyes, which was duly dispatched. However, the thrill of seeing game in its natural surroundings in the African bushlands lures us away to the country as often as we are able to go. Packing the car with safari, gear we spent many weekends looking at and photographing with the cine camera the game for which East Africa is world renowned – elephant, giraffe, buffalo, rhino, hippopotami, zebra, lion, leopard etc. The thrills we experienced when my husband was near Lake Tanganyika, which separates the Belgian Congo from Tanganyika, will have to be told another time. My six short weeks there were filled with adventure; the biggest thrill was when we stood examining a dead antelope and were suddenly made aware of a snarling lioness in a tree above us!

Just to finish. The reports of people's experiences with game make the daily paper out here a little more exciting to read than the newspapers in most other parts of the world. These reports come from all over the territory and could be anyone's story as wildlife is scattered throughout the greater part of Tanganyika. A recent report concerned a traveller who was having engine trouble so he stopped to investigate the cause. Busy with his head buried under the bonnet, he was suddenly conscious of another presence and looked up to see an Elephant taking playful swipes with its trunk at the rear mudguard. Fortunately, and much to the traveller's relief, it then sauntered off! Another person travelling home with a truckload of goats heard a commotion and turned around to see a lioness devouring one of the goats! The lioness stayed put on the truck whilst he raced for home, then well fed, disappeared into the bush before the owner returned with a gun!

This last story is a gem, I think and is actually in today's paper. A little girl, Monzi, was standing in a river washing her clothes when a crocodile grabbed her leg. She bent down and bit the crocodile's nose. When the croc let it go, so did Monzi!! I asked Yasini what he thought of the story. 'Labda' (perhaps), he said.

Darvall at Cambridge University

Lila, Ida, Darvall and friend touring in the UK

Darvall and Ida holidaying in Africa with their chaperone, Jeffrey Crellin

Ida and Darvall in Sumbawanga when first engaged

Darvall and Ida wedding

Darvall and his beloved Austin station wagon in Africa

Darvall and Ida, work lunch in Dar Es Salaam

Darvall filming

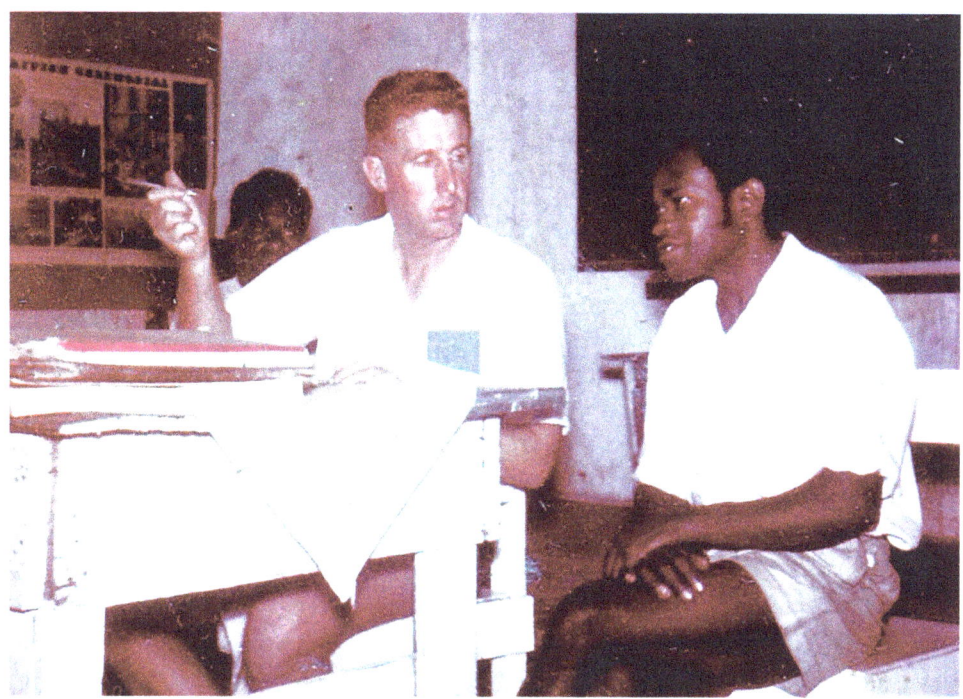

Darvall holding court in Africa

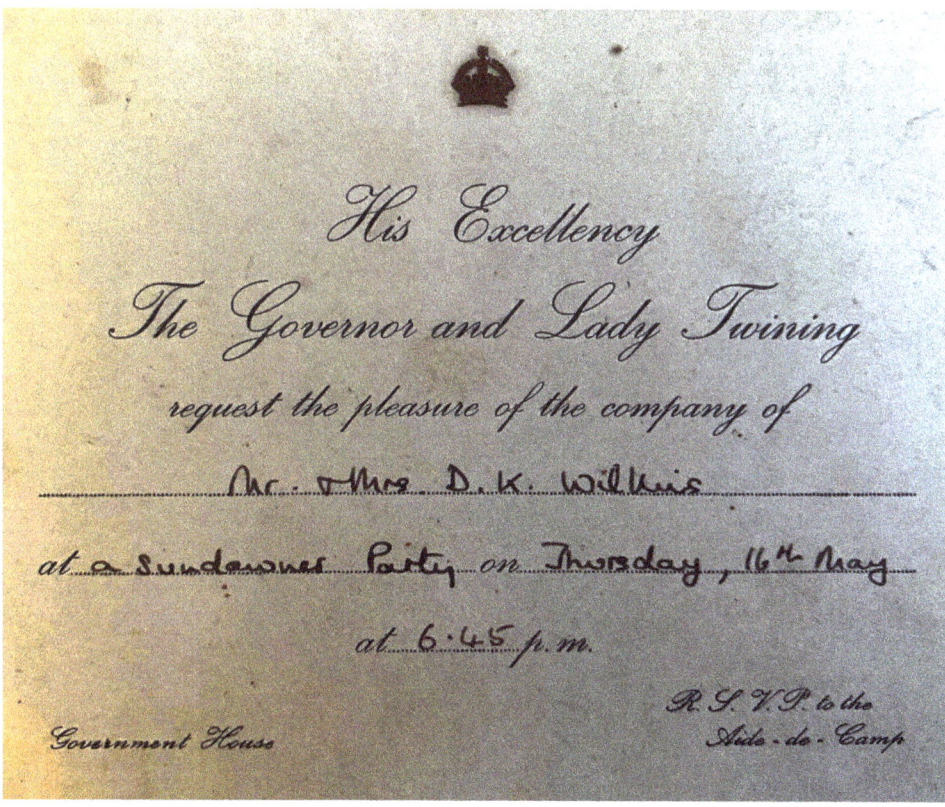

Invitation to a party in Dar Es Salaam from Darvall's boss, Lord Twining

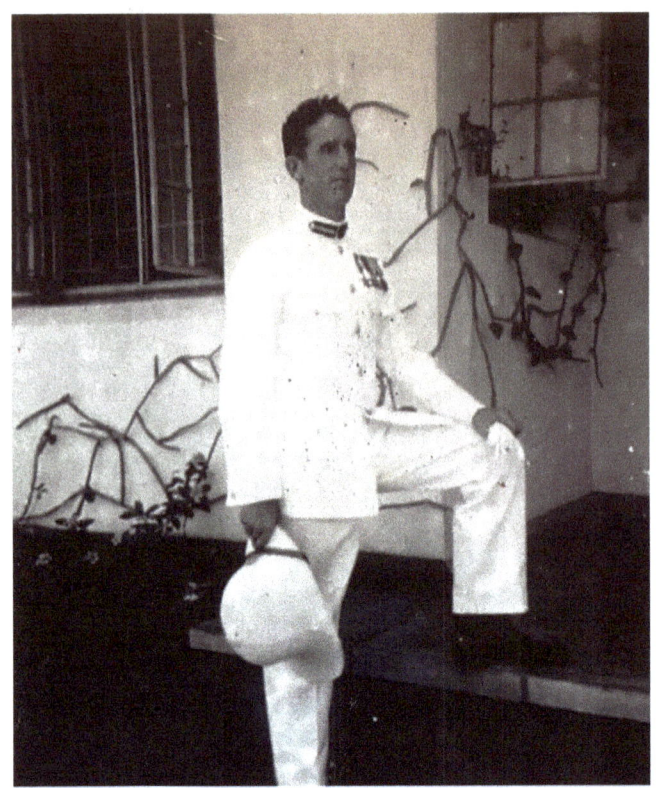

Darvall in colonial uniform, Dar Es Salaam, Africa

Darvall, Ida and Karen on holidays from Africa

Darvall's touring camp in Tanganyika, Africa

Darvall on tour in the New Hebrides

Tanna agency views

Tanna agency

Darvall, unidentified, M.Duc Dufayard on Tanna

Simon, 'smol masta', with policeman on Tanna

Ida, Karen and Simon on Tanna

Darvall, Ida, Karen and Simon on Tanna

Santo family shot

Ida and friends at a party in Santo

Karen and Simon dressup party

Karen and Simon Santo English School

Darvall BDA CD2 takes up residence at Bushmans Bay

Original CD2 Agency at Bushmans Bay

Alan Samson, Darvall, Tinsley Lulu, unidentified, Tabia Kalsakau at Lakatoro in the early days

Lakatoro offices being built

Lakatoro first Agency, the original plantation house

Darvall's first office at Lakatoro

The new office at Lakatoro

The old Norsup airport

Seven

1957 South Pacific
Vila, New Hebrides

After four months leave in Dubbo and Sydney, we set out on a new venture to the Anglo-French condominium of the New Hebrides in the South Pacific. On a beautiful sunny Saturday morning, we sailed from Sydney Harbour on 'The Caledonian', a maritime vessel of about 20,000 tonnes. The sunlight twinkling on the waves, the ship sailed slowly towards the heads, whilst we waved frantically to my mother, Lila Wilkins, and Ida's mother and father, Marjorie and Horace Mackay, who had waited patiently on the wharf until we were out of sight.

We had a very comfortable cabin, quite large, and a bathroom attached. I think there must have been about 20 passengers of whom the majority were French and some English. One of them was an actor whose name unfortunately I can't remember, who played the leading part in a well-known Australian play *Summer of the Seventeenth Doll*. We were also later to become very friendly with an elderly couple, two lovely gentlemen who lived in Neutral Bay.

The sea lived up to its Pacific Ocean name and in smooth seas we sailed on without any problems up to New Caledonia. Karen was as good as gold. She was then about a seven-month-old of big blue eyes, very blonde, and very friendly. There was always someone willing to watch over her so we could go to meals in peace without worry at any time.

It was a lovely fine morning when we entered Noumea Harbour and after Karen had had a sleep, we went for a walk around the town, splashed with Poinciana trees and dominated by the Roman Catholic Cathedral, the nickel mine and smelting works. After lunch, I went off taking photographs of the area and then going on to the popular swimming Vata beach and the South Pacific High Commission Headquarters. The latter comprised all the Pacific island nations and Great Britain, France, Australia, and New Zealand.

Arriving

The next day, we sailed for the New Hebrides. We were fortunate to enter Vila harbour in bright sunlight, a large harbour with heavily clad forest on the hills on both sides. The inner harbour comprised a small settlement on the foreshores and offshore the tiny island of Iririki (where in the Presbyterian Mission Hospital, my last two children were to be born), and beyond Iririki, Fila Island.

On arrival, we were met by Keith Woodward (Keith was to become a very close friend in the years ahead), and taken to the British Residency on Iririki Island. We travelled from the mainland to Iririki (about 200 yards) in a small rowing boat. We then climbed 200-odd somewhat daunting steps up to the residency itself. Staff carried baggage and all we had to carry was Karen and our personal bags. The British Resident Commissioner John Rennie and his very charming wife met us; both of them were Scottish with a lovely accent. Mr Rennie, a dour Scotsman, was an academic with no fame to physical achievements, in contrast to his French counterpart Pierre Antonioz. He was later to become Governor General of Mauritius.

Lady Rennie, or Mrs Rennie as we then knew her, showed us to our personal suite which was on one side of a very large wooden house of British India bungalow-style: very wide verandahs of about 12 feet and our own large room and bathroom, and small kitchen. Mrs Rennie made us very much at home and at night we sat down to a rather informal dinner in the formal dining room. It was a very large room with a table which would seat 24 and lit with silver chandeliers.

In the next few days, we stayed at the residency very comfortably and I made formal calls, donning my one and only suit and going first to the British and French High Court judges and then to Mister Rennie's colleague Pierre Antonioz, French Resident Commissioner. After struggling with my schoolboy French, he put me at ease in fluent English. He was an extremely interesting man with a small stature and an arm crippled from polio. He had an extraordinary reputation, being highly decorated during the war when he served with the French Maquis liberation forces. He had evidently had some extraordinary adventures and was then in the process of training to swim across the headlands of Vila harbour—about a ten-mile swim in shark-infested waters. He had gathered a lot of his cronies, some somewhat reluctantly, to partake of the adventure. The one British representative was Keith Woodward who still had reasonable eyesight, although he was rapidly losing it from some terrible disease. Days after the event, Keith said his face looked like a piece of pickled pork.

Vila Life

After three days at the residency, our house was finally vacated. It was called 'Mile End' (the British staff houses were all named after Underground tube stations in London). We found it very comfortable, but we were rather overwhelmed from the word go with invitations to dine. All we wanted to do at the beginning was to unpack and settle Karen in. We were offered the help of a young village girl but she didn't really settle down very well and later we found Miriam, a New Caledonian girl who spoke fluent French but no Bislama and, of course, no English. She was a godsend—very intelligent and a lovely girl and we became extremely fond of her.

Three days after we moved into the house, the couple from 'The Caledonian' came to see us and offer assistance. They were a tremendous help in the next few days, coming each day to make meals and look after Karen whilst we unpacked. They obviously enjoyed it, especially Karen's company, and we were sorry when a few days later, they sailed for France.

Life in Vila was very social but I had not yet been designated a particular job, which eventually turned out to be relieving the British Commandant of Police. I just checked into the office each day, dealing with files and records and meeting up with the rest of the British staff. I think within a couple of days of settling into the house, we were invited to the Police Commissioners' evening. It was a Western Pacific evening and guests were very casually dressed in coloured short-sleeved hangout shirts. I was embarrassingly dressed in more formal attire. It was a very pleasant evening and we met a lot of people, had delicious food and drink, and the local police-force band played. The local doctor and his wife who had previously worked in Tonga, and was a friend of Queen Salote, asked their house girl to perform a traditional Tongan 'Hula', dressed in frangipani leis and the traditional grass skirt; it was most spectacular.

The few stores were not well-stocked, the principal establishments being Burns Philp and Ballons (a French supermarket-style store). Most Europeans put in monthly orders to an Australian grocery firm and the Burns Philp vessel 'Tulagi' would call every four to six weeks, so one of our first jobs was to work out an extensive grocery order.

Our only way of obtaining fresh fruit and vegetables was from the Vietnamese women. A number of them who had been brought in by the French in the early days to work on the plantations, would come round past our house every day with baskets slung on a pole over their shoulders, carrying fresh food—tomatoes, lettuce, cucumbers, parsley, and so on. Fresh meat was more of a problem. At that stage there was no local beef and apart from the odd scrawny chicken which might be offered at your door by one of the New Hebrideans, the only meat came from Burns Philp when they had it, and availability was not assured. We did have fresh milk, which was a blessing. I would boil it for three minutes before giving it to Karen. The Vietnamese evidently chewed betel nut pretty regularly and had blood red teeth so when they smiled, it wasn't a very attractive sight.

A casualty from our voyage across from Australia was the piano, which we had brought back from Tanganyika. On unpacking we found it was quite severely damaged. The sounding board on the iron frame had cracked which was greatly disappointing. We were told that there was someone in the town who could repair pianos. This turned out to be Monsieur Dupurtuis a defrocked Catholic priest from France with a lovely Tongan wife. Monsieur Dupurtuis persevered with the piano and finally got it into playing order. Alas, when we arrived at Tanna, the piano was inadvertently dropped into the sea and never sounded like a piano again.

We had reached Vila three days before Christmas and inevitably were flooded with invitations. We decided it would be preferable to have a quiet Christmas, just the three of us. However, we made up for it with the New Year, which is the biggest festival time for the New Hebridean people. We'd been out to dinner that night and returned after midnight to go to bed and at about two o'clock there was an unholy noise at our front door with shouting and screaming, and I assumed that it was a case for police action. To my relief, when we opened the front door, we found a large crowd of New Hebrideans bedecked in flowers, faces white with flour and/or powder. They proceeded to shower us with powder and flowers actually taken from our own garden, with much joviality, singing and shouting. The crowd proceeded on down the road, leaving us to go back to bed.

The British district agent for the Vila district and surrounding islands suggested that I might like to go with him for a tour around the island, which I did. This was Dick Hutchinson, another administrative colleague whom I was to get to know well over the years ahead. We set out in his Land Rover and the going was rough. The road got progressively worse until we came to an enormous banyan tree on the northern side of the island, about 100 feet high and about 60 feet in diameter which had fallen across the narrow track so we had to hack our way around it with bush knives, reminding me of Mpanda, Africa when Enriko used to regularly do a sterling job clearing road obstructions with a little axe from the back of my Peugeot. We proceeded on calling at a number of villages, the houses very neat with clean white coral floors, bamboo thatch walls, and most seemed to have a coral path to the front door.

The impression I was getting was that in many ways other than politically, the local people were well ahead of the Africans, but they seemed a fair way off independence—I believe still drugged into a benevolent stupor by mission influence. Despite best efforts to date, both the British and French governments still had some way to go to bring the local people to independence.

Farther on we stopped for a meeting of the local chiefs. The proceedings were in Bislama, which of course I did not follow. Following the meeting we squatted on mats under a large mango tree for an impressive feast. Masses of food was presented—the local traditional dish, *laplap*, (grated root vegetable pudding, wrapped in large leaves and cooked between hot river stones), pineapples, and banana—the highlight, a platter of cold fatty hunks of pork: a local delicacy! Dick and I arrived home at dark after a long and very bumpy ride.

I was appointed temporary British Commandant of Police—certainly a job I had never done before, but it didn't prove too arduous. Local crime was not extensive and sub-inspector of police, George Kalsakau from Fila Island, was very competent. We did deal with several night-time calls, several road accidents, and assaults, but at no stage, thankfully, was there anything serious. We lived very comfortably in our new home for three months with work not too laborious. We socialised regularly, meeting more and more people: planters, traders, and missionaries, whilst I waited anxiously to find my final appointment. This I was glad to say was in charge of the southern islands of the New Hebrides, with its headquarters on Tanna Island.

Eight

1958 Tanna

At the end of March 1958, we began packing our belongings, including the piano, and loading them onto the 'Darnley', a local Burns Philp vessel that visited about every six weeks to two months. We would travel on the 'Rocinante', a condominium vessel under the French captain, Guenet. We set sail one evening at dusk, sharing the only cabin with Madame Jocteur (wife of a deceased French administrator). The Rennies, Keith Woodward, and several other new friends came down to the wharf to wish us bon voyage.

Alas, having set sail into peaceful waters, no sooner had we rounded the headland than we met raging seas, which continued until we reached Erromango 24 hours later. There we had a little respite, resting in the harbour for about half an hour while goods, chattels, and deck passengers were unloaded. An hour later, we set out again for a final dash to Tanna, the seas even heavier now, with hurricane-force winds. Madame Jocteur, Ida, and 11-month-old Karen took turns to be violently ill. I had strapped all three down in their bunks to avoid being thrown onto the deck saturated by massive waves, and then spent the night holding on with one hand and a bucket ready in the other. Karen's reaction was frightening—her eyes rolled back in her head, her pallor deathly white, falling into a comatose state until we arrived at our new destination. I experienced tremendous relief when finally at dawn, after 36 hours at sea, we reached the protected bay of Lenakel on the Tanna coast.

What a sight it was—heavily timbered green hills, coral reefs, and best of all, just solid land! We came in fairly close to the shore but then had to wait patiently, the 'Rocinante' continuing to roll horribly, whilst the mail was given priority and sent ashore. Meanwhile we saw that a whole host of Europeans were gathering on the shore to greet us. Trying to disguise our very bedraggled appearance, poor Ida bravely pulled herself together and ashore we went. Fortunately, everyone had guessed what a trip we had had. They had watched us tossing and rolling into harbour.

On the beach were the renowned French district agent (FDA), my colleague-to-be and his wife, Monsieur and Madame Duc Dufayard. Also, there were the senior policeman and French and British residents and their families, planters, mission hospital staff, the doctor and his wife, and a crowd of natives—we had heard all of the names before, but it was difficult to know who was who. It was also difficult to decide on the spur of the moment, whether you said, "how do you do" or "Bonjour!"

As it happened, I said, "Bonjour. Comment allez vous" to a man dressed all in white. He replied, "Cut it out, mate. I'm Australian." He was vastly amused by it, but I think that was the only slip. So all in all, it must have been quite an amusing landing! But we were rather flattered to think that everyone had come down to meet us. It was quite an event for Tanna, of course, as we heard later that we were the subjects of discussion for some days afterwards all over the island. Monsieur and Madame Dufayard were impressed with how "*fraiche*" Madame (Ida) looked after such a terrible voyage. There was also a report from the other side of the island that said that, in fact, it was the High Commissioner for the Western Pacific, who had landed. This rumour (the island is prone to rumours) arose because of the large crowd on the beach to welcome us! We were hurriedly introduced by Michael and Barbero Challon, the current District Agent and his wife, and whisked up to our new home. It was about two miles from Lenakel Beach where ships unload. We followed a winding track in a very ancient and rattling Land Rover through an avenue of coconut palms and up onto the hills, out of the trees, and there in front of us was our home of the next four years.

It was about 11 in the morning when we arrived, and Barbero showed us into our tiny room, with Karen's cot and our two beds, the guest room. I must say our hearts fell at the sight of it! We really would have loved a hot shower, a cup of tea, and then a sleep after our trip, but alas, no. Instead we had Swedish coffee and then discussions for the rest of the day. Michael had mobilised a force of prisoners (locals convicted of a crime working and helping around the British government stations instead of being locked up) who began unloading our boxes of belongings from the Land Rover along with the assistance of Dr Ian Reid and the mission utility. But woefully, the first three boxes landed were dropped into the surf including our piano! So as soon as they came up I had to unpack, to try and dry things off a bit, and within the day we had things strewn everywhere. It was rather heartbreaking to see our books dripping wet! Barbero and Michael had already started to pack their things, so all in all, the house was quite a mess for a while.

We found to our consternation, that Barbero had no less than eight cats, that almost always were inside the house and poor Ida began to sneeze! We said that they worried her, feeling that we couldn't put up with them for a fortnight, and they did their best to keep the cats out. But that was, in fact, impossible. Karen was the only one who appreciated them and crowed with delight whenever they came near. The cats didn't appreciate her though!

Adding to our discomfort, there were flies, millions of flies. And what was worse was that Barbero, who ran the house, wasn't a bit perturbed about it. The Angelonis, who had been here before the Challons, had had parts of the house gauzed. However, we found to our horror that the gauze had, in fact, been removed and the gauze doors were used on the chicken yard. So we had a constant battle to keep flies away from Karen. Miracle of miracles, none of us went down with diarrhoea, and I can only think that the good Lord was keeping a weather eye on us, because under normal circumstances, with the flies as they were, we would certainly have done so. I was just itching to eradicate the flies with spray and gauze etc. I was sure that it wouldn't take much to get them under control.

The house seemed to be full of helpers—two prisoners in the kitchen pottered about washing a spoon, putting it away, washing a knife, pondering about where it might go, hunting the cats out, bringing in some wood for the kitchen stove, washing again, and so on and so on! It was hopeless chaos, and there were more flies in the kitchen. We met Makia, wife to the police corporal Joseph who became our permanent house girl. She was a serene, dignified lady who adored our children and was extremely capable in most respects. Barbero, although shrieking out in a high-pitched voice from all parts of the house, was very nice from the very first day. Karen was thrilled with her and the prisoners, for whom she always had bright smiles. Then later in the week, we got in yet another girl to help with the washing. So we had a tremendous staff falling over themselves and the cats, all the week. There was no organisation or system at all. That too we were itching to remedy! Anyway, the important thing was that there was no shortage of staff, and what a luxury it was.

From Monday to Sunday, we didn't leave the house either. Michael was flat out on his handing over notes, and annual report on the district. After unpacking and organising our luggage as far as possible, thereafter in my spare time I read reports, files etc. And checked with Michael as I went along. I did glean a lot of information from Michael who after three years on Tanna knew a lot about it and the other nearby islands. We seemed to be late to bed each night, because we sat and talked or had visitors like Ian Reid, the doctor, who on Tuesday brought up the piano in his truck. Bob Paul also dropped in; he was an Australian planter and trader, with an Australian wife, Kath, and five children. They lived about two miles from us and dropped in on and off to see how things were going.

We also had a good look round the station and the police lines, prison, gardens, etc. The British District Agent's house was referred to as either the residency or the agency, and we thought of the two we preferred the former, although it sounded a bit pretentious.

Thursday saw the first of the "bun rushes" as my uncle Bill would say—the first round in the social swirl—to farewell the departing agent, and to welcome the new one!!

I had been hearing a lot about the Duc Dufayards—how difficult they were etc. And so we were well prepared when we were asked over to their place for dinner on the Thursday night. In fact, we had a most luscious spread—a seven-course meal, and really delectable, that included mushroom omelette, roast chicken, and ice cream. Madame, about forty five only spoke French, not a word of English. The Duc, as he was obviously called, was about fifty and they were very hospitable. We all thoroughly enjoyed it. I could see in further meetings with him that he might well be difficult, got the impression that Michael had got a bit overwrought over the wrangling which he and the Duc had had. Certainly it was a task for me to patch up the rather bedraggled, international relations, which at present existed. The Duc spoke good English, thank goodness, but we certainly had to pep up our French if we were to win over Madame. They had no children, but she seemed interested in Karen. I was hoping that they would not be that difficult.

Certainly one of the peculiarities with this condominium set up is that the smallest decision had to be referred to one's colleague before anything was finalised. You really should be on good terms, if you are going to get anywhere! Michael said that both the Duc and Madame had a bee in their bonnet about being corrected, and doing the right thing!! He said that their formality, especially in such a small community, became trying.

For instance, there was almost an incident over whether the Duc or Michael should throw a cocktail party to welcome us and to meet the European population officially. No doubt, in a place where informality is the obvious answer, that must get a bit trying. Anyway, the question of the cocktail party was finally amicably settled and Michael and Barbero threw the party on Saturday evening, to which the whole of the European population on the island was invited. In fact, only one of the traders and missionaries from the east side of the island about 25 miles away, and over a pretty high range of hills (about two thousand feet) did not come. It was a pleasant evening, quite cosmopolitan, with French and English language spoken from the four corners of the room. The Duc and Madame came half an hour late and went early.

Everyone wanted to entertain Michael and Barbero before they left. And, of course, we were invited too. So we were meeting the same people over and over again all in the space of two weeks! We were quite relieved to find that this normally would never happen and there was not that much entertaining, except at Christmas!

On the Sunday, we went off for a picnic, leaving about 11 o'clock. Karen woke early, and so we set out as soon as she was awake, and we were back about four. We drove to the other side of the island and picnicked on the mountainside with some picturesque views to the east and to the north and south, the island off Aniwa in the distance.

Tanna is a lovely island, with some beautiful scenery. We had a glimpse of the volcano on the other side of the island, an extraordinarily eerie sight to see this mountain, bald and black rising out of the mountains, massed with green jungle, pouring forth a deep blue smoke. And the volcano was something that we saw more of anon—a magnificent subject for the video camera—and quite a tourist attraction apparently.

Each day Michael and I had been dashing about the island trying to see as much as possible, and meeting as many natives as possible. Monday morning, we went south by Land Rover to the European planter in that part—a Frenchman, Jocteur, who was married to a Norfolk Islander and descendant of the Bounty mutineers. In the afternoon we met the Pauls at their place for a few moments, then went on to another French trader, the Rollands, and finally, a bachelor English trader, George Bright. He was rather a rough diamond, but a good-hearted one, they said. We were quite glad to get home again.

At night, we just talked to the Challons who were anxious to hear something about Tanganyika. Tuesday was a long day. In the morning we called in at the hospital (run by the Presbyterian mission) that had been especially tidied up before my visit. We had a formal inspection and a nice cup of coffee with the Reids and the two nursing sisters—they all seemed very nice.

Later, Michael and I went across to the other side of the island and saw the two European establishments there—the Coopers with whom we had lunch, they were Australian and Presbyterian missionaries, and another Australian trader.

On Thursday I took the old Land Rover with a policeman orderly to the north of the island and looked at a site for the airstrip, which I was pressing for early completion. We met some more of the chiefs. It was almost dark when I got back. That night we went to the mission hospital and were given a buffet supper with some of the native nobility. It was a tremendous spread, but I felt a bit wonky next day, as did Ida—something must have disagreed with us. It was very hot too because they had kerosene lights, which threw off a tremendous heat!

The next day, Friday, we went off again to the other side of the island. Michael, Barbero, and I leaving Ida and Karen. This was for a council meeting and also to meet some more leading natives and to go to a farewell lunch on that side. I was glad Ida had not come, because it was a long and tiring day. The road was rough, and the Land Rover had no springs, and I felt thoroughly bumped about by the time we got home.

On Saturday, 29th of March, 1958, the 'Rocinante' arrived unexpectedly in the morning. Michael and Barbero were to go back to Vila that night at nine, so you can imagine the rush. At five-thirty, we went to the Dufayards' for a glass of champagne, and the Challons made their fond farewells, then on to the Pauls' for dinner, which they were giving jointly with the Rowlands, and from there down to the beach, which was only 200 yards from the Pauls' house and the Challons went aboard the 'Rocinante'.

When Michael set a foot in the dingy, I became the British District Agent, Southern District and the Resident Commissioners had been so informed that day by telegram. The Duc wanted to have a ceremonial send off with our police forces six-man side, presenting arms, but we managed to dissuade him!

We did not know ourselves with a quiet house, but best of all no cats. I'd never been so fed up with cats in all my life.

On Sunday, we were longing for a quiet day. On Monday, we settled down to reorganise and systematise a lot of the work—but the pace was obviously more leisurely here—such a treat that was. I'd noted that Michael never got up till about eight, though of course he worked till later as a result of it. But that suited me and I followed in his footsteps.

The Agency

Our new home was certainly not an imposing edifice by any stretch of the imagination—desperately needing a coat of paint on the exterior at least—weatherboard construction and galvanised iron roof. The garden, too, at a glance disappointed me—a tiny suburban garden surrounded by a high hedge! Furthermore, the flagpoles, the Union Jack, and tricolours were too close to the house. The setting for the district agency, however, was superb with large banyan trees on either side. From the verandah you had the most magnificent view—below, the green mass of jungle, coconut plantations stretching to the shore, and beyond the white surf crashing onto coral reefs, the background azure-blue sea, and a winding coastline stretched to the north and the tips of green hills beyond us to the south. As I say, I was rather disappointed of my first glance of the garden but was soon cheered with the prospect of endless possibilities and I reckoned that in a few months there would be some radical changes.

A disadvantage was that with the prevailing easterlies, the Yasur volcano (so named by Captain Cook) would regularly shower the house with ash, and the entire contents would regularly be covered with black volcanic grit. The evenings were often cold and we would be glad to warm ourselves in front of the wood-burning kitchen stove.

In my first few days of taking over the district, I had the hedge removed and my flagpoles moved a farther 50 yards from the house. The repositioning of the flagpoles immediately led to my first contretemps with my colleague—the Duc. In a very flowery letter, the gist of which took me some time to fathom, he complained that my flags were flying higher than his. Wanting to avoid an early argument and having carefully stood back and observed both sets of flags, I found that this was true. Accordingly I moved the flagpoles again to a lower position, thus retaining the spirit of joint administration. Over my four years on Tanna, I had many such notes pointing out that my action on such and such a matter was not within the spirit of the joint administration. Nonetheless, we worked reasonably well and harmoniously on our quarterly joint tours in the 'Rocinante', establishing the first local council in the district at Aneityum with Jean Marie Leyhe as first president, later to become a President of the Vanuatu Republic, and to present me in 1996 with the Vanuatu Medal of Merit.

Flagpoles, however, continued to be a source of friction. Later our joint offices were completed and my intention was that we abandon our own sets of flagpoles and just have the Union Jack and tricolour fly over our joint offices. For some reason or other, the Duc would never agree to take this action. Each time I suggested he move in, there was always an excuse. The 'elder statesman' Dr Armstrong commented sourly that it was probably because Madame would not let him. In the event, my colleague never used the office adjoining mine except that following our practise of a Saturday morning discussion of district affairs we would take turns to use each other's office. Each morning he would come in to greet me by shaking hands and should he or I meet during the day, we would again shake hands. I confess I found this rather trying.

Reverting to the district agency layout, the main road, instead of going to the back entrance, now swept past the front garden with a path winding up the slope to my entrance. It was a tremendous improvement, looked most attractive, and met with the approval of the expatriate population.

I retained my own flagpole with its Union Jack in my garden and each morning, Corporal Joseph with his detachment of five police in full uniform would march smartly up to the flagpole and stand at attention whilst Joseph raised the flag. The procedure was repeated in the afternoon. I never knew my colleague's procedure but we felt that probably his police were too busy on 'domestic duties'. We knew, in fact, Madame made no bones about it that the French Sergeant Tom's duties included cutting the flowers for the house and working in the kitchen.

The house was of a style I was to see later in other areas of the archipelago, mostly mission stations, probably prefabricated in Australia in the 1920s. It had a wide front verandah, a central dining room, bedroom, and office to one side, sleep out on the other, a passageway with pantry storeroom on one side, and a bathroom on the other. The passage then led by open walkway to a large kitchen. The kitchen was luxurious, equipped with a kerosene refrigerator and a wood stove. It was deliberately set apart to prevent the danger of fire spreading to the rest of the house. In the winter months, we greatly appreciated the wood stove and would frequently sit in front of it for our tea and to read before bed.

Our lighting initially was dependent upon kerosene lanterns; later we progressed to pressure lights. These were something of a nuisance, preheated with methylated spirits and delicate mantles which often broke, but at least they threw a reasonable reading light. Finally we bought a small generator, which also provided light for the clerk's house and police barracks.

The little office at the front of the house, hardly big enough to swing a cat, was reputedly haunted. A young district agent, pre-war, had committed suicide there and the legend grew that the poor young man's ghost returned from time to time. We never had the pleasure of meeting him.

During our second tour, I was determined to improve our living conditions by having our own en suite. I raked up the necessary funds—quite illegally, as I recall—and inveigled Dr Armstrong, our multi-skilled retired doctor, to build it. It was a very prolonged and laborious process and I should have been aware that it would involve very many lengthy lectures from the elder statesman on just about everything except the building of the bathroom. Because the house was on stilts, it was easier to build the bathroom at ground level and this necessitated steps from our bedroom down to the bathroom itself. It was a luxury indeed, even to having gas hot water.

However it, rather like the office, was to have a sad story attached to it. One of my successors, Guy Wallington and family, took over in 1970. Apparently on one occasion, the family had a vicious attack of flu and were extremely ill. Guy, smelling gas, struggled down to the bathroom and found Susan in the bath unconscious. He attempted to lift Susan out of the bath and collapsed, then crawled up into the bedroom and outside to call for help. It was too late, and Susan was already dead. Poor fellow—what a terrible experience.

Guy had already undergone an equally terrible experience on Tanna. Paul Burton piloting an aircraft with 14 passengers had crashed into the hinterland mountains when crossing the island from west to east. An alert was given and Guy organised the search party immediately, firstly without success. A villager on the south-west coast later informed him that she had heard a tremendous bang and was sure it was not thunder. This led to the discovery of the aircraft, smashed literally to pieces on a steep mountainside. Investigators subsequently decided that he had underestimated the power of the aircraft to climb over the high mountain. Poor Guy had the responsibility, with the team from Vila, of trying to identify the dead—an almost impossible task. What a job that must have been for everyone, but especially Guy.

The Southern District

The Southern District for which my French colleague and I were totally responsible included Aneityum, Futuna, Erromango, Aniwa, and Tanna. The principal island was Tanna, approximately 40 by 20 miles wide. Ten miles to the east lies Aniwa, the 'orange isle', so called because it produces masses of the most delectable oranges. Futuna—the population has a distinct Polynesian strain, the people have lighter skins, and are overall more robust. The island, quite small—about five miles square—is virtually a plateau rising steeply out of the sea. The most frequently used approach is by ladder, involving a climb of about 200 feet. Aneityum is famed for its kauri forests and kauri is still exported to Australia. It includes a tiny 'Mystery Isle', which these days is frequently visited by cruise ships. Erromango, the 'Martyr Isle', so called because it was at Dillon's Bay that four of the mission family of John Williams were murdered in the 1850s.

The district administrative headquarters was at Isangel on Tanna. Here the British and French agencies were based within a stone's throw of one another and between a jointly occupied administrative office. Tanna saw the first successful Presbyterian mission base established by John Paton in the 1860s and was put on the map by Captain Cook when the 'Resolution' was de-barnacled there. Overlooking Port Resolution is the active volcano I mentioned, Mount Yasur. In theory, at least, the district was administered jointly. That was, any administrative decisions—policy, road building, councils, etc.—were to be jointly agreed upon between the French and British agents.

My agency comprised of a small police detachment with a corporal or sergeant in charge, two clerical assistants, a prison, and a condominium radio with communication with Port Vila headquarters twice daily. Transport—one Land Rover. The District Agent's principal duties were firstly to maintain law and order and secondly to promote self-reliance. Medical facilities comprised a Presbyterian mission hospital with a Caucasian doctor, two fully qualified nurses, and a small dispensary on the east at White Sands. Later the French administration established a small hospital with a French doctor at White Sands. Education was limited to rudimentary Presbyterian village schools in the vicinity of Isangel and White Sands. They were only classes one and two. The Roman Catholic mission had a small village school north of Lenakel. The European population comprised planters at Lenakel and on the east coast, missionaries at Lenakel and White Sands, and district administrative staff.

Administration

No clear directives or guidelines appeared to have ever been given to British District Agents and one made up one's own policies. My personal policy was firstly, to obtain the confidence of the indigenous population by making direct contact with the people in their own environment rather than in my office; secondly to encourage the development of self-reliance, which I saw as being through the establishment of viable local councils. We submitted quarterly and annual reports of our achievements and developments to the British Commissioner HQ in Vila. Looking back, it seems extraordinary that we were not instructed to give priority to the advancement of the local population towards independence.

In our joint offices we each dealt with a constant stream of paper. I never really seemed to be able to sit back and say I had nothing to do in the office because there were always files to be dealt with. My primary work, whether I was touring by truck or on foot, was the hearing of court cases and dealing with land disputes and bride prices. We held native courts under the condominium Native Criminal Code, of which the most common offence was adultery. The other common offences were assault and drunkenness. A case would be brought forward mostly by the village chiefs and I would hear it assisted by two local assessors, appointed jointly by the District Agents. The assessors would be leading members of the community, more often than not chiefs or village elders. The police would bring cases before me sometimes, but on Tanna this was rare because the police were very inexperienced. On my return to the office from tour, I would write up the cases and they would be approved in Vila but 99% of the time, action was taken against the offender before securing this approval. Sentences were normally not more than three months imprisonment or sometimes a fine of money or goods.

Two other matters constantly involved a court, these were land disputes, which sometimes took days to resolve, and disputes over women and bride price and '*esjenis*' (exchange). In my experience, the practice on Tanna (but not elsewhere) was that if a man took a girl from another village, his family had to in turn provide a girl for someone in the bride's village. This led to many heated and lengthy disputes but more often than not, bride price (kava, mats, and pigs) were amicably resolved.

Local councils were slowly being established in most cases with much opposition and suspicion from traditional villages and Jon Frum supporters (more on this later). The Presbyterian and Seventh Day Adventist followers were the ones who assisted us in setting up some councils and these were supervised by my colleague and I.

National services, British or French, were dependent upon allocation of funds from their respective administrations. In my case, allocations improved each year. In 1959, funds were provided for a replacement of the prison in permanent materials and to order a replacement Land Rover. Needless to say, the old one was on its last legs and only kept moving by Dr Armstrong's stalwart efforts. By 1962, I had funds for dispensaries in the north of Tanna (Loanengo), Aniwa, and Aneityum, new joint offices, new police barracks, new quarters for my clerical assistant, and other improvements to my agency.

Our fieldwork included public works, extremely limited in the Southern District at that time. A small fund was provided by the condominium for manual road labour and that was about it. Under the chiefs, villages would be organised to contribute labour and provided with wheelbarrows and shovels they would use to fill holes and improve drainage.

Touring

When transferred from Tanganyika to the New Hebrides in 1957, I always bore in mind the strictly enforced maxim of the then governor of Tanganyika, Sir Edward Twining, that all administrative officers were to spend a minimum of 14 days on safari per month—thus ensuring that the administration were brought into regular close touch with the people whom they were serving. In Tanganyika, a lot of the safaris were done on foot with an enormous entourage carrying all manner of things to ensure the officer concerned bedded down comfortably at night.

On my arrival in the condominium of the New Hebrides, 'Touring' as it was known there, was normally carried out on the ship 'Don Quixote', captained by Jack Barley from Fiji, or occasionally by chartering a commercial vessel like the stout little launch 'Trudy'.

One of the first things I decided I should do was follow the practice I'd been taught in Tanganyika. This was, as far as possible, to tour on foot and sleep in the villages. The principle being that the local population were who you were supposed to be working for, and touring in this way enabled you to create a relationship with them and they in turn would become confident in you. I felt it was a very sensible practice. I was accompanied by a policeman and two porters, a far cry from the Tanganyika safaris where one took a team of 30 or 40 porters, but even so my approach caused quite a stir among the local population.

At the end of a tour, by foot or sea, I would outline briefly in note form events and matters requiring action on my return. These would serve me as a reminder when I got back to my office and equally importantly, they would serve to keep the British office in Vila au fait with what I had been doing. Later I was astonished to find that while this was set down as accepted practice in Tanganyika, it was largely not followed in the New Hebrides.

My first safari, or tour, after we were established at Isangel, was to the far south-west of the island. I took my Land Rover as far as Port Resolution where the road ended and set off with my personal possessions in a haversack. I had deliberately not asked one of my police to accompany me because I felt that the local people might construe his presence as a protection for me against the 'dangerous bushmen'.

By evening, I had reached the village … a small one with a population of not more than 50 souls, where I experienced my first taste of Melanesian hospitality which was to be regularly showered upon me for my ensuing 20 years of touring in the New Hebrides. I asked for shelter for the night in my best pidgin (very limited) and was allocated a small thatch hut on the outskirts of the village. I was given a coconut leaf woven mat on which to sleep. Whilst unpacking my victuals (tin meat, 'Marie biscuits', and a bottle of water) I was conscious of a woman standing outside with a large basin in her hands. This she handed to me. It was full of large hunks of steaming hot yam (which of course I soon found was the staple diet). I was staggered by the quantity of the gift and after hoeing into one piece which was more than sufficient, I thought to myself, what do I do with the rest? I obviously didn't want to offend her by returning the hardly touched dish, and I couldn't very well dispose of it in nearby bush without discovery, so I took my only course of action and stuffed it all in my socks and bag. When the woman returned, I handed her the empty basin and thanked her warmly. I couldn't miss the look of astonishment on her face as she walked away. Years later, I related this story at one of my farewell parties, and the audience was convulsed with laughter. They knew very well that the basin of yam was destined for the whole family and as a guest was offered firstly to me!

On my return from tour, Ida on unpacking my bag was equally astonished to find the haversack and contents saturated with cold yam, one of the many odd things she was to cope with in future times.

Sir John Rennie Visit

On a visit to Tanna by Sir John Rennie, he expressed a desire to do a tour on foot so I took him overnight to the south-west of the island. I also took an extra porter to carry a small portable camp stretcher I had from my safaris in Tanganyika. I desisted from taking another piece of Tanganyika safari equipment: a wooden toilet seat with screw in lugs which the porters would rig up over a small pit, drive in stakes, and erect a hessian screen to make a very comfortable and upmarket toilet. This, I felt, was stretching it a bit too far in the New Hebrides and it would be less discriminatory if we used the oh-so-awful pit latrines sometimes shown us with great pride by our hosts.

We were just about asleep (or I was), when Mr Rennie turned over with a grunt and over went the bed, him wrapped (smothered would be a better description) in the overhead mosquito net. The next morning, by eight o'clock he had not stirred so I woke him gently and he seemed mightily displeased. I really never did get to know Mr Rennie as he was then. He was intellectually so many streets ahead of me that I used to feel a nincompoop in his presence and believed that my conversations bored him.

It was not until we met the Rennies after his illustrious career as Governor of Mauritius and Head of UNARA in London in 1990 that I realised what a really nice man Sir John was. He talked easily and was very relaxed while he pressed us to a sherry. He was human, after all.

Joint Touring

Joint touring was considered by both governments to be an essential part of our demonstration of the Anglo-French condominium's togetherness. So on arrival in the Southern District, I followed my predecessor's example and joined my very senior French colleagues in the most frustrating touring of my life.

About every three months we would be allocated the 'Rocinante' and set out from Isangel Bay to visit Aneityum (say, two days), Futuna (one day),

Aniwa (one day), with an absolute maximum of eight days, which was more than enough for me. We would arrive after an inevitable rough crossing, to Aneityum, Anelgeh Bay, at dusk in time for a shower, change, and then sit at length over dinner whilst Captain Guenet and Mr Duc Dufayard would carry on an interminable discussion in French, of course, on some topic or other. Our police aides (one each) would have been despatched ashore to alert assessors that we wished to meet them and the villagers at eight the next morning. Several bottles of red wine with dinner and I, at any rate, was glad to hit the sack.

My colleague always arose very early and would greet me with a *"bien dormi?"* when I stirred, just in time to throw on some clothes, swallow Captain Guenet's hunks of bread and evil coffee, and be ready to go ashore. We would normally return for lunch unless asked by Artie Kraft or others. We would jointly sit for a court case or two, with one or the other presiding, the other simply listening in. We would discuss the proposed local council; the French at the time were equally supportive of the establishment of councils. At the end of the day, we would return to the smelly 'Rocinante' for supper. That was our typical day when jointly touring. These whistle-stop tours I found most frustrating with my domineering and scheming colleague and was always thankful when they were over.

I observed these niceties and this joint touring procedure for the four years I was on Tanna and was seldom able to visit without being accompanied by my colleague. When, therefore, I was posted to Santo to take over Central District Number 2 (CD2), with my colleague based at Lamap, it was an ideal time to follow my own inclinations and as far as possible, go it alone. There was certainly no danger of my colleague joining me on some of the copra vessels I travelled on from Santo to get to my district. In this way, I established the practice (no doubt wrongly in the eyes of the condominium) of touring alone.

Nine

Vignette – Tanna

Healing and Witchcraft

There were rumours at a village in south-west Tanna that a woman was vomiting up money—a profitable sort of soul to have around, I thought. Anyway, a specimen of the money that was genuine was handed to me and I was asked to investigate. They said she also produced stones (with magical qualities) from her ears. An unusual woman it would seem. My vehicle took me to the end of the south coast road and from there on I walked. She was a little wizened up thing but was quite happy to talk to me. Yes she could vomit money and produce magic stones from her ears but they were sidelines to her 'profession' which was to help the sick. She did admit to having done some harm in the past to certain people, upon payment from clients.

At a meeting with the surrounding villages I was told that she was 'a clever' (a witch doctor) but she had healed a lot of the sick that 'white medicine' had not been able to cure. After prolonged discussion, she agreed that there would be no more sideline activity and she would stick to her medical role. Everyone shook hands quite happily and home I went.

Perhaps the most sickening sight I had was to see yaws and its effects on human beings. It began as an ulcer eating away the flesh and leaving a revolting cavity on leg, arm, or face. There was no cure amongst the indigenous population and it was not until the introduction of penicillin that it was eradicated. The WHO organised a team in 1961, which systematically covered the entire archipelago. On Tanna it met with strong opposition from the Jon Frum movement and it took long and patient negotiation before the yaws teams were reluctantly accepted to operate in their villages. Even today, one sometimes sees the scars from this horrible disfiguring disease.

Nangalat

In the early days of our sojourn on Tanna, I decided to do a walking tour on Erromango. Incidentally by this time my foot tours were being applauded by

Dr Armstrong, the elder statesman who said caustically that it was time the British began to know something of the indigenous population which they were governing. The 'Darnley' landed me on east Erromango with a young constable called Kaikai. There were not more than a dozen little settlements on this coast so we soon set off westward.

It was a much longer walk than I had anticipated and by dusk we were in heavy bushland with no trace of a settlement or a human being in sight. We came across a copra-making bed where underfoot the ground was dry from extensive fires. We took off our haversacks and had just sat to relieve weary limbs, when we suddenly heard a movement in the bed above us and there curled up in the rafters was a very large python. Kaikai turned quite pale and made a dash for the open. I was aware that there were no dangerous snakes in the New Hebrides and with a bamboo stick prodded it gently until it slowly moved away. With some coaxing, Kaikai carefully returned.

We were hot and sticky—I could hear water trickling close by and decided to wash. I stripped off and with a towel around my neck, pushed my way through the undergrowth to a delightful little stream. The water was clear and cold and I had just begun to enjoy it when I began to itch. I got out hastily and hurried back to our shelter. By this time my whole body felt as though it were on fire, and I returned desperate to the water's edge, again pushing through the undergrowth, to bathe again. I repeated the procedure several times without relief. My policeman, still a little nervous after the snake episode, was sympathetic but offered no solution. I smothered myself in Johnson's baby powder from my pack but this was unsuccessful. I tried to sleep under my blanket but the itch was unrelenting. Time and time again I went down to the stream to cool off, still without relief. I think it was the longest and most miserable night of my life.

With the break of dawn, we packed our bags and began to walk again. Towards the end of the second day, the itch was subsiding and by the time we reached the coast and settlement it had gone. I slept very soundly that night.

On talking to the elderly Erromango clinic dresser, he chuckled and said, "Ahhhh, nangalat. Mi savvy." The nangalat tree, with its either red or white veins and serrated edged leaf, is a stinging nettle well known by all New Hebrideans and always carefully avoided! Evidently, I had brushed against the same branches of the nangalat each time I made my way down to the stream to cool off. Water only serves to exacerbate the terrible, relentless itch. It was only later that I learnt that the antidote was cool sap of the tree branch itself, which gives a considerable amount of relief. The discomfort can continue for days. My policeman was evidently a 'city boy'!

I seemed to have less contact with Erromango than any other part of my district, probably because it was a very small population who seemed to be very law-abiding and cooperative. A small local council was established at Dillon's Bay (named after a well-known trader in the early days). I remember being shown a cave on the seafront which had literally hundreds of skulls strewn around. In the hinterland hills there was a sheep farm with a very Australian-style farmhouse, established in the early days by an Australian. The sheep farm still operated and it was from the owner that I procured my little flocks of sheep, first on Tanna and later Malekula.

Air Services

It needs to be borne in mind that at this stage of 1958, there were no air services whatsoever in the New Hebrides, apart from flights in and out of Vila by the French airline TAI. The first internal air service which began from Tanna was solely due to the tenacity and ongoing enthusiasm of Bob Paul, manager of the Burns Philp plantation at Lenakel since the 1950s.

Early in 1958, he began talking of his dream to establish an internal air service. And by the end of that year, he had befriended Paul Burton, an accomplished pilot in Australia. Talk had spread throughout the island of an aircraft for Tanna. Bob had chosen an airstrip site on BP land, not more than a mile from Lenakel which his Futunese labour began clearing. How he found Paul and where he mustered the money to purchase a small twin-engined Dornier Rapide I simply do not know, but the next thing we heard was that Bob and Paul were heading north for the New Hebrides.

There he faced the problems of officialdom and the Anglo-French administration. From the very beginning, the French government was strongly opposed to Bob's initiative basically because it wanted to ensure that, presumably with TAI (*Transports Aeriens Intercontinentaux*), it would establish an internal group service. The French Resident Commissioner Monsieur Favreau, a newcomer, refused adamantly to give joint permission for registration of the aircraft to operate in the New Hebrides.

Meanwhile, I had been pestering the British administration (in coded telegrams) to do their utmost to support Bob's initiative. There were two very valid reasons for their support. The first and obvious one was that this isolated region desperately needed speedy and regular contact with the mainland rather than the painful 36 hours by sea.

The second was that the potentially subversive Jon Frum movement was gaining kudos from the delay in the arrival of a plane, saying that it was Jon Frum who would eventually bring in his own aircraft. This gave considerable impetus to the movement.

Finally it was found that by registering the aircraft in a British colony, for example the Solomons, there was no valid reason for preventing the aircraft from landing on New Hebridean soil. The British administration was rightly concerned about air safety, the airstrip, firefighting control etc.

In the event, the Rapide landed at Vila, and Bob's Futunese—aided by my prisoners—continued to clear the site for an airfield at Lenakel. During these developments, my colleague Monsieur Daniel (fortunately not the Duc who was on leave at that time) had remained very discreetly silent. No doubt, having a young daughter, he was particularly aware of the benefits of an air service.

The big day finally came when Bob informed us that they would land. The entire Loval population turned out onto the strip and waited, and waited—Kath Paul (Bob's wife) most of all with her heart in her mouth!

About four in the afternoon, the Rapide appeared out of the sky and circled the airstrip three or four times. I began to wonder whether Paul Burton was feeling doubtful about the strip. Then he came in to land, trundling over a very rough service and, frighteningly for us watching, hurtled towards the coconut stumps at the end of the strip that had not yet been removed. The plane came to a stop no more than 20 yards from the finish of the runway and Paul said later it had been touch and go. Subsequently, before the plane took off again, the remaining coconut stumps were removed and the strip lengthened.

My first trip in the Rapide was a few days later when Bob said they were going to look at the north of the island and asked if I would like to come. It was an exciting little trip and I was able to peer down on some villages I had trekked to on foot and others I'd not yet seen.

The saga, of course, was not yet over. The French government issued an instruction forbidding its own or condominium personnel to travel in the aircraft that was now making regular flights to and from Vila. It also forbade the raising of any charges on passengers who did travel.

Bob said on one occasion a plain-clothed French policeman flew down to Tanna and on alighting, offered Paul Burton five dollars that, naturally, Paul refused. The policeman then went to Bob's store leaving the five dollars with Kath saying it was payment for his return ticket. Kath hurriedly sent the cash to Paul who again refused payment saying his trip was "on the house".

We, on the other hand, were paying for our seats and making full use of flights to Vila. About this time, M Favreau was replaced—we thought probably because the French administration in Paris were not happy with him. Monsieur Delauney took his place and negotiations were made much easier. Talk of amalgamation with a New Caledonian airway collapsed and at last the French administration gave in, recognised Bob Paul's air service, and began making every use of it. Regular flights to Vila (speedy regular trips—75 mins instead of 36 hours on a rough sea) had a big impact on island life—for government matters, business, medical attention, and even shopping. Years later, Bob's brave little venture developed into Air Melanesie, the first inter island air service.

Emergencies

Dr Ian Reid was called upon to deal with many emergencies. The most horrific occurred when a small boy on the island of Aneityum climbing an orange tree to look for fruit fell and was impaled on a broken branch. Fortunately the 'Rocinante' was at my service on this occasion and we sailed immediately to Aneityum. The child had been recovered from the tree; I hate to think how, and was barely conscious. He was taken back to Lenakel hospital and miraculously recovered very quickly.

One evening, Corporal Joseph reported to me that one of the police was very, very sick. I hurried down to the police barracks to see for myself and sure enough, he was writhing in agony. Corporal Joseph was dispatched post-haste to the mission hospital, and Dr Reid returned some short time later to examine the patient. He said that he would have to operate immediately, much to my alarm. Fortunately at this stage we still had electric light (the little generator was to pack up a week later), and as the mission hospital had none, Ida set to work preparing our kitchen table for the operation which Ian said was a ruptured hernia. By this time, the sisters had arrived with all the necessary implements and Ida and I were much relieved to leave the job to them. By midnight, the operation was over. The policeman, still out to it, was taken back to the barracks. When the kitchen had been cleaned up, Ida gave the medical team a cup of tea before they went home.

Because no hospital bed was available, our policeman remained in his barracks, a sister from the hospital coming up regularly to dress his wound, and Ida taking him regular meals. He soon recovered. Not long after the policeman's emergency and whilst I was absent on tour in Aneityum with my colleague, Ida developed appendicitis—I was so informed by radio. I had visions of her being operated on atop our kitchen table as well, but in the event she was safely evacuated by sea in the 'Rocinante' to Vila. And thence to The Whiston Hospital at Potts Point, Sydney by air for treatment. She was operated on there, continuing to feed three-month-old cute baby Simon, who became a hospital favourite.

Simon and Sallie

Karen was a year old when we arrived in Tanna. Simon was born in the nurses' quarters adjoining the Lenakel mission hospital in August 1958. The sisters felt the old hospital was too antiquated for his birth. He had to be induced and I well remember sitting under a banyan tree close by for a long afternoon and finally hearing him cry. Dr Ian Reid had delivered him with the help of the two mission hospital nurses. He had a shock of long red hair and a very pimply, blotchy face but he was a sturdy perfect baby. Simon was to be known by the Tannese as smol Gavman (small government), my French colleague and I being referred to as Gavman.

With our third child, Sallie, there were many early complications and much discussion with local and visiting doctors about whether Ida should have the baby on Tanna or at Presbyterian Mission Hospital (PMH) in Vila. By this time, February 1962, there was a French army doctor based at White Sands on the east coast of Tanna. In the event, it was very fortunate that the senior doctor at PMH, Dr Anderson, said emphatically that Ida must come to Vila. It was just as well because there were difficulties with the birth including severe blood loss and had there not been full hospital facilities, both mother and child could have been lost.

Ida stayed with the Rennies for several weeks awaiting Sallie's arrival. When the time came, she was carried down to the hospital on an old sedan chair. They kept me posted through a long and traumatic day with me listening and waiting on the radio at the Met office on Tanna. Manipulating the radio was Kalarimanu, husband of Nesweiyu, adopted daughter of Dr Armstrong. Mrs Rennie conveyed to me as gently as possible that all was not well and it subsequently transpired that the birth was indeed a very difficult one and life-threatening for Ida. Then finally on the last radio schedule at ten, Mrs Rennie's voice came crackling over the air—Sallie had arrived and Ida, though very weak, was okay. I walked back to the agency to check on Karen and Simon, relieved and so elated, and to weep a little.

Ida was advised to seek specialist advice in Australia. And a month before the end of our Tanna tour, she had to fly off—this time, thank goodness, for a sojourn at the Prince Alfred Hospital with the three children. Unfortunately I was not permitted to accompany her so it was a very trying journey with an overnight stop in Noumea including two-hour bus trips to and from Tontouta Airport.

I had a very lonely Christmas, returning to Australia on long leave in April 1962 just after my fortieth birthday. Ida had organised Kath Paul to ask me to dinner on my birthday and she went to great lengths to provide a delectable meal!

Health

Overall, the children remained remarkably fit but of course the ever-present malaria was from time to time a problem. We would give them Malocide regularly and when an attack occurred, Dr Reid or one of the nursing sisters would inject Nivaquine. These attacks would not normally last long and after a couple of days they would be full of beans again. However, when the attacks were more severe, they left them and us feeling listless and fatigued and it would take weeks to recover. Sallie remembers being delerious from very high temperatures. In those days there was no panadol to reduce a dangerously high temperature. In our third year, it was decided that Malocide had become resistant to the local strain of malaria and we went on to Atebrin tablets. These were vile tasting and Simon particularly always resisted vigorously and had to have his tablet forced down his throat.

Simon at the crawling stage, was a great fossicker and we thought that we had stowed most things out of his reach, but one morning there was panic. Ida found him stuffing rat poison into his mouth, which had been left in a saucer in a dark corner of the built-in pantry. I held him up by the legs and tried to make him vomit without success. So, Ida holding him, we raced down to the mission hospital at unusually great speed. Dr Reid took over and assured us that there was no indication of rat poison in his stomach and that all would be well. Simon suffered no after-effects and following that incident, the rat poison was kept high up in the shelves.

On the first occasion that we found worms in their stools we were horrified. This over the years became not an unusual occurrence. Each time worms were detected, we dosed the children with great difficulty with what must have been pretty revolting stuff, but it did the trick. Much later on, in Malekula, Simon produced an enormous worm—probably ten inches long—which he proudly discovered swimming in the toilet. A revolting sight, but this too was dealt with by the necessary tablets. Over our sojourn on Tanna, poor Ida faced some difficult medical problems and when she had to be evacuated for better medical facilities, transport was always a worry.

The following year, there was a widespread outbreak of Hepatitis in the community, and both Ida and Karen succumbed. In later years on Malekula, Sallie at the age of 9, became very ill with Hepatitis.

Daily Life

As a fully trained kindergarten teacher, Ida could not resist setting up a little kindergarten "in her spare time". It included some European mission children, local children from our closest village, Bethel, and our own. They all loved it and looked forward to classes on Wednesday and Friday afternoons. The Bethel children would be brought up to the station in Jack Usamoli's old Jeep. The appreciative shouts and yells on arrival and departure of the visiting children were very rewarding. Jack Osamoli, who had Fijian connections, had a little bakery—an oven built with cement and beach stones—which worked very effectively and we usually procured our bread from him.

By the beginning of our second tour, (January of 1961) the tennis court was taking shape. I had begun clearing the site with prison labour and from time to time organised the expatriate population for working bees, Ida, of course, always providing the afternoon teas. Fortunately, the Duc's relief (when he proceeded on leave) was M Daniel, a man of my own age and a keen sportsman. He and his wife were both avid tennis players and he agreed readily that we use condominium public works labour to finish the job. The tennis court was a great asset; apart from the joy of tennis, it brought people together socially, resulting in many happy gatherings.

In the early days on Tanna, I borrowed a 16 millimetre cinema projector from headquarters and began showing my own films and some documentaries borrowed from Vila. There was an enthusiastic response and within a month, I would have as many as 1000 villagers attending the show.

Later I was provided with funds to purchase a projector for the district. I would laboriously lug it with the screen and a portable generator on tour to the outer islands and to regions accessible by vehicle on Tanna. As I say, it was enthusiastically received by the local population but it was something of a strain on the projectionist—me. It meant operating usually until midnight and at the end of a long day of discussions, court hearings, and negotiations over land disputes, it became quite a struggle. However, I felt that it was well worth the effort and gave not only pleasure but also some inkling of life in the western world to my audiences. I think the most appreciated were my own films and rather hackney cowboy films that became very tedious.

One of our great joys as a family was to drive down to Lenakel, sit on the beach and watch the whales migrating on their way north or south. It was always a magnificent sight; these enormous animals would approach almost to a stone's throw of the beach and again on the return journey south accompanied by their young. They would just play waving their enormous tails up in the air, tossing their large babies to somersault back into the water. We never ceased to enjoy the spectacle, a magnificent performance.

Dr Beaglehole

During this time, Dr Beaglehole from the University of Wellington NZ arrived in the 'Moama', bringing welcome mail. He was a historian and the authority on Captain Cook. He came to visit Port Resolution where Captain Cook in the 'Resolution' spent several weeks having his vessel careened and procuring fresh vegetables in 1779. Dr Beaglehole had almost completed his work *The Life of Captain James Cook*. He was a most charming man and we found him no trouble at all. I took him on various occasions to Port Resolution to leave him there for hours at a time, soaking up the atmosphere. He stayed for several weeks and later in a thank you letter he said he very much regretted that he had been unable to thank us for our hospitality in his preface to his book.

Queen's Birthday

The Queen's Birthday was and remained until independence the most important social event of the year. It was an occasion to 'show the flag' and in this respect the British made more of the annual celebration than the French appeared to do for their equivalent, Bastille Day. On Tanna we made elaborate preparations. The most important event of the day was the *kaikai* (feast) for which fairly substantial government funds were always made available. Prisoners killed and cooked two head of cattle and cooked ten bags of rice, using empty fuel drums. Usually up to 2000 people would attend. After feasting, local bands would strike up and dancing continued until daylight.

In the early days, liquor was not allowed but this was abolished in 1963. I vividly recall many years later on Malekula sending an army of prisoners out to collect en masse the empty Foster's beer cans.

VIPs including the French District Agent and wife and staff, all the European population including missionaries, planters and traders, and leading members of the indigenous population—chiefs, assessors, and government staff—were invited.

On Tanna, on each of the four Queen's birthdays for which I was responsible, we planned a garden lunch that included pre-dinner non-alcoholic drinks with savouries, a main meal, and sweets.

In our first year, we procured 20 chickens and made an enormous curry to go with rice. When the day dawned, to our horror we found that the cauldron of curry was bubbling alarmingly and had gone off overnight due to lack of refrigeration. Thus the only alternative was to raid our stock of tinned meat carefully hoarded in the pantry—ten tins of canned sausages. Everyone politely said it was delicious. The savouries and the sweets which Ida had toiled over for over a week were indeed delicious—such delights as lemon meringue pies, coconut cakes, and fruit salad.

At one stage of the proceedings before I had asked for a toast to the Queen, I noticed assessor Nieri filling his felt hat which he always wore with lemon meringue pie and taking it over to the garden fence to feed his multitude of children. I was fortunate on that first occasion to have received on loan the 16 millimetre projector and showed a mixture of travel films and comics. And the audience, not having seen film before, were transfixed.

Isangel Storm

We had just settled down for the night when we heard a loud knocking at the door—Elijah had a message for me from Vila: 'Tropical Storm SW, speed 50 knots moving NE. Advise precautions'. I hurried over to the office and looked for its position on the map and found that it was heading straight for us. I raced home again, got out nails and hammer, and started to batten down. Just as well I did so because before I had finished, a window in the spare room blew open and the glass smashed.

The wind was literally roaring overhead by now and I finished nailing up in between gusts, taking shelter every time it got too wild. Coconut leaves were flying everywhere, limbs snapping off, and iron roofs flapping. I had put the dressing table against the door to Simon's room that would not stay closed. Every so often, the dressing table would go spinning across the room so eventually I nailed that up and put Simon into a pram by our bedside, which seemed the most sheltered spot. I brought everything into the west verandah with rain and wind streaming in. By this time, both Karen and Simon were both wide awake—it was such a terrific din, neither could nor wanted to sleep.

Finally, I had everything secured. I reckoned wind speed must have been 60 knots, too fast to be comfortable, and the old house was shuddering on its foundations with each big gust. I decided to brave the gusts and go across to the Met station to get its midnight report. I dashed between flurries from spot to spot. The poor garden had already laid flat, and passing our joint offices, I found the roof had been lifted neatly off its posts, 50 yards from the building. The radio office door was wide open and not a soul in sight. I located Elijah eventually in the new brick police barracks, snoring his head off where he had found company and reckoned he was safe. I told him off suitably, it was too late to get another report. He probably would not have been able to get it anyway.

I nipped back to the house where there were some terrible noises and was relieved to find that it was only the guttering hanging like wet socks over the electric wiring. Sheltered behind the full water tank, which I felt was secure, and between lulls and flying branches, I dashed out to remove guttering. I was relieved to get it off and go back inside again.

We decided there was no point in staying awake, so we huddled into bed with Simon on one side, Karen on the other. We listened to the flapping of loose iron and the shuddering of the house every now and then. I felt most anxious for the roof as the wind was now coming from the west and beginning to lift the verandah. I decided that if the roof went, we would make a hasty retreat to the police barracks, probably the strongest building on the station. We drifted into a heavy sleep and did not stir until five. There was no sound at all, a bright sky, and enormous seas pounding the shore. The poor garden, what a mess—branches were down, two mango trees toppled, and the native store flattened. Thank goodness the new garage and Land Rover were still in one piece.

Gradually the station came to life to survey the damage. The Duc said that he'd thought his house was going to go. It lifted off its foundations from time to time. Our prison gangs started cleaning up.

Dr Armstrong came at seven-thirty, full of excitement about the tremendous seas which had come up to within 50 yards of their house, which is about a quarter of a mile from the sea's edge. We drove down a road littered with leaves and deployed two prisoners to remove them as we went to view the damage. What a sight—the beach strewn with rubbish, dead goats and fish, trees etc., the sea having come more than 200 yards inland.

There were crowds of Tannese collecting fish, some alive, many dead, from the bush. Bob Paul's 'Corrigan' was lying badly damaged on its side on the beach. His and other boat sheds were flattened. We went on to look at the Catholic mission station. It was unbelievable—heavy seas had swept hundreds of yards inland taking away coconut trees and other big shady trees. Père Sacco said he had been sleeping despite the heavy winds and awoke to find his room awash in a matter of minutes before he had time to call for help. He'd had to run for higher ground, no time to rescue anything except his glasses.

The little church made of concrete had just crumpled up, he said. His house had lifted up and been dumped and buried in the sand. His Land Rover rolled 100 yards from its site; practically everything had been completely ruined. Poor Père Sacco. We felt so sorry for him.

Lots of native homes along the beach were just completely destroyed. Houses had fallen on top of families, thatched ones of course, as they struggled to safety. Further north, we learnt that three children had been lost when the house they were in just disappeared. It seemed to me that it must have been a tidal wave, but it seems that it was just a coincidence with the very high tide and powerful winds.

The Met station in Vila told me that only the south had been hit. Two ships had gone out that night—the 'Concorde' and the 'Lakeleo'—nothing was heard of them for two days and I had really begun to think that they had been lost. I organised an aircraft to start searching and they were found on the coast of Erromango. Miraculously, they had found some shelter, but were terribly battered and were having to make repairs before going on to Vila. Their radio was out of action.

So that weekend was taken up organising relief with blankets, food, etc., in Vila. The vessel 'Don Quixote' was dispatched with food supplies which were badly needed on Aneityum. I had planned to go on to Aniwa but then the new French Resident Commissioner arrived down on the Concorde and the 'Don Quixote' was recalled. I took a poor view of this as I felt that we should at least have seen how Aniwa had fared—we had had no radio contact with them. In fact, I subsequently found that the damage had not been so severe there.

Tidal Waves and Earthquakes

One afternoon after torrential rain for a few days I received an urgent telegram from Vila—'tidal wave your area imminent, take all precautions'. I posted Ida on the west verandah with binoculars to keep watch and sent Corporal Joseph along the north coast with the Land Rover, and a policeman on foot to the south warning villagers to take shelter inland. It was four o'clock; he got back and there was still no sign of the tidal wave.

Kath Paul, whose house was situated close to the Lenakel passage, had moved her family up to the mission station. I had visions of the recent tidal wave that had destroyed parts of the Chile coast and Hawaii so I was relieved to be sited on high ground. The evening passed without event—the sea looked greasy and there was a big swell and high winds. It felt ominous and I thought we were in for a bad night. The rain fell in torrents for the rest of the night. There was no sign of driver Jimmy who had been sent to the east coast to warn the population there.

We were up at dawn the next morning but still no tidal wave, thank goodness, and the day proceeded normally. Later we heard that there had been considerable damage in Hawaii and Fiji but we fortunately had escaped.

Minor earth tremors were a regular occurrence but at no stage did we experience anything serious. Yasur continued to rumble and throw red-hot boulders up into the sky from time to time and to shower the whole island with black ash. When the wind was coming from the east, it was Makia's first job each morning to dust down the ash from all exposed surfaces.

During this time we had a visit from a French Government-financed team of volcanologists, led by Monsieur Tazzief who was apparently a world's leading authority on the subject, to examine the volcanoes of the group. Firstly the underwater volcano off Tongoa, then Ambrym's Marum, Samuel Bembo, and Lopevei, and Yasur on Tanna. We housed the party in the rest house but poor Madame Duc Dufayard had to feed them, calling on Ida to assist from time to time. We had them to dinner one evening and found Monsieur Tazzief a charming man and an amusing raconteur.

Ten

Vignette – Pirates and Poachers

Illegal shipping and fishing coming into our sea space regularly posed a problem. Most of these ships were from the Far East, such as Formosa, and they were looking for Trocas and Green Snail shells, which at that time were worth $500 per tonne. A law had been promulgated preventing the fishing of shell for a period to allow the crop to regenerate. On one occasion, I was told that a ship was loading shell and working on it day and night on Aneityum. I reported it to Vila and a Lancaster was sent dropping a note on the vessel, ordering it to Vila. This was done at three in the afternoon and my colleague and I set out in the 'Rocinante' to see that the order was followed. Not unusually, there were heavy seas and we arrived at Aneityum at dawn to find the ship had fled.

On another occasion, a Japanese vessel was reported on the reef at Aneityum. Artie Kraft radioed me to say he had a crew of 28 and that they did not speak a word of English and what should he do. While I was talking to Artie, the French warship 'Francis Garner' appeared on the horizon. Apparently she only dropped some supplies and hurried away again, which wasn't very helpful in assisting our crisis.

I chartered Bob Paul's plane and we flew over the site to find that the ship was breaking up. There was nothing much we could do at this stage but on return, Vila told me that a local Japanese vessel was on its way to pick up the survivors—so Artie Kraft's problem was soon solved. For the villagers at Aneityum it was like Christmas—the ship's cargo of pears, peaches, tinned meats etc., were strewn over the beach ready for the taking. When I went back to Aneityum a month or so later, big seas had indeed broken up the vessel and nothing of its cargo remained.

Another incident occurred on the 10th of April 1962. I had been away for the day at Sulphur Bay, and on my way back when negotiating a washed-out road, I broke the centre pin of the front bearing of the Land Rover. With my front axle ending up at right angles to the chassis, I abandoned the truck and walked. That afternoon, I eventually arrived at John Cooper's and used his radio to ask for a French truck to come and pick me up. We continued on but there was no sign of the truck and I eventually walked right through to the hospital, arriving at seven in the evening. We were just finishing our meal at the hospital with the Peermans when Kath rang to say the radio station had been trying to contact me urgently as there were reports of a foreign vessel shelling at Aneityum. I confirmed with Aneityum that there was indeed a vessel, probably Japanese, so I got onto Vila through the Met station who were still on duty and finally talked to Colin Allan. Bob had offered his launch of the 'Corrigan' for charter if I wanted it.

Meanwhile Colin, after ringing the French residency, called me back to say they would discuss it in the morning and would probably send a navy patrol vessel of air force Lancaster. Having visions of the previous year's raider—which as soon as the Lancaster appeared, set sail and was never heard of again—I asked if I should charter the 'Corrigan' and proceed down to Aneityum at once and rendezvous with the Lancaster there. More telephone discussions took place with Colin and Mr Rennie, before finally an instruction arrived as follows: 'I have discussed with the Resident Commissioner. If you are satisfied Paul's boat is in satisfactory condition and has good radio communication, please proceed as quickly as possible to Port Patrick and report before taking further action. It is essential that you are in a position to communicate with Vila on sighting the vessel. Signed, Allan'.

By now it was ten at night. Bob went off to recall the 'Corrigan' which was fishing just up the coast, and I got the police organised. I took Corporal Norman and policemen Kaikai and Ahten, who were my best men. We prepared nine 303 rifles, a box of ammunition, and all five of my handcuffs, as well as supplies of water and food. I regretted not having a pistol but could not locate one to take. By this time it was midnight and I had arranged to be on the beach at three-fifteen, so I went to bed for a couple of hours of fitful sleep, wondering how mad I was.

When I woke to the alarm, Norman was loading up the borrowed truck. We went straight down to the beach. Bob Paul and Peter Johnstone, who had asked if they could come, were also loading up and refuelling. This all took some time and we did not sail till five—the first light of the dawn was just breaking as we left the bay. Before leaving the beach, I'd walked into an overhanging branch and gashed my forehead which did not make me feel very happy. I'd dashed up to the house to patch it up and take some aspirin and as the day went on and with all the excitement, I forgot all about it, thank goodness.

We were extremely lucky to get a reasonable sea and a lovely day, the first in weeks, so the gods were with us. We discussed plans of attack and at seven called up on the radio to report our position. We maintained regular contact thereafter until ten when I got onto Colin Allan again. I enquired news of the Lancaster or naval vessel. He informed me that the French Commissioner had not seen fit to ask for either and that we must "go it alone". He said if I wished, he would organise Paul in the Dragon to patrol with us at zero hour, so I accepted, feeling that even moral support was better than nothing.

It seemed that the French RC was piqued that Mr Rennie had organised the dispatch of a patrol (mine) without French agreement. The Duc was in Vila with the French RC anyway when all the telephone conversations had occurred. He was also mindful of my previous experience with the 'Yung Chin' which had also been shelling illegally and had simply got away when warned by the Lancaster without ground action to stop it.

I was determined not to have French police on board who would have been more dangerous than they were helpful. At least my policemen were accustomed to some discipline. I also had Bob and Peter to contend with, because though they were loyal and helpful, both could be somewhat trigger-happy and scatterbrained. In fact, Bob could not have been more helpful and cooperative throughout the whole expedition, abiding by what I said without question.

So we rolled on. I had a little doze but the sun was hot and the launch too small for comfortable resting. Lunch was bully beef and tea. Bob had his tape recorder and we made a recording of the venture from time to time. We sighted Aneityum clearly by midday and thereafter arranged radio schedules with Vila every half hour, then every quarter hour, then a ball by ball description. For an hour we raked the coast with binoculars but could not see anything and began to think that they had got wind of us and flown.

Suddenly there was a flash of light, probably the sun on the bridge windscreen, and there it was, anchored close in. We reported sighting back to Vila, by which time the whole of the group was obviously listening in. The usual programmes had been stopped so that we had constant clear communication. By 1 o'clock we could see it—an old shaggy-looking vessel about 100 tonnes, we thought.

The police now donned their uniforms and hid below. Rifles were loaded and hidden at convenient easily accessible points about the boat. I changed into clean whites so that I would look official and Peter lent me a little .22 automatic which fitted into my pocket without being obvious. I had strife getting my clothes on as we were rolling hard. I too stayed below for a surprise boarding. We rolled on. My heart was beating fast I can tell you. I just hoped that there would be no strife. I felt pretty sure there would not be but with visions of the possibility of a Chinese crew or even a tough pirate crew, I did not feel too happy. No sign of Paul in his Rapide overhead and I wished that he'd hurry up.

At half-past one, we could see that there were very few people on board and probably the crew was out shelling in their small boats. It looked as though we were lucky. Bob was giving a running commentary to Vila over the radio and loving it! At 1.45 Bob called out, "Okay!" and I popped up on deck. We were right alongside and there were about six Chinese men standing about on their deck.

The surprise boarding failed, however, as Bob's coxswain was so nervous that he kept misjudging distance. We circled three times at close quarters before we got close enough for me to jump. As I did, Norman followed in full uniform and swinging his little silver-topped cane and looking very smart. The other two police, Peter and one of Bob's crew, pulled out rifles from under tarpaulins. The captain and crew of the raider looked horrified and I knew the day was won! Bob called as I jumped aboard with rifle in hand, "Keep your back to us, Darve. We've got you covered."

I demanded from the captain the name of his ship etc., but he obviously couldn't speak a word of English. By this time, most of the crew as far as I could see were on deck. I sent one policeman forward to guard from the forecastle and one aft. Peter with one of the 'Corrigan' crew went forward to search the ship and hustle anyone else on deck—there was only one other—six in all. All the rest, 21 all told, were out shelling. We were lucky. If they had all been there, they might have tried to throw us overboard.

The radio operator, a Chinese man, spoke a few words of English and I found out that the ship was the 'Ah Whan' from Formosa. He admitted to shelling for trocas and green snail, and had no authority to enter the New Hebrides, no flag flying, and no ship identification. Bob was still giving his running commentary—I heard snatches of his report; "Mr Wilkins is talking to the Captain, the police are searching the vessel, the 'Corrigan' is circling nearby and the two other crew members are standing with rifles covering the ship". I hate to think what would have happened if someone had fired a shot!!

There was still no sign of the the Dragon Rapide aircraft and I kept thinking the shelling boats might appear at any moment around the point with their crews. Bob kept reminding me to "watch my back" and the like; he was loving every minute of it! Conversation with the captain was difficult, however, I got him to understand we were going straight to Analgahaut, Aneityum's main anchorage, where Artie Kraft was with more people to assist if necessary. The captain was obviously reluctant but the engineer had started up the fuel burning engines with a terrific noise! The ship stank to high heaven of shellfish and then there was strife getting the anchor up. I thought we'd never get moving. Finally we did, heading for Analgahaut with me guarding the bridge, Peter patrolling the vessel, a policeman forward and aft, and Bob calling out again, "Keep a check on the crew members". He had a lot of sensible advice really, and went on ahead. I told the captain to follow and off we steamed with no strife! Half an hour later, we heard the Dragon overhead. Paul came down to swoop and buzz us then flitted about, darting overhead like a fighter pilot for the next hour.

Ahead, we sighted three launches with crews returning from their day's shelling. By now it was three in the afternoon. They were completely taken by surprise. We decided to tow them rather than having them all on the ship. This we did but the last crew refused. Bob fired a shot over their bows, the first shot of the day, and they came up smartly with no further dispute. Thus we proceeded into Analgahaut. At this stage I sent a telegram to the British Resident: 'Ship and crew now in custody, proceeding to Analgahaut'. I gathered that all of Vila heard about it!

As we steamed into Analgahaut with Bob proceeding in his launch, towing three launches full of shells and Chinese crews and with Paul swooping overhead, the entire village turned out to watch us. Bob towed the crew ashore where they were guarded by the villagers and I piloted the ship to anchorage (shades of sailor!). We took the captain, engineer, and radio operator ashore, leaving only three crew aboard.

At a council of war, we decided to keep the three key men under arrest ashore and the rest of the crew aboard the boat where it would be easier to guard them and feel more secure. A guard of three villagers and a policeman was with the three key men and a patrol of villagers were on the beach to see that none of the crew would swim ashore to attempt a rescue. All the three launches were anchored well away near the beach where they could be watched.

It was now five in the evening and I arranged a call with Vila from the Met station. I talked to Colin Allan. He said that both the Resident Commissioner and the French Resident Commissioner sent their congratulations. Subsequently, I had messages from the Duc and John Longoton. Mr Robinson, the radio engineer, said he could hear the disappointment in Bob's voice when he reported "Mr Wilkins now aboard, there is no fighting".

The French RC had arranged for a detachment of marines to be flown down to Vila and then Tanna from Noumea as there was no escort vessel available. From there they would be brought down to Anelgehot on the 'Trudy' which was leaving the next night. "Which confirmed my theory that all the French Navy is useful for is giving cocktail parties," said Bob. We had a long wait.

Guarding by day was not a problem but by night it was not so easy. I did not feel comfortable with all those Chinese aboard and with inexperienced guards on land. There was a risk that they could swim ashore, overpower the guards, and flee outside territorial waters where nothing could be done. So we did not get much rest. Bob and Peter were exhausted and went into a dead sleep but I kept waking up and checking. It was another long night but it passed without incident.

The next day, I had council meetings, courts etc., with incidentally a nice little stack of paperwork to do as a result—writing up court cases, tour reports, and so on. So the day went without a rest. Thursday they confirmed from Vila that the 'Trudy' had left for Tanna and the marines would arrive on Tanna on Friday morning. By this time the Duc was back on Tanna and organising everything, as you can imagine. Thursday night again was restless. Feeling responsible, I was up every few hours checking. I managed to have a rest on Friday afternoon which was good. Our captives were very docile, poor fellows. I felt very sorry for them really.

Friday night the village decided to have a farewell party for me as I was soon to be leaving the district. I would much rather have gone to bed because the marines were due at ten that night and we could then hand them over and have a sleep. They arrived, all sick and exhausted but ready to take over. They took everyone on board and locked them below deck and guarded the ship. They were armed to the teeth and I was hoping that they would not be unnecessarily tough. They seemed to be okay. It was 11 am by the time plans for departure were sorted out and the dance in my honour could begin. I could see right from the start that it was going to be a daylight job and it was! We planned to leave at five in the morning. At four, there were speeches and I was presented with baskets and a grass skirt. I was quite touched though as they seemed genuinely sorry to see me go.

I had a soft spot for Aneityum as I seemed over the four years to have been involved in a lot of emergency visits to them. Once with Dr Reid for a child who was seriously hurt and evacuated on 'Don Quixote' just after my arrival in the district. Then the tidal wave visit, another time to collect a chap who had gone mad and threatened to kill his family, then the abortive 'Yung Chin' and now the Formosan ship.

I heard the roar of the 'Ah Whan' and knew that the marines were getting the crew to start up ready for departure. So I gathered everything together. Bob, in order not to miss out on arrival back at Lenakel and his boat being slower than the 'Trudy', had left at 3 in the morning. Peter stayed to come with me in the 'Trudy'. We went down to the beach just as the first rays of light were touching the eastern sky. The villagers sang and played their guitars and ukuleles as they lined up big and small to say goodbye. We rowed out to the 'Trudy' and moved out of the bay with the 'Ah Whan' obediently following. It was dawn once more. I had a cup of coffee and toast before leaving. Sitting up on deck I could see there was no trouble and about 8 am went below to sleep till about midday. When I came on deck, the 'Trudy' was rolling hard, the 'Ah Whan' was still astern, and we could see the 'Corrigan' rolling well in front of us.

At 2 o'clock we were all just off Lenakel and Bob went aboard the 'Ah Whan' to pilot her in. The whole world and his wife were ashore to meet us. The Coopers had come over for the day and also the Brisbanes, so there was a crowd of Europeans. I could see the French police in uniform and as we came ashore, the Duc ordered a present arms for me (typical of the Duc)! There was great excitement, congratulations, etc., as we recounted the story. I was glad to let the Duc take over arrangements with the help of the other half of my police, while the marines came ashore to eat and swim. They left the next morning at six for Vila. Kath was expecting me for dinner—a delicious roast. We were all famished, not having eaten since the night before as it was too rough to cook anything on board. By the time we had finished dinner and discussions it was four in the morning.

Then Marge and co arrived and Bob played the tape recording of the radio conversations which were most amusing really. By this time I was keen to get home, bathe, and sleep. I did not stir till nine next morning.

Jon Frum

Cargo cults sprang up in the Solomons and later, in the New Hebrides after the end of WW2. The massive influx of troops and materials, aircraft, vehicles, guns, and an inexhaustible supply of clothing and food must indeed have had a tremendous impact on island people. American troops had easy access to all these luxury goods—why not them?

The first cargo cult, as anthropologists called it, started up in the late 40s on Malaita in the Solomons. It was known as 'The Marching Rule', was opposed to a white government, and willing to wait for the arrival of goods and chattels that the Americans had had. This movement did not die out until the mid 60s.

In the New Hebrides, there were two somewhat similar outbreaks. The first on north-west Malekula where a European trader, Donald Gubbay, gained some influence in the region promising trucks, refrigerators etc. The New Hebridean leader was Paul Tamlamlam. Not surprisingly when only a couple of dilapidated American army Land Rovers were landed at Tontar in return for all local copra produced there, enthusiasm quickly waned and the movement, such as it was, died a natural death.

The second movement on Tanna, however, was a different story. There were obscure stories of a figure dressed in green with a felt wide-brimmed hat appearing mysteriously from time to time in the south-western region of Tanna, and the name 'Jon Frum' took hold.

It was on the east coast that the movement gained momentum. Its headquarters were at Sulphur Bay within the shadows of Yasur, the volcano. It became widely believed that the enormous wealth of goods and chattels held by the American troops would start to flow and from which the messianic figure would appear. At Sulphur Bay, a high bamboo fence protected the village entrance with a wide entrance gate patrolled by Jon Frum 'soldiers' carrying bamboo rifles. The leaders here were Nampas, a tall imposing white bearded man, Moiles, short and stocky, and a very effective speaker, and Boite, insignificant—an aide-de-camp to the other two.

It was Nampas and Moiles with whom we always negotiated. About the end of 1959, red painted wooden crosses began to appear at strategic sites in different parts of the island and rumours spread that Jon was about to appear. He didn't, but this did not put an end to rumours. We were told that Sulphur Bay was now closed to the government and my colleague and I went over to investigate. At the entrance to the village we were told by the guards to wait and Nampas and Moiles were called.

They informed us that it was Jon Frum territory and government was forbidden to enter. We pointed out that we were on Tanna to help its peoples' progress and must have access to the entire island. A long discussion between the leaders ensued, at the end of which we were refused entry. This was a somewhat tense moment because most of the village had turned out to listen to the discussion.

Fortunately my colleague and I were in agreement. We took a pretty deep breath, pushed our way through the crowd, walked slowly through the village, turned back to the gates, shook hands with Nampas and Moiles—who did so very reluctantly—waved to the villagers, and drove off!

The movement was a constant threat to our jurisdiction and over the years it continued to pose the problem of holding back developments, even down to opposing the construction of roads, dispensaries and schools. But on each occasion, with no more than verbal pressure, the opposition would collapse. Probably the biggest blow to the movement was the arrival of Bob Paul's aircraft in late 1958 that they had maintained would land with Jon Frum aboard.

It was an ongoing source of irritation because we were regularly called out by the progressive elements and particularly the Presbyterian Church followers to deal with Jon Frum opposition to their plans.

Kava and Copra

Kava played a big part in the social life of a man on Tanna. I was keen to experience the effects of kava and so on my first walking tour into the isolated north of the island, I camped overnight in a small village and set up my small tent. I had a bite to eat and then went down to the *nakamal* (meeting place), traditionally under the shade of a banyan tree. This tree was some 100 feet in diameter. At the *nakamal*, there were eight or ten men of the village squatting around a fire watching three young boys of about 12 or 14, prepare the kava. Kava is made from the roots of a shrub, *piper methysticum* and the shrub is dug out very carefully so as not to break the roots. These are washed thoroughly and the boys who have not yet reached puberty masticate the roots into a soft pulpy substance. The pulp is then spat out onto the outer bark of the coconut palm, which serves as a strainer. Water is stirred into the pulp, which is then sieved through the mesh, poured into coconut shells, and swallowed in one gulp.

The old men were still sitting comfortably on their haunches and the kava was passed around to them. As each man took his shell of kava, he would turn away from the fire, walk to the edge of the *nakamal*, and gulp down the contents of the shell. Having finished, he would hawk loudly, spit the remnants of fibre from the kava, and clearing his throat, then amble slowly back to his seat.

My turn came. I was politely handed a shell and so followed suit. It was something of a trial as I had seen these youths masticating the root and had visions of some terrible disease like tuberculosis, but comforted myself that it must be reasonably safe because of the powerful disinfectant content of the root itself. Nonetheless it took a great effort to swallow the brown syrupy liquid, which looked and tasted like muddy water—a vile taste I must confess. As it went down, and it was an effort to get the whole shell down without a breath, I could feel my throat constricting and I had a horrible fear that I might throw up at any moment. I felt a strange numbness on the lips and throat and this increased after a few minutes. It definitely had an anesthetising effect, which I knew was one of kava's qualities. I moved slowly back to my seat—I was privileged to be seated on a log—and talked or rather whispered to my neighbour as the numbing effects increased.

The second round was so difficult to take and I felt slightly weak at the knees. With the third round, half an hour later, I was feeling distinctly unsteady. By this point all was quiet. There were certainly no loud voices (a far cry from the Australian pub scene) and periodically one of the men would get up to stoke the fire and push in the hot logs with which the fire was initially set.

About this time, one old man moved over to the fire, took a burning stick, waving it slowly from side to side to shed a little light, and wandered slowly into the night. This was repeated over the next hour or so, each man taking it in turns to quietly take an ember from the fire to act as a torch and slowly move off into the night. I felt strangely content as I lay back on the ground looking at the stars twinkling through the leaves of the banyan tree. It was deadly quiet now and I began to feel, I suppose, my spirit leaving my body. It was a most extraordinary feeling and as the natives say, when you drink kava "yu harem wan samting". I must have slept very soundly and did not stir until dawn when I went back to my tent.

The next day passed with me hearing a court case over a land dispute and other routine matters. I felt no after-effects at all of the kava except to feel slightly sick when I thought about how it had been prepared.

Copra was and remains one of the principal export crops and money winners of the population of the entire archipelago. It is made from the white flesh of the ripe coconut. French and Australian planters initially established coastal coconut plantations throughout the islands and very quickly the indigenous population began establishing their own; often hard up against the European plantations to act as a barrier for further expansion by the white owners—a practice which often happened in the early days.

Copra beds haphazardly constructed with local material and thatched roof are found throughout the native gardens and the copra made from their palm trees provides a cash flow for most villages even to this day. The copra having been dried out by fire in the copra beds, is bagged and taken to the closest seaport for purchase traders. The price of copra like any commodity varies tremendously.

The 'Duc'

In a note from Duc Dufayard, he complained that one of my policemen, Kaikai, was playing up with one of his house girls. I punished Kaikai with several days stoppage of leave and thought that that was the end of it. Then Kaikai wrote an abusive letter to his rival, a French policeman. Evidently the French policeman complained to the Duc, who promptly sent a note back to me demanding more action. I decided I had taken sufficient action against him and that was that. The Duc came to my office the next day very annoyed with me for not having done more. After a heated argument, the matter was dropped—just an example of the trivial matters which constantly interfered with our joint administration.

Another example was one Friday when sparks flew. I had written to the Duc suggesting that work be done on a certain section of the road and it was his month for responsibility for public works. He wrote back criticising my work of the previous month and raking up several other incidents we had argued about previously. I felt the criticism was quite unjust and childish; I was very angry, marched over to his office, plonked his note on his desk, and said, "Don't you think it is time, M. Duc Dufayard, that we stop writing these ridiculous notes?" This started him off but by this time I really was angry, grabbed the note, crumpled it up, and threw it on the floor. I said, "I'm too angry to discuss the matter further," marched out of the room and down the garden path. He was evidently left speechless. I was so cross I had to sit down for a while and cool off.

The embarrassing thing was that we had arranged to meet that afternoon on the other side of the island for discussions with the Sulphur Bay Jon Frumites. I was tempted not to turn up. But having promised to pick him up at the volcano crossroads, I promptly did so. He was very polite and tried to make chatty conversation so I gave him a cool reception. The discussions at Sulphur Bay went well and we got the 'big men' there to see some reason.

Saturday was the usual weekly meeting, this in my office, and so at 9.00 over he came. Richard was there typing so we discussed humdrum things first. Then when Richard departed, my colleague said, "Mr Wilkins, I can see you were very angry yesterday but I cannot understand why." So I said, "M. Duc Dufayard, if you allow me to explain," and then did so with the Duc trying in customary fashion to interrupt from time to time. He said that his last note had not been intended to be critical etc., and to cut a long story short, we became pals again.

No doubt there are always language difficulties, and notes can often be misread. Anyway I took the opportunity of making the suggestion that if he would only move into his own office immediately adjoining mine there would not be so much misunderstanding and we could deal with problems jointly as they came up. He agreed about this. He remarked it was just a case of getting down to it but his wife did not like having guests in her house—which would have eventuated if he had evacuated his office, thus making room for guests, which Madame would not tolerate. I had him on the defensive for once.

Duc Dufayard was in fact a very senior officer in the French administrative service, serving his last tour before retirement. Apparently in the French Overseas Civil Service, the farther away you are from Paris (and on Tanna you could not get much farther) the higher the salary, and he had, I believe, refused offers of governorship in French African territories. He was a very determined man used to having his own way. In other respects he was a good administrator and overall we worked more harmoniously together than I was ever to find with other colleagues in the next 16 years of joint administration.

Madame 'Duc'

Madame Duc Dufayard, a rather forbidding but kindly lady, had been a midwife in French Equatorial Africa. Apparently she originated from a well-to-do French aristocratic family in Alsace-Lorraine.

Language was always a barrier. She spoke no English, practically no Bislama, and our French was poor. She used the small French police detachment as personal servants and it was not unusual to see poor Sergeant Tom with a tea towel over his arm serving at the table and working in the kitchen. She was a marvellous cook and served vast quantities of the most delectable foods. She enjoyed having guests to meals but not to stay. She had a wonderful vegetable garden and a menagerie of poultry, pigs, and goats.

Madame was incredibly kind to both of us. More particularly to Ida and later, despite an age difference and language problems, they became close friends, exchanging recipes and kitchen equipment quite regularly. She adored our children.

I remember on one occasion after a sumptuous dinner, I planned to set out on a walking tour the next day. And just before my departure, a large parcel arrived of cold French pancakes which I had enjoyed the night before, to aid me on the journey.

Local Characters

Jimmy Tasiriki, I think from North Efate, had been imprisoned in Vila for some years and was transferred to my prison. He had been sentenced to 20 years for poisoning his mother-in-law. He was extremely capable, a good driver and mechanic, and both on Tanna and later on Malekula, he proved himself invaluable.

As I've mentioned, Dr Armstrong was very appropriately known as 'the elder statesman'. A short, stocky man with a bristling white moustache and white hair, he must have been about 60. He was a terror to talk to and one had to always allow time to listen. He took offence very easily, for example, he hadn't spoken to my predecessor for some time before his departure and he detested the Duc. On the other hand, he was extremely kind and helpful and we got on well, although there were times when his chatter became somewhat wearing. Although a fully qualified medical practitioner, he could turn his hand to almost anything—from repairing motor cars to electrical work, from carpentry to lawn mowers. He was thus equally invaluable.

His wife was a charming, kind lady who to my amusement always wore white socks and sandshoes (a missionary habit). I regretted over the years that I never seemed to have the opportunity (probably because Dr A would never let me) to talk about their past. He had been the mission doctor at the Lenakel hospital during the war, and retired soon afterwards to a small cottage built principally with native materials on the edge of the Presbyterian holdings. They had adopted a Tannese baby girl, Nesweiyu, who married Kalarimanu, the radio operator from North Efate. Nesweiyu worked for us in a domestic capacity from time to time.

Mrs Corowa, who arrived on our shores from Northern Queensland in 1958, took the island by storm. She was a direct descendant of a Tannese from south-west who had been blackbirded to Queensland sugar cane fields in the 19th century. On arrival she wore a smart blouse and skirt, high-heeled shoes, and stockings and a black hat. She spoke good Australian English. She immediately came up to my agency to ask if she could get assistance in going south to trace her antecedents, but could she first have accommodation for the night.

We asked her to dinner and talked well into the night. She planned to set up a school on south-west Tanna after she had traced her family, to teach the children English. The next day she went off and we only heard by rumour that she had made a considerable impact and was creating great interest everywhere.

A few months later, she turned up at Isangel again, looking a little bedraggled and without the stockings and high heels. It was rather a sad story—she felt very discouraged having not got very far with the school idea, and she thought the local people were almost bushmen. Could she have a job? Ida was pleased to take her on with her staff and for some time she was most helpful. Then she became restless again and struck up a liaison with George Bright, a local trader.

This lasted a few months, until she came back to tell Ida that things were not working very well and she was thinking of going back to Australia. She drifted about, sometimes with George, sometimes in a village, and sometimes with us. She was always willing to help in a crisis and Ida was grateful to be able to call on her for VIP visits etc. Finally she went back to Australia and we heard no more.

Artie Kraft was a genuine Australian bushman who had spent most of his life in the timber industry. He had apparently left his wife and perhaps children and taken up abode on Aneityum to work the kauri forests. He took me into the mountains to show me the work he was doing. It was hair-raising—precipitous mountains and enormous kauri being felled and dragged to his sawmill on the coast by his bulldozer. The logs were exported to Australia from time to time. He lived in a thatched cottage by the beach at Analgahaut. He was always hospitable and greeted you with open arms.

The story goes that in 1974 the 'Britannia', with the royal family aboard for a formal tour of the group, crept quietly into Analgahaut on its way north. Artie came down from the hills as usual to investigate. He saw the beautiful ship anchored and activity on a spit of land, an island within the bay itself. He found a party picnicking happily on the sandy beach. He squinted, and said, "'Pon my soul, it's the Queen." Apparently they invited him to join them, which he did.

Paul Burton, middle-aged and clean-shaven, was apparently befriended at some stage by Bob Paul whilst in Australia. To Bob's delight it transpired that he was a skilled pilot and from that meeting began a perilous friendship which ended in the formation of the New Hebrides Airlines Ltd. In Bob's battle to establish an air service from Tanna, Paul played a key role, piloting firstly their Lockheed Rapide aircraft to land for the first time on Tanna. The problem was, however, that he was a playboy and irresponsible with money, to Bob's regret. On one occasion he was financed by Bob to take the aircraft to Fiji for repairs but apparently wasted the money. He had a weakness for the girls, especially the Tannese, but he was an excellent man nevertheless.

I remember on one occasion flying with him from Vila to Tanna—it was a beautiful sunny calm day and he flew all the way almost tipping the waves. On our first landing on Futuna, the strip was not more than 400 yards long and stopped at the end of a cliff—some 200 feet above sea level—I thought my last days had come. However Paul, unperturbed, brought the aircraft to a halt just in time.

Tragically some six years later, flying a twin-engine aircraft with 14 passengers, he crashed into the mountains trying to cross from south-west to east on Tanna. Only a boot was found with which to identify him.

I met Richard Tarileo on my first day on Tanna. He was the Isangel British office clerk and his wife was Kwaisi. They had one little girl who became great mates with Karen. Richard was from north-west Pentecost and I found him to be a goldmine. He helped me to struggle with pidgin, he advised me on local custom and generally administrative procedures, and stayed with me as clerk for our full four years on Tanna.

Later when I was well entrenched at Lakatoro on Malekula, I arranged for him to be transferred to my new office there. Again he was most helpful. There he asked Ida to assist with making his liaison with Kwaisi a legal one and to have a formal marriage. Ida sewed up a wedding frock and veil and the bride wore bright white sandshoes. I performed the wedding in the office and later there was a wedding feast and dance at the Lakatoro Metemet Club.

Lofmanteni was a village chief who I appointed as a court assessor. He had a tall imposing build and a white beard and I always found him not only knowledgeable but very wise in his advice on everyday problems dealing with the local population.

Tanna Summary

Overall I found the job of administration in the Southern District very discouraging. There was insufficient transport to service the outer islands, and on Tanna the Jon Frum cargo cult movement held sway. Even those not supportive of this movement appeared to doubt my motives when I tried to encourage the establishment of local councils, schools, and medical services. Suspicion was widespread, the 'big men' (the leaders in the various communities) would listen politely, discuss proposals at length, and come back with the inevitable, "I gud ia be mifalla no wantem" (that's fine but not for us).

Eleven

1962 Santo

On our return from leave in October 1962, I was appointed British District Agent (BDA) for Central District Number 2 (CD2) that comprised the islands of Malekula, Ambrym, Paama, Pentecost, and at first, Epi. Because there was no longer a residence on Malekula, I was to be based at Santo.

On arrival, we were met by Dick Hutchinson, BDA for the Northern District. And after lunch, we were taken to our new home at the southern end of the Luganville settlement that faced the canal, as the anchorage was called. We were sadly disappointed.

A far cry from our Tanna house, it comprised two small bedrooms, a very small lounge, a narrow front verandah, and tiny kitchen and bathroom. It was shabby and needed painting inside and out. A pretty depressing start as we spent the next three days unpacking our crates of personal effects that had been brought up from Tanna. The backyard was tiny, overgrown, and like so much of Luganville, littered with remnants from the USA wartime occupation. To the south of us was the British Office Radio Station with Tom Layng in charge, and to the north were dilapidated American Quonset huts occupied by local people.

Dick Hutchinson was anxious to have a reception for us to meet the local population but the French frigate 'Dunkerquoise' had called in to show the French flag and invited us aboard for cocktails. As Dick said, this was a saving on his entertainment funds because we could be introduced to Luganville locals there.

I was almost immediately thrown into my diplomatic role because the next day the Swedish ambassador from Australia arrived and paid a courtesy call. I felt obliged to entertain him, so provided my new Land Rover and driver to show him the town and take him to lunch at the Santo Hotel. He was very agreeable and that night insisted on taking Ida and I back to the Santo Hotel, virtually the only suitable place to dine out.

My office joined my British colleagues at the northern end of the town. Tom Layng, who lived next to me, told me about a Bantam motorbike for sale. I had never ridden a motorbike but decided it would be useful not only on Santo but later on Malekula, and made the purchase. Tom generously offered to maintain it for me. Later when I had sent my new Land Rover down to Malekula, the Bantam did prove useful, thus allowing me to go to and from the office leaving Ida with our small car. It was a Simca, which I was able to purchase very reasonably, and which gave Ida freedom to ferry our own and neighbouring children to and from school, and also to visit her friends.

Luganville was a small town, its main street comprising the Santo Hotel, a small French Ballandes Store, the Burns Philp store (a little more impressive), and a number of small Chinese operated stores. We were immediately thrown into a very extensive social life with dinner parties and dances, quite often continuing on till the early hours. The occupants who became close friends were mostly younger than Ida and I, nearly all in their late twenties or early thirties. It was nice for Ida to have the social contacts but I began to find them somewhat trying because one would return from tour to face yet another dinner-dance party. We usually managed to sneak away from these no later than one or two, very occasionally we lasted till dawn.

I remember at one party, the guest was the captain of the 'Polynesie' a French Messageries Maritime vessel that plied between Sydney and Vila/Santo every six weeks. At daybreak, the captain asked us aboard the 'Polynesie' for a delicious breakfast of croissants and coffee, and bacon and eggs. We returned home to find Simon and Karen sitting on the front steps anxiously awaiting us, and Sallie still asleep, with Mary our house girl from Tanna hovering in the background.

CD2 (Central District Number 2)

For me, it was a different world at the office. Domiciled in Santo town and with an office attached to BDA Santo, Central District No. 2 presented a real challenge. With no base in the district itself from which to make contact with the district and its people, I was determined to meet the challenge and find a suitable site for a headquarters as soon as possible. I was soon to see that Dick Hutchinson, District Agent, Santo, looked upon me as adjunct, and was going to do his best to rope me in whenever he could. I took a firm stand from the beginning and began almost at once non-stop touring, which of course I had to do to get into the district to be able to work in it.

My initial tour was on the 'Mangaru', captained by a Fijian, Filimone Bataweti, with a Fijian engineer, Bill Smith, and three New Hebridean crew. This British vessel was allocated to the Northern District and when not required by Dick, it was available to me. The 'Mangaru', with a crew efficiently trained by the British Marine Superintendent Captain Kirkwood (an ex-naval Captain), was scrupulously clean; it had a comfortable bathroom and toilet, four berths which would fold down to make lounges with a central folding table, large windows instead of port holes, and steward Joseph to bring me a cup of tea whenever I came on board. Captain Filimone would steam down the channel close into the shore near my house and would sound off the ship's siren whilst I waved furiously. Karen and Simon on the shore thought it was wonderful.

On my initial tour, I was to quickly set foot on all four islands and to make contact with my French colleague at Lamap Port Sandwich, Monsieur Fabre. He and his charming wife whose forebears were from Algeria, asked me to dinner when I called. He was to prove a very cooperative colleague. I looked with interest around his station but could see no possibility of an adjoining site for my headquarters. My next stopover was at Bushman's Bay where stood the remains of the old CD2 agency surrounded by a mere acre of swampy land.

CD2 was administered at this stage principally by the French District Agent at Port Sandwich and until about 18 months prior to my arrival, his British counterpart was Michael Allen based at Luganville. The old British District Agency at Bushman's Bay, Malekula had been abandoned in the early 1940s with its last occupant Mr Adam in charge. Apparently in those days the British District Agents were often locally recruited with no particular qualification or training. With Adam's departure, there was no replacement and the agency at Bushman's Bay very rapidly fell into a state of disrepair. I later used the old agency as a temporary campsite for my operations.

At Port Sandwich, the French District Agents—certainly after the war—continued to be appointed. But as far as I could see, they concentrated almost entirely on supporting the fairly extensive network of French planters. When the British residency decided to reopen a representative for CD2 in 1961, Allen was sent up to Santo. The need for a British representative became more apparent and urgent because the joint condominium court was beginning to deal with land claims on Malekula—these claims were very extensive. Allen described himself as living something of a "Jekyll and Hyde" existence and I quickly found how true this was living in Luganville and working in another district.

For the next 18 months, I was almost constantly on tour. Occasionally, I had the good fortune of the use of the 'Mangaru'. But as I had no specific vessel at my disposal, this meant chartering whatever commercial vehicle was available and that usually resulted in my travelling on copra boats and sleeping on copra bags. Funnily enough, most people hate the smell of copra, but for me it had and always will have a very nostalgic effect. And being a very good sleeper, I slept extremely comfortably even on copra bags.

I would be unceremoniously 'dumped' on whatever island I chose to tour. Then it would be a matter of proceeding by foot or cadging a lift, or occasionally hiring a local vehicle, though my travelling funds were very limited so it was not often that I was able to have that luxury. Vehicles were very few and far between on any of the four islands for which I was responsible (Epi was included as part of Central District No 1 not long after I took over), and the roads were poor and road connections very limited. The vehicles most in use at the time were Land Rovers and the old American Jeeps.

Travelling with only a replete kitbag (a few luxuries like a tube of condensed milk, salt, biscuits, and a tin or two of soup) meant that I moved about cheaply but always with the luxury of a porter. I had no hesitation in doing this since having walked all day I would usually sit up with villagers till the early hours of the morning dealing with land disputes, women problems, gun licences, requests to cease debts, moneys to banks, and always, of course, local government matters—either checking the cash books and minutes, chasing tax defaults or proselytising its advantages and importance. Porters and vessel charters, including speed boats, I always paid immediately from my travelling imprest.

Having begun by taking with me a policeman or two, I soon realised that they had insufficient to do and were better employed on their own. So I instituted police patrols of two police at a time from my detachment of 8 to 12 who would have a specific route to follow, officially investigating crimes. More usually they'd report civil debts, but quite often petty crimes too, especially any sexual abuse, assaults, etc. And above all, they'd be 'showing the flag' as it were.

For myself I found it easier and more satisfactory to tour alone. I could work the hours I pleased without having to feel guilty about holding up others who had finished their work … and without a policeman standing guard by my shoulder, I felt I soon became more approachable and perhaps less awesome because one had to admit that the average Melanesian in the village was still slightly in awe of the government. Many times I had heard of the days when Mr Adam, my predecessor from Bushman's Bay, would stride into a village accompanied by a detachment of police probably to arrest someone in a neighbouring village and "oli shek shek"—everyone would start to tremble.

In the early seventies, the district had its first rest house strategically placed on a sandy spit of Peskarüs sand in the Maskelynes. This comfortable touring headquarters was based on the Tanganyika models, a simple rectangular room with a small verandah. A water tank was attached to catch the water from the galvanised iron roof and a small bamboo clad toilet was 20 yards away. There was a bed, chair, and table from Vila—written off by the British works. With a small Primus stove and some crockery and cutlery, this was indeed a home away from home. It was a base for the occasional police patrol to work from in the southern part of Malekula, for education officers to inspect and work with teachers, the agricultural department officers, and medical officers. It encouraged the junior officers, many of whom did not like touring, to stay longer and get into the villages.

My second rest house along similar lines was built as an addition to the dispensary at Magam, North Ambrym. Tim Lang, the cooperatives officer, built a similar one at Lawa, South West Bay. I later worked with the South Pentecost Local Council to build a rest house at their headquarters at Pangi.

The money to pay for these buildings (which the condominium would never pay for, knowing that my colleagues or their staff would never stay in them) came from my 'goat bag'!—a practice in Tanganyika where the District Commissioner would quietly put away for district use any surplus funds which he did not have to account for when the auditor made his annual inspection.

I have written at length about touring as I believe it was the most important factor in district administration. Many tours were made with the comfort of a ship as a base; the 'Mangaru', 'Euphrosyne', and the 'Ida'—though the 'Ida' was not exactly luxurious accommodation. The temptation to return aboard for the comfort of a comfortable bed and cooked meals was often so great, but it was in the evenings at the end of the day that the villagers relaxed and chatted. Touring brought you into constant contact with the people you were administrating. Their trust was built up and we became more and more aware of their problems, their worries, and their thoughts and aspirations.

On my first visit south, I was landed on the little offshore island of Rano, with its white sandy beach and crystal clear blue water. I camped here in an empty hut given to me by the villagers and had a superb swim each morning. I had meetings every day on the mainland, being paddled across by canoe to deal with land disputes and minor criminal offences. On my first day, I was brought a delicious chicken and rice curry, and the sweetest pineapple I have ever tasted—presented by one of the locals who had worked as a chef on a local ship. As I ate, I had to ignore the blowflies buzzing around my face the whole time, ultimately it didn't deter me from enjoying my windfall.

The next day, I crossed to the mainland again to visit the Roman Catholic mission there headed by Father Soucy, an American citizen. He had been able to organise funds from America to build an enormous cement brick church which, painted white and located on a small headland, was most imposing. On the third day, I walked along the foreshores passing but not visiting the little island of Atchen and after another two hours, I crossed over to Vao Island. A large Catholic church dominates the island of Vao but there was not time to visit the villagers because people wanting to talk had held me up en route. At Vao there was the 'Mangaru' with my family on board. They were having a lovely swim with the local children but we had to call them back to the ship with some difficulty and return to Luganville. The family had had a wonderful day.

Occasionally I toured with my French colleague aboard the 'Concorde', a French government vessel. I never really relished touring in French vessels—French conversation was exhausting and French food seem to vary in quality. The 'Concorde', like its sister ships, always looked like it needed a good scrub out. However Fabre was easy to work with, much more so than my Tanna colleague the Duc, and was the only colleague I was to have who supported the British system of local councils.

French Colleagues

Nevertheless we did carry on some occasional joint tours in CD2, first with my colleague Fabre, then with Boileau. My subsequent colleagues, Teppe and then Lecuyer, I never toured with.

Boileau was forceful, energetic, and intelligent, and naturally was always pressing *la gloire* and influence of *la belle* France. We toured jointly when necessary, for example, to deal with the Conzinc Rio Tinto efforts to exploit or search for copper on south-west Pentecost. This ended in failure (much to my admiration of the locals who refused, saying they would wait for the children of their children to exploit the minerals if they wanted to). Other reasons included: to establish local councils, for the annual general meetings, to announce currency changes, and to hold elections.

Prior to the arrival of Boileau, I more or less ran the district as I wanted. But Boileau obviously had instructions to slow down my growing influence in the district and one of his first proposals—to which I could only agree—was that we should tour in turn, to deal with all the court cases which he seemed to think was where most influence could be executed. This did not preclude me touring independently, of course, as he did on national matters, visiting the planters and developing the groundwork for French education.

On a joint walking tour with Boileau (yes walking) to the coastal settlement of the Big Nambas on the north-west coast—where both of us were individually trying to consolidate our respective national interests—he admitted to me to my astonishment that independence was shortly inevitable (this was in the 60s), and that English was obviously the language that should dominate.

Finally there was Datchary, whom for want of a better phrase I can only describe as a very smooth operator. I do not recall ever touring jointly with him in the strict sense. I would rendezvous at a prearranged location as necessary and then we each would go our separate ways. Even these joint public meetings were reduced to very infrequent ones as political events changed, and it obviously became a faster race to press our national interests.

On my first tour together with Fabre, we visited the well-established north Pentecost local council at Abwatuntora, shared by Dr Phillip Ilo—the first New Hebridean to qualify as a doctor after training in Fiji. From Abwatuntora we moved south to Melsissi Bay to visit an extensive Catholic mission station there. Thence across to Ambrym and finally back to Port Sandwich, where I had dinner with the Fabres and an overnight stay there. Next day I set off on foot northward on a three day walk along the coast and finally home by a chartered vessel from the north coast of Malekula.

On my second visit to Ambrym, I was landed by a copra vessel at Craig Cove in the early hours of the morning, about three, on a very sandy black beach. It was a beautiful night. All I had with me was my kitbag jammed with my necessary clothing and a packet of Marie biscuits. I often depended on these, being the only things you could get in the local stores that were edible on many of my tours. On this occasion it was a superb, moonlit, balmy night and I stretched myself out on the sand and went into a deep sleep.

I woke to the chattering of a lot of people and opened my eyes to see a group of village women staring at me. They had seen my prostrate body on the beach and assumed that at this hour of the morning I must have been drunk. It was a good start for the new BDA.

After several days in that area, I decided to continue on to south-east Ambrym. I employed three porters to carry my baggage and thank goodness I did so. It was a long and arduous walk crossing ravines at regular and frequent intervals, and then steep rivers of solidified lava that had poured down from the Marum volcano. It really was hard walking. There was no track, of course, and no beach so we just ascended and descended with difficulty getting a foothold. I was thankful at dark to see coconuts, and then a track, and then village fires. I was made most welcome and well fed with *laplap*. I spent the next few days here at Taveak hiring a Tonkinese-owned dilapidated Jeep to tour the villages.

I had arranged for the 'Mangaru' to meet me at Taveak, the only workable passage, and was glad to get home, in time for Dick and Katie's dinner dance. There were about 60 people, with table and chairs out on the lawn. The French guests seemed to be au fait with the latest dances, of which the most popular was 'The Twist'. It was useful here to meet a lot more people and we packed up about 2.30 am.

Over the next few months, I was to do a lot of this landing in various parts of the district and visiting as many villages as I could in the time available to me. I'd introduce myself and just get to know the chiefs, the assessors, and the people. It was always the same procedure at the end of a long meeting. I would say, "Well in a couple of months' time I will be back," and I would be making notes of the various complaints which might arise or which needed attention, but I always got the impression that they viewed my assurance that I would return with great scepticism. This was understandable because for as long as most of them could remember, there had been no British District Agent living in the district and visits had been extremely few and far between. In fact, many of the areas had not been visited since the time of my renowned predecessor.

My work plans were regularly thrown awry by reports for urgent action on one score or another. Planning to spend a few days on office work I received an urgent message from Rev Good on Paama, 'severe ash fall causing extensive damage. Exodus imminent'. I had visions of 3000 Paamese seeking safety and Mr Wilkie who was staying at the time remarked that he could imagine the Rev Good leading 'the exodus' like Moses. Of course I had to go and investigate, was able to procure the 'Mangaru', and off I went.

Sure enough it was very serious. Although no exodus was imminent, the ash from the Lopevi volcano had been consistently showering the subsistence gardens on Paama for some weeks. The weight of the ash was breaking off leaves and branches and would certainly have a disastrous effect on the food supply. I tramped up and down valleys all day looking at gardens and returned to the 'Mangaru' hot and dirty from the ash fall. In the event, the ash fall suddenly ceased and there was no need for action, for which I was thankful.

The next day, we circumnavigated Lopevi. The volcano rises, cone-shaped out of the sea, and from time to time molten lava pours from its vent at the top, or in this case just ash, carried by the wind to Paama. Several months later, Lopevi erupted again. I was fortunate to be on south-east Ambrym at the time and had a magnificent grandstand view. I sat on the beach for most of the night watching molten red larva slowly make its way down the mountainside towards the coast. By four in the morning, it reached the sea and shot columns of steam thousands of feet into the sky. Virtually the whole northern side of the island was covered in the molten red larva—a sight I shall never forget! Fortunately the island population had been evacuated in a similar eruption some two years' prior and settled on Epi.

Easter Cyclone

I had promised the family that we would do something together and as I had been invited back to Epi by the Presbyterian mission staff there to stay whenever possible, we set out on the 'Mangaru' on the Easter Friday. The sea was glassy-flat and being a 13-hour voyage, we travelled overnight and awoke to find us anchored in Lamen Bay and the mainland. Sister Mary Wall from the mission hospital came down to meet us in her Land Rover and insisted we camp in their little rest house where we were most comfortable. I made use of some of the time to visit reasonably accessible villages and plantations but mostly we lazed and swam on the local white sandy beach. On the Sunday, we went across to Lamen Island to meet up with the Presbyterian Resident Missionary, Graham Horwell, and his large family. We attended the service there and had, as usual, a nice lunch. It was then time to pack up, go aboard, and head for Santo and home.

Mary had given us seasick tablets, and to ensure a good night's sleep, I dosed Ida and children with them. Again the sea was glassy-smooth but the air was heavy and forbidding. Captain Filimone had checked with the radio office in Vila—there was nothing ominous around, but by the time we turned towards the large gap between Malekula and Ambrym, there were rising seas and high winds. An hour later, we were obviously in the teeth of a hurricane and as the night wore on, the seas grew bigger and bigger.

I lashed the three children down in their bunks with sheets and packed them with pillows, and we rolled on. By this time, Filimone was finding it hard to keep on his feet and had to hang onto the wheel for support. As we rolled, I would look out my window and see from time to time nothing but sea. Visibility was non-existent. Incredibly Ida and the children slept on but keeping the window open a fraction for air, I was drenched by saltwater spray.

It was not safe to go from cabin aft for'ard to Captain Filimone's wheelhouse because of seas flooding both sides of the ship as we rolled. I began to wonder whether our last days were coming. Filimone said later that towards dawn he had completely lost his bearings and was worried that we might end up on Malo, so he had to wait for an opportune moment with raging winds and high seas to turn and go back until he had such time with daylight to establish his position. As we rolled, saltwater poured over us, but we made the turn safely and at daylight when we could see Malo, we turned back towards Santo. Finally the entrance to the canal appeared and as we entered the bay, there were tremendous seas running and we could see the 'Polynesie' being buffeted about against the wharf. By this time the wind had dropped to about 60 knots but coconuts were still bent right over. The next problem was to get ashore, so we left all our gear aboard and piled into the dingy, soaked to the skin. The children were all extremely good. About ten yards from the shore, the crew jumped out and carried the children one by one onto the beach where Mike Dumper, the police commandant, was waiting, having seen us enter the harbour. As the dingy could not be taken right to the beach because of the heavy sea, Ida and I got out in deep water as the boat almost turned over us. At one stage Ida was swept under the dinghy whereupon I dived under the water to help her regain her footing—it was a close call. The 'Mangaru' went farther up the channel to find shelter and Mike drove us home.

High winds had burst most of the windows and much of the house was drenched with rainwater. I hurried around, nailing up windows and doors. By this time the wind had reached about 80 knots, but exhausted, we all were able to sleep. Later I found that the town had been quite badly damaged but there had been no loss of life.

Ambrym Volcano Eruption

Not long after this trip I had an urgent message saying that villages on south-east Ambrym were being inundated by a lava flow and people would have to be evacuated. So reluctantly I had to call on the 'Mangaru' to retrace my steps as far as south-east Ambrym. After a rough trip, we arrived off south-east Ambrym about midday Saturday. It was too rough to land on the beach near the reported damage so we cruised by and observed a lot of unperturbed people who gave us a wave and no sign of smoke or lava. Obviously the report was false so with the crew's disgust we turned about. There had in fact been violent eruptions on Lopevi adjacent to Ambrym and Paama. The senior geologist from Vila was on board with me so we decided to check it out. I went with him ashore and it was rather an inspiring and frightening sight. What had a few weeks before been a fertile coast was now burnt to cinders and a mass of black ash and dry crackling lava.

The little cove where I had been ashore before was now entirely obliterated and a peninsula of lava had completely filled it, all trace of vegetation had gone.

We stumbled over lava, still feeling the waves of heat and looked down on cracks of red-hot lava under us. I must say I felt pretty uncomfortable but Arthur assured me there was no danger. The summit still puffed black ash but there appeared to be no other activity. Nonetheless I was quite relieved to get back on board.

Santo Life

At Santo, I continuously faced a dilemma; unless I was on tour, I could not do my job. On the other hand I felt guilty that with my constant touring I was not taking responsibility for my family. The children seemed to undergo a series of illnesses at this time—frequently malaria, colds, and then measles. This put a great strain upon Ida who coped with it all admirably. She would call on the French doctor at the French Hospital, Dr de Carfort, who was always extremely helpful and understanding. The treatment was often injections of one sort or another and suppositories that the French seemed to be keen on.

Coming back from a hospital treatment, Simon or Sallie would say in relieved tones, "No more bities, Mum". Despite sick bouts, Ida enjoyed the companionship of some very nice women, particularly Pam, wife of the BP's manager, Middy, wife of the police commandant, and Denise Gubbay, wife of Donald Gubbay, manager of the Palekula Fisheries.

In the Christmas period of 1963, our 12 year-old nephew, Ian Pettit, had arrived to stay armed with paraphernalia to preserve his forthcoming collection of sea life. For a number of weeks our bathtub became a holding tank for various live specimens which intrigued the children but was alarming in other aspects. I don't think he ever collected anything dangerous, however the potential was there.

We had a lovely Christmas party that year. Ida and I wrapped 30 little gifts for a children's party, which after the usual children's eats I showed a black and white film. As our departure for Malekula was now nearing reality, we decided on a Christmas farewell and we had some 30 guests finishing at a more reasonable hour than was usually the case. The next evening, two days before Christmas, I had just finalised a court hearing in my office where a Japanese from Palekula Fisheries had clobbered a fellow countryman on the head with a beer bottle—one month imprisonment. The phone rang and it was Ida saying Sallie had drunk one of Ian's preserving concoctions and to come quickly. I dashed back to find Sallie in great discomfort. We hurried to the hospital with the empty bottle as evidence where Dr de Carfort, having sniffed the bottle, gave her an injection and she vomited and retched for an hour.

Ida returned home to the children and I remained for the night, a restless one, checking her at regular intervals. Sallie was exhausted but had fallen into a heavy sleep. I was awakened next morning with a cheery "DAD, DAD". Dr de

Carfort checked her again; he said it could have been very nasty and we were lucky. Sallie showed no after-effects.

New Year's 1963, our last on Santo, Ida and I had been heavily involved in the New Year's Dance—a fundraiser for the Tennis Club. Plans included attending in fancy dress. The idea was well received and for the evening we had something like 800 revellers in Mao's bar, which had ample provision with its Quonset hut taking a large crowd. I had wriggled out of a party the night before in order to be fresh for the onslaught.

With the children to bed and Mary our good old fallback house girl to keep an eye on them, we were able to relax. At this time I was again acting District Agent for the Northern District because Dick was very unwell and was to be shipped off to Vila and then on leave. I had enlisted the 'Mangaru' crew to assist with the evening but seemed to spend most of the night behind the bar taking money from door, bar, and gambling etc., and transferring it up to my safe in the office. Some of the fancy dresses were extremely good and Ida gave out prizes at midnight, at which point we also let loose 250 balloons that had been blown up during the day.

After the hullabaloo had subsided a little, I announced the New Year's honours which included a local Geoff Wilson, a previous BP's manager, and Keith Woodward from the British Office. Keith's award was particularly gratifying—he was the greatest supporter of the district agents, and with an incurable eye disease was then rapidly losing his sight. At 31 it was thought his career was almost over but he then began to teach himself Braille and continued on at the British Office in Vila as a key administrator almost until Independence. Celebrations continued inevitably until dawn when we got to bed. Sallie welcomed us, just awake, with a "hello, Daddy and Mummy".

In February 1964, a joint tour had been arranged with my colleague and I left on the 'Mangaru' for Malekula and joined him on the 'Bonite'. We had a very successful tour, the seas like glass, though as usual it was something of a strain with the inevitable French chatter. The Captain and my colleague seemed to like noise from the radio regardless of whether it was messages or static and music.

I had to return to Santo to meet the High Commissioner passing through to Honiara and then to deal with some pressing court cases and the usual paperwork requiring action.

By this time, Simon had a very nasty attack of the measles and I was reluctant to leave Ida with him unwell, to tour again until he had improved. I was thankful that I had not gone on tour. We had very restless nights. Simon, "When will morning come?" Me, "It will come soon." Simon, "When is soon? Why doesn't it hurry up? I'm itchy. Is it daylight yet?" And so on. Quite laughable really.

Poor Filimone and his wife, Agnes, from the 'Mangaru' were severely poisoned from eating what was locally known as "red fish". They were both hospitalised and were quite ill for over a week. Back on board, he said that for months after his arms and legs would ache.

This incident rather frightened us off eating locally caught fish, though we were told there was no danger with deep sea fish and from time to time were given and enjoyed enormous tuna from the Japanese Palekula Fisheries Ltd. Also when touring on the 'Mangaru', Filimone would often tow a line and catch barracuda or tuna for our meal. I also remember one pleasurable item on the 'Rocinante' menu, made by Captain Guenet, and that was tuna cooked in red wine—delicious.

Despite commencing at the French school, after much thought we had decided to move Karen and Simon to the newly opened British Primary School in Santo. The French school had really been a disaster. The treatment of children there was appalling. Simon had obviously been nervous about going to the French school and was absent a lot of the time. The New Caledonian teacher was known to mistreat children—the children said that he had locked pupils in a cupboard and this had happened to Karen. She complained that he had hit her three times on the back because she could not reproduce a blackboard illustration of his. Children had been known to have water poured into their ears. At the new British school they both settled in very happily and began to thrive. They were reluctant to leave when we finally moved to Lakatoro in September 1964.

Events

The annual Presbyterian Assembly which brought together its representatives from all over the group was, in 1963, held on Malo Island on the eastern side of the canal, not more than four or five miles from our house as the crow flies. I was on tour and Ida was asked to stand in for me as government representative, attending one session. She and the children were collected by a small local boat and taken across. Whilst the children, with hordes of others, had a wonderful day and were well cared for, Ida attended an assembly meeting after which there was the usual feast.

She thoroughly enjoyed the day and at about 4.30, set out for home in the same boat she came across in. She said she felt sure that they headed south instead of north but did not like to interfere. By dark they were lost. They looked to Ida to take command. She rightly turned north but it was pitch-dark and it was very difficult to pick up any landmarks. Finally they pulled into the shore to find that they were still not home. Out they went again, and by this time the police commandant's wife, Mrs Sankey, and guests at the assembly were becoming very agitated. Ida had no choice but to keep going north, which she did, and finally with great relief all round saw the lights of our house and all were safely landed. She hoped the poor crew would find their way home again.

At Malo, Ida had met Len Stephens and his wife Eleanor, long time settlers on south Santo. Len was a descendant of the original Stephens from Tonga and a relative of the infamous Jimmy Stephens (who led the Coconut rebellion during the independence years). They invited us south to their home one Sunday where they gave us a most magnificent island spread ranging from oysters and lobster to tropical fruit salad. They had a beautiful tropical garden which ran down to a white sandy beach and a view to close-lying tiny islands.

In the afternoon, they took us on to the Tangoa Training Institute where Presbyterian teachers were given basic Gospel and scholastic training. The principal was the Reverend Paddy Jensen. It was a lovely day and we were home by dark.

Mid-year 1963, I had to go to Fiji to represent the New Hebrides at a pacific island housing conference of all things. The conference, a ten day affair, I found pretty boring but it was an experience to see how a multilingual event worked. We were accommodated in luxury at the Grand Pacific Hotel in Suva, a fine colonial-style building, and at the end of the conference attended cocktails at the Governor's residence. I was glad to get back to work but the visit proved useful in that a few years later, I knew my way around when I had to take a group of ni-Vanuatu to do a traditional dance at the Western Pacific Arts Festival.

High Commissioner for the Western Pacific Visit

Dick, representing the Northern District, accompanied me south in the 'Mangaru'. Along the coast we collected representative chiefs and anchored overnight at Tisman. The High Commissioner for the Western Pacific, Sir David Trench, and his wife arrived in the 'Euphrosyne' from Vila. I had had a late night preparing notes ready for his speech, setting out relevant points and matters to be raised, and was late to bed.

The official party landed at nine in the morning when he opened the new British Dispensary and watched some spectacular custom dancing; we then observed preparations for a custom Kaikai, the cooking procedure etc., after the consumption of which there would be 'danis go go catchem daylight'. We adjourned to Oscar Newman's for lunch which in Oscar's usual style was an extraordinarily lavish one—champagne of course, Tahitian salad, roast chicken and suckling pig, and of course the usual wines and other post prandial drinks.

Oscar, an excellent raconteur, entertained us with some fascinating stories. We returned to the 'Euphrosyne' and sailed down to Port Sandwich to change for dinner. On landing we were met by M Fabre. His Excellency (HE) inspected a guard of honour and walked around the French administrative centre. Madame Fabre gave us a delicious dinner—lobster again—and after a dinner chat, all of course in French with Dick and I translating (HE spoke no French), we went back to the 'Euphrosyne'. HE travelled through the night arriving at

Santo in time for breakfast. Here my responsibilities ended and Dick took over responsibility for HE and party. HE was a most vital and interesting man who later became the Governor of Hong Kong. The next morning, I had to change into a suit to say goodbye to Sir David and his wife at the airfield.

Move to Malekula

By mid 1963, after being based at Santo, it soon became very apparent indeed that I had to do something about basing myself on Malekula. Apart from anything else, it was impossible to expect the family to live in Santo whilst I spent 90 per cent of my time touring and camping in the district. The most obvious site was Bushman's Bay on central Malekula, where my predecessors, pre-war and immediately after the war, had been based. The old agency was a dilapidated old timber house on a two-hectare rectangle carved out of the Corlette estate and facing the black-sand beach.

I had looked at many areas with the view to selecting a site for a headquarters but had made little progress, principally because either the land was not suitable or the owners were not willing to my leasing it. So I decided to domicile myself at the old agency at Bushman's Bay. The fine old weatherboard house was in a sad state of dilapidation. It had been shaken off its concrete pillars by many an earthquake and the garden was so overgrown that it was practically impenetrable. I did manage to cut my way through to the verandah and found that, in fact, one of the rooms inside was still intact. This was where I was to base myself for a few months, periodically going up to Santo to see the family.

Mr Adam had originally occupied the house and then I think Crozier and finally Tom Harrison of *Savage Civilisation* fame—who in 1937 (or so the story goes) absconded with Douglas Fairbanks and Mary Pickford in their yacht after having taken them up onto the mountains to visit the Big Nambas. The story also goes they took a lot of the files with them. Whether that is true or not, I don't know.

The Agency land fronted onto Bushman's Bay itself: black sands with a very exposed anchorage and plagued by mosquitoes. Beyond the actual agency boundaries the old plantation, which originally belonged to Mr Corlette and now the Gidley family, was completely overgrown. In the garden a few enormous Croton plants and the odd red hibiscus still survived, but for the most part it was just a jungle. The separate kitchen joined originally by a walkway had collapsed entirely and was completely unusable.

The biggest argument against Bushman's Bay was that the Corlette estate to the north and west and the Fleming, now SFNH, French-owned estate to the south surrounded it. Thus it made it difficult for the Melanesian population to have easy access, having to pass through the European plantations. It was not so bad with the Corlette estate, which was badly overgrown under the Gidley ownership, but the SFNH plantation was reasonably well-maintained and the entry of Melanesians into the property was not welcomed.

Two hectares was far too small for future expansion and future expansion was going to be necessary. The terrain beyond was unsuitable—flat, mosquito ridden, and swampy. The soil was sandy and above all, there was the problem of access to fresh water, vital to any developing station. So I began a search for a more suitable site. This was not easy because I had to be within easy access of a good harbour and this restricted me to the Port Sandwich, Bushman's Bay, Sarmet, or Norsup areas.

The other obvious position was on the southern headland of Port Sandwich, where my French colleague had been ensconced since the 1920s. My colleague at this time in 1963, as I have mentioned, was Jacques Fabre—a very nice man, a gentleman and very co-operative. I spent several days based in that area and in fact, he provided me with accommodation for those few days whilst I negotiated with the local people with the intention of either renting or purchasing land.

Although the local villagers were obviously dominated by the French and had been for many years, they were clearly quite keen for me to come in. This was not surprising because it was certainly a practice amongst most New Hebrideans to play one District Agent Officer off the other. This was an inevitable measure and frequently a very useful one from their viewpoint. The problem was that the land in that area was very densely populated and heavily planted so that it was not easy to find a suitable site. I did in fact pick an area of about two hectares right on the point, which would have made a lovely house site, but in the long term would have been quite impracticable because of the lack of space for future development.

Fabre seemed quite helpful but it soon became apparent that the French residency in Vila was not very keen on me moving into Port Sandwich. This was an extraordinary attitude because quite obviously in a condominium, a joint administration would supposedly be expected to work jointly and in Tanna, Vila, and Santo, the other District Headquarters, British and French District Agents lived and worked side by side.

There was a small portion of Burns Philp land farther into the bay and this also was a possibility but again limited in size and I soon came to the conclusion that it would not be a very healthy spot because of the mosquito and malarial infestation. The next land that I inspected was on the northern headland of Port Sandwich, Point Hasuk. This was a magnificent site looking out across to the island of Ambrym and in the distance Paama and Pentecost, and where there was plenty of suitable land.

The whole of Point Hasuk down to the river on the northern side of the point (the name of which I can't recall at the moment) was owned by a Frenchman (again, whose name I can't recall) who lived farther inside the harbour and had quite an extensive plantation. He seemed quite co-operative and I spent a few days ploughing through fairly thick undergrowth with a view to looking at an exact position and within that site, locating suitable flat land for building purposes.

Again water was going to be a problem and as I saw it, the best possibility would be pumping fresh water from the river at Black Sands. I continued negotiations quite successfully having also the co-operation of the Black Sands' villagers, who in fact were claimants to the land, which had been alienated to the French much earlier in the day and they also were very keen for me to settle there. I got to the point where I was able to ask for Vila to support me in the enquiries and Colin Allen, who was then the Assistant Resident Commissioner, came up and we spent a day in Port Sandwich. He arrived in the 'Euphrosyne' and we negotiated with Monsieur Blank. No decision was reached as to cost but this was to be taken up by Colin Allen in Vila—where negotiations stalled and evidently again, it was the influence of the French residency in Vila putting its foot down about having land made available to the British Agent.

On one of my routine tours about this time, I spent an overnight at Tisman—the plantation of CFNH managed by the renowned Oscar Newman. Oscar was extremely familiar with the whole of the coast and he suggested to me that an ideal site for a British Agency would be where Gaby Lamoureux owned a plantation. Oscar thought this would be suitable principally because it had a good water supply and it faced quite a reasonable anchorage at Port Stanley, and above all because Gaby was in dire financial straits and was anxious to sell. So on my next tour of Malekula my landing was at Norsup and from there, to save my travelling expenditure, I walked along the track through the PRNH coconut plantation to Gaby Lamoureux's land.

Within a couple of hours of exploration, accompanied by the local leaders concerned—Simo, Kilman and his father, Sauli, Bomani (Wanhan), and Chief Rion of Litzlitz—we had walked around the boundaries of the land and I decided that this was the site for the future district agency. Locally at Norsup there was the PRNH plantation which included an indeterminate head of cattle, a fine workshop and an experienced and very skilled Italian mechanic, Monsieur Migotti, a foreman who was a Fijian and therefore English-speaking, Peter Wright, and the manager. He was a Frenchman by the name of Monsieur Tanguy who spent perhaps six to nine months on the plantation and the rest of the time in Paris. Finally, there was a store run by the plantation, which had all the essential food: sugar, rice, flour, tea, tinned foods, and periodically they sold bread and fresh meat killed on the plantation. As to Gaby's land, 80 hectares, it was a rectangle with its west-eastern boundary facing the sea and a quite reasonable little passage facing into the Port Stanley harbour. The second-best harbour in Malekula, Port Stanley is protected farther to the east by the beautiful island Uripiv and a headland running along the eastern seaboard called Uri, with several small coral islands in the harbour.

The land stretched back up the mountainside as far as the track running north and south from the PRNH plantation to Bushman's Bay. To the east of this road, the land was flat and partly planted with coconuts, the balance to the sea still virgin bush. To the west of the land, it was also flat and still planted with coconuts but I could see an ideal site in the future for a sports oval. It sloped upwards with a small creek dividing the land virtually in half to a first plateau densely covered in *kassis*—the notorious weed brought in by the early missionaries as building material, which had rapidly overtaken tremendous acreages of land on most of the islands of the group. Amongst this *kassis* were planted young coconuts, I suppose about four or five years old. To the north of the creek sat a small galvanised iron cottage comprising a long narrow lounge with two bedrooms and then a further bedroom and a lean-to kitchen, shower, and laundry. It had a gravel floor but the main part was on a cement base. The building was reasonably sound.

Apart from that building, the rest of the land was virgin bush rising, then rising again after about 200 metres of gentle slope, steeply up to the mountainside where there was a second plateau. We explored the water supply. This was a source spring about two miles up in a valley in the mountains to the south-west; a beautiful source with a permanent steady flow of crystal clear water. I could see any number of possible building sites when the land had been cleared. And above all, the entire acreage was surrounded by native-owned land with the village of Litzlitz some half a mile south, and the small village of Blackgate immediately between the Gaby land and the PRNH plantation where Bomani and Simo lived.

Having made up my mind that this was it, the next step was to begin negotiations with Gaby Lamoureux. This was initially opened by Oscar Newman, who was a very skilled negotiator, and then taken over by the British Residency. Gaby was asking £4,000 but we finally clinched the deal (I think this was about June 1964), for £3,500, which was a pretty good buy.

The negotiations were very forcefully pressed by Colin Allen, who right from the beginning had supported my insistence that we should be based within the district which I was to administer. Finally, there was exciting news from Vila—the Colonial Office in London had by telegram confirmed agreement to purchase Lakatoro and the provision of funds to establish the new district agency. After 15 months of searching and waiting, a new beginning was assured.

From this time until our permanent departure for Malekula, I was pretty constantly on tour. The first was with Mr Brian Pearce, Private Secretary to the Under Secretary of State, Mr Fisher, from the Colonial Office. This was an important contact because it was he who shuffled the papers up to the Under Secretary to approve the allocation of funds for the development of an administrative base on Malekula. We virtually toured the whole district, but most of all I wanted him to see Lakatoro and appreciate my situation and the necessity to be on the spot and not somewhere else. He was most receptive and obviously understood my problem. I am sure that the tour reaped benefits and that it was through Brian Pearce that monies were released so quickly. During our visit to Ranwadi on Pentecost, he was amused by an incident recounted by Mrs Smith, the large, jovial Church of Christ missionary there. Apparently, soon after her arrival years before, she had set out with an entourage to visit a village in the mountains. She became desperate for a toilet visit and whispered accordingly to one of the girls. The latter went up to the leader of the group and whispered to him. He then turned around and called out in a loud voice, "Missus i wantem pispis." So Mrs Smith scuttled off into the bushes.

On return to Santo, I was met by yet another VIP needing similar treatment and took the Australian Consul, Ivor Bowden, on tour with me. When we returned, I found that Karen had developed chickenpox, was a mass of spots, and fairly quickly Simon and Sallie followed suit. Poor Karen had only just recovered from chickenpox when on her first day back at school, she climbed a frangipani in the playground, bumped a large wasp's nest, and fell to the ground screaming and covered in wasp bites. It must have been very painful, taking almost a day with calamine treatment to recover.

Keneri

I cadged a lift down to Malekula in one of the Paama-owned vessels—the Liro chief's I think it was. After a very, very rough trip, I was landed thankfully on the reefs opposite Tautu village. A fine specimen of a man came striding down to meet me, shirtless. He possessed enormously wide shoulders (built up from loading copra, I was to learn) and a really quick, bright smile with strong, dazzling white teeth and a hearty guffaw. This was Keneri Williams, whom I was to know probably better than any other Melanesian and whom I still look upon as a genuine friend. And he remained a great friend of the family for all his life.

At our first meeting with the North Malekula Leaders at Sanwir, Fabre and I were to officially inaugurate the North Malekula Local Council, and Keneri was elected its first secretary. Keneri and I did many tours together, promoting the council and collecting head tax. He was full of information about Malekula and Melanesian customs and held me spellbound with some of his tales.

The first time that I stayed at Bushman's Bay, I was landed at the PRNH plantation at Norsup and there hired a vehicle before calling at Tautu to collect Keneri and moving down to Bushman's Bay where we camped for the next few days to visit neighbouring villages.

On my second visit to the villages of Lingarak, Hatbol and to the other side of the island at Vunmavis and Tisvel I was able to introduce Keneri as the new Local Government Secretary who would be collecting head tax. This was not always very favourably received, but I was able to present the principle of a local council as being the basis of the preparation for self-government.

Independence, of course, at that stage had never been heard of. The fact that I talked about the island being eventually run by the Melanesian people themselves was met with a lot of scepticism.

Over the next few days, we really roughed it—walking to and fro from the villages. We'd bathe in the sea at night and then settle into the one and only room which was mosquito proofed and cooked with a borrowed saucepan and a Primus stove. Keneri always spoke about a particularly good meal in Lingarak village where we were presented with a chicken and some yam. We chopped up the fowl with Keneri's pocketknife and made a delicious stew.

Keneri was a staunch Presbyterian and was extremely suspicious of my French colleague and the French government generally. He served as Council Secretary from 1964 until the mid 1970s and did a good job trying to keep the council afloat, and eventually became Air Melansie's permanent agent at Norsup Airport.

Twelve

1964 Lakatoro

Lakatoro Base

At the end of 1963, I had been greatly cheered by the Colonial Office's approval, in principle, to the establishment of an administrative station on Malekula. But it was to be many months before funds would be forthcoming, permitting me to start work there. I had my camp at the old agency at Bushman's Bay, but now with official blessing I felt that I could at least take some steps towards preparing for a permanent base at the Gaby plantation. At the beginning of 1964, I moved my Land Rover and BSA Bushman motorbike to Gaby's ramshackle plantation house which became the sole base for my operations, and began camping there along with a few prisoners and 2 police. The police supervised the prisoners clearing the bush, mostly kassis which had completely covered any land which Gaby had previously cleared for his plantation. The house was far too primitive for the family to live in. There was no communication, no shower, laundry, nor airfield, and I had to depend on merchant trading vessels for a lift to visit the family in Santo whenever one was available and this was not particularly often.

Still officially based on Santo, of course, I continued to have obligations both personal and administrative there. It was not until March 1964 that I was able to hand over the Northern District to Alex Mitchell and this at least left me free to concentrate on my own district. Alex's wife was not able to come up to Santo, so he called upon Ida fairly regularly to host receptions and organise such things as the Queen's Birthday celebrations. This added to pressure to Ida's already very busy life.

The prison gang continued to make good headway on the Gaby plantation and were not cutting out any trees, thank goodness. The British Office produced from somewhere an elaborate canvas tent and this I used as my first office. I had been allocated funds to employ a clerk some months previously and I now arranged for him to join our small team. Paul Binihi from Pentecost had been based in Santo and had worked partly with the British District Agent, Dick Hutchinson.

He became my personal assistant and one and only staff member. With a new radio in the tent, I had regular communication whilst on tour or in Santo.

Once based at the Gaby plantation, eventually to be named Lakatoro, I was able to begin planning and development. Despite the fact that the Colonial Office had given its blessing, the frustrating part for me was that funds were not to be released for any work there until after the 1965 financial year. Nor were there funds forthcoming from the British Office in Vila for any work on the newly acquired property. This was very trying indeed, and I did not yet have a goat bag, so my only resource without money was prisoners.

The main problem was housing. The only building on the land was the plantation house and it was necessary for me to use this for all the staff I had. So I took the main bedroom, Paul took the next one, the police the third bedroom. Then came the question of housing prisoners and for the first few months, the prisoners shared the fourth bedroom. We were a fairly mixed and egalitarian family, sharing the cooking and the bathing facilities and generally having great fun in between a lot of hard work.

The next most encouraging development was the arrival of a 17.5kVA Lister Petter generator, but this had to await a technician from Vila to install it. I had funds now to also employ a Fijian carpenter, Zackery, who began to renovate Gaby's old house. He was a very slow but meticulous worker and I was able to manipulate funds to buy timber and cement etc. from Santo, to add on a bathroom and kitchen to replace the lean-to we had previously used. The house's occupants—prisoners, police, and myself—were moved out into prisoner-built thatched quarters and a prisoner started painting.

At that time, the local population including the surrounding villages like Uripiv and Tautu and Litzlitz were delighted that I was moving and I had tremendous support. The most support of all being from Sauli and his son, Kilman, who was later to become my right-hand man and personal driver. Sauli, whose land was on the northern side of the original Gaby land, had agreed that I could lease a further area for future extensions if required. Later, I was to take up this offer and it was a tremendous boon because it gave room to the north for expansion for the move into the headquarters of the condominium public works and other ancillary staff.

Prisoners became the lifeblood of the station, in a sense. Touring during this time, I would be holding courts under the Native Code and assisted by two assessors wherever I might be. I would hear these cases, normally fairly trivial matters, but sufficient to warrant short prison sentences, so that I was accumulating prisoners and bringing them back with me to Lakatoro.

The first step was the clearing of future housing sites—the foremost being a prison, and this meant cutting out the kassis, which is one of the hardest woods you could ever imagine. It became a standing joke in later years that when I sentenced a prisoner, there would generally be a chuckle in the audience and a murmur of, "Hem i go katim kassis," (He is going to go and clear the bush at Lakatoro). In between my touring and occasional visits to the family at Santo, all my leisure time was spent in walking around the Lakatoro land and envisaging where I was going to develop. It was an exciting and challenging job and my first selection of a site was for my own British District Agency and office. This took a long time and the locals were most amused because they would quite often see me climbing or perched in one of the many trees trying to find the best outlook.

I finally selected what became a superb view and was insistent right from the beginning that no tree was to be cut without my permission—they were needed not only for beauty but for shade. This also was to become a source of amusement amongst the local population. After many hours of surveying, I finally had an overall plan for the station laid out in my mind; on the flat land at the bottom near the road, the football field, the oval, and future use for a school and club. To the south of the creek on the first rise, a police barracks and a prison. And on the northern side of the creek, my own agency higher up overlooking the whole station, my own accommodation, my own house and below it an office and whatever staff accommodation was required for clerks, education officer, and so on.

I gave a lot of thought to the naming of the station and finally decided on Lakatoro, this apparently being in the local dialect the word for 'dark bush or place of burnt out sugar cane stumps'. Apparently before Gaby had cleared the land and planted coconuts, it had been quite a substantial sugar cane area for the local villages and these occasionally would be burnt out to stimulate new growth. So Lakatoro it became, and I became known as BDA (British District Agent) CD2 (Central District No. 2), Lakatoro.

My first most valuable piece of equipment after the Land Rover and the motorbike was a radio. This was housed in the plantation house and gave me regular contact with Vila and the rest of the group without having to traipse up to PRNH—the local French plantation headquarters where they also had their own commercial radio. The next bit of equipment that was a tremendous boost was a tractor. Both the Resident Commissioner, Mr Wilkie, and the Assistant Resident Commissioner, Colin Allen, were anxious to look at progress at the new site on Malekula. As a result of these visits, I was delighted to learn from Colin that somewhere the British Residency had found sufficient funds to purchase a Fordson tractor and blade. This was to be a Christmas present. I couldn't believe it, but sure enough it wasn't very long before a Fordson Major tractor arrived and subsequently I was able to buy, with the government funds, a front-end loader and later a small grader blade.

The next thing was to find a driver and I began making enquiries for someone who would be reasonably efficient in driving a Fordson tractor and being able to use a front-end loader. Here again fortune smiled on me and I found what was a goldmine of a man in Wilben Willie, son of the chief Willie from Atchen Island. He was a devout Seventh Day Adventist, and was recommended by the Seventh Day mission station a little farther to the south of me at the end of Port Stanley Bay. I was finally able to track Wilben down, he was working on Malo Island. When he arrived I soon found that he was a goldmine—not only could he drive a tractor, but he could maintain it. He had also driven and was accustomed to using a front-end loader. He was enthusiastic, loyal, and he had an aptitude for being able to think and plan ahead, which was not common amongst the local population at the time. A good example was regarding fuel. It was the usual thing for the police or the medical or education departments to come along to me and say, "Masta i finis," (Sir, we've run out). But with Wilben, he would say "Masta i gat wan drum i stap yet," (Sir, we have one drum before we're out), so that I had time to order fuel before we ran out.

1964 High Commissioner's visit

Mid-year of 1964, the new High Commissioner for the Western Pacific, Sir Robert Foster, and his wife made a formal visit to the New Hebrides. After formal proceedings in Vila, the official party was to be the guest of my district and go on to Santo. Because the Resident Commissioner's wife, Mrs Wilkie, was in the throes of packing to return to the UK on leave, Ida was invited to join me to do the CD2 tour on the 'Coral Queen'. About the size of a Sydney ferry, she was a luxury vessel in comparison with the various little ships on which I was used to travelling.

After the cocktail party at the residency, we all adjourned on board, travelling through the night and arriving at Lamap about ten the next morning. To my consternation, the 'Coral Queen' was only doing 8 knots instead of the usual 12, thus my programme was behind schedule from the start and we had to abandon our first scheduled stop at the Maskelynes. I felt very badly about this because the previous week I had been there to arrange HE's visit and no doubt they would have made considerable preparations. There was no means of informing them and thus I made a special trip the following week to apologise.

At Lamap, M Fabre waited to greet us in full ceremonial uniform, with a guard of honour and the singing of both national anthems. And we then proceeded to the administrative centre to inspect the station, accompanied by local notables. We had a "vin d'honneur" and were away again by 11.30, back on schedule. After lunch and a siesta, we arrived at Lakatoro, anchoring opposite the station in Port Stanley. At our passage, my Land Rover—spick and span and pennant flying—and the local villagers awaited us. They sang "God Save the Queen" lustily, after which we drove up to Gaby's house and saw a little of the land being cleared.

Thence on by Land Rover northward to Wala where there was a tremendous crowd of about 2000 waiting for us. After I had presented the local chiefs, counsellors, and the local missionary, Father Soucy, we sat to watch custom dancing. The dancing was very spectacular, mostly in the enormous head gear which they wore—conical-shaped helmets about six feet high and colourfully decorated with fowl feathers. Here I was to note, as elsewhere in mission influence areas, the traditional penis wrapper was not worn. "Mifella i shem tumas," (It's too embarrassing). The dancing went on till after dark, lanterns being produced for the last session.

Unfortunately the 'Coral Queen' had not been able to anchor nearby but had moved to a sheltered anchorage off Wala Island, so again my planned schedule was disrupted. A strong wind had sprung up and the 'Coral Queen' tender, a small one without cover, was not the best for ferrying guests, chiefs, and notables across to the ship. Three trips had to be made. I had mustered all the raincoats and umbrellas that I could find and explained that guests did not have to feel any compunction about coming aboard. Evidently everyone did, but it was 8.30 and not 7 when the last guests arrived. It went off very successfully, finishing at 10 instead of 8.30. I was concerned that HE would not be pleased, as his predecessor, Sir David Trench, would have been extremely exasperated. HE, however, was unperturbed. He and Lady Foster sat on the deck for a final drink afterwards and he said how he envied me and my job.

We had good seas as we travelled overnight and I was called at 7 am to go to the bridge and advise the captain on berthing at the Santo wharf. At Santo, there had unfortunately been torrential rain, the first in weeks, and there was still rain falling. Nonetheless the well-advertised British School Fete was already attracting outsiders and the parade led by the Solomon Islands Brass Band created a lot of interest. Again there was a guard of honour, the national anthem sung, and Alex Mitchell, BDA, to do the honours. On board, we were keeping an eye out for our family whom Pam Kidney had so kindly looked after during our absence. We took the children around the ship and they were delighted.

Lady Foster, attended by Ida (because Alex Mitchell's wife was still in the UK), opened the fete, and despite the rain we cleared about 500 pounds. There was the inevitable cocktail party aboard that night with the Solomon Islands Brass Band playing, attended by about 60 notables.

HE and party were not due to depart before 11 the next morning by Fiji Airways, so whilst Alex and I talked with HE on board the 'Coral Queen', Ida took Lady Foster on a shopping expedition around the town. Ida found her a delightful companion and in a note of thanks a few days later, she and Sir Robert said how they hoped they might one day be able to have a couple of days in our proposed rest house in Lakatoro.

Lakatoro Home

By mid-September, with the children recovered from their chickenpox, I was able to fix a date for our final departure—3rd of October 1964—and Ida began packing. Inevitably we were also flooded with invitations to dinner. I was going up and down to Lakatoro by sea or by air. Paul Burton was now running a twice-weekly service, Vila–Norsup–Santo, on the just recently completed little airstrip. This meant that I could keep a close eye on activities in Lakatoro between routine district work, and urge Zackery on with the carpentry. The last hold up was plumbing but Vila came to the rescue with an efficient plumber, and having made several trips with furniture and personal luggage on the morning of the 3rd of October, I sailed for Lakatoro aboard the 'Mangaru'. On arrival, I dispatched a telegram to the Resident Commissioners at Vila: "BDA CD2 Lakatoro now in residence".

I had equipped the house with a reasonable amount of furniture—bed, refrigerator, etc. And had built two staff quarters; one for the clerk Paul and the police, and a small office—all in local materials i.e. bush timber, thatch roofing, and bamboo walls. The family came on the 'Euphrosyne', the British-based Resident Commissioner's vessel, along with the personal effects.

I think it was a bit of a shock to the system, especially for Ida, to move from a reasonable European house in Santo fitted with mod-cons to the very basic plantation house at Lakatoro. But they settled in very happily and very well; glad to be together with me, and me with them. From the word go, the children—Karen, Simon, and Sallie only a baby of some three years—loved it. They loved Lakatoro and enjoyed the freedom and the space in which to wander and play. We had lots of fun in that first house.

In the run up to Christmas 1964, both air services were out of action. NHAL's aircraft was awaiting repairs and Fiji and Hebredair's service in New Caledonia, thus we had no air service for almost a month. While the services were greatly missed, it was rather nice to have a break in the flow of visitors. Burns Philp's 'Manutai', a substantial local trading vessel equipped with an on-board shop (the equivalent of the local corner store), fortunately paid us a visit before Christmas with supplies. It was well stocked with most needs and the whole world and his wife came aboard to shop.

Ida was able to stock up with small items for our Christmas party and the usual groceries. Karen, Simon, and Sallie each had five shillings to spend on Christmas presents for their friends. Simon bought a football and crackers but on reflection after we returned, had decided to keep his items for himself.

Thirteen

1965 Settling into Lakatoro

In late 1964, we returned to Australia on six months long service leave and we were relieved by BDA John Leaney and his wife Caroline. This wonderful benefit was a standard fixture for the British Colonial service and accrued every two years. We were very lucky to have this and it kept us in touch with Australia and the family in a wonderful way. We had a marvellous leave, which we particularly enjoyed because we were able to have a Christmas at home.

The months flew by and in April 1965, we flew off to the New Hebrides via New Caledonia. We had the usual hassles in Noumea, a one-and-half-hour bus trip from Tontouta Airfield to Noumea town itself and a 4 am start the next morning back to Tontouta, finally arriving Vila at 3 pm. We were given a warm welcome and at 8 o'clock set sail in the 'Euphrosyne' for Lakatoro. I had dosed the family with Mazine and despite the roll we all slept, anchoring off our passage at Port Stanley about midday in pouring rain.

John Leaney met us in my old Land Rover. We got halfway up to our house and got stuck in the mud, and so trudged in pouring rain to home, all soaked to the skin. I spent the afternoon debriefing with John and Ida took over the house from Caroline and began unpacking. The 'Euphrosyne' was ready to depart at 7.30 pm so I drove them down in pouring rain after John had done several trips with their luggage which included two crates of ducks, one of pigeons, one of parrots, one of dogs, and another of cats. Captain Kirkwood refused to take their canoe, which they bequeathed to us. By this time I could feel an attack of malaria coming on and Ida unpacking our musty belongings was disturbed by asthma.

We had a restless night but thankfully the children slept well. The next day it was still pouring with rain. I dragged myself out of bed to look briefly at the station but by this time the fever was raging and I went back to bed. We all felt a little despondent and unsettled. However, the next day the sun shone, the children located their old friends, and were soon content. Helped by a prison gang, we got our house into some sort of order. It was pleasing to see that the two buildings for which I had left funds were underway; both office and our own house had the foundations well started.

We quickly settled down to routine and I went off on tour in the 'Mangaru' to visit Ambrym and Paama. A new inexperienced captain unfamiliar with the region had replaced Captain Filimone and arriving at Paama, we hit a reef. There was great panic and for a few moments I began to think that we might be losing our ship. No sooner had we hit and stuck with a sickening thud and crunch than a squall blew up and rain started pouring down, obliterating visibility. I dashed up to the bridge where there seemed to be chaos—the captain waving his hands and giving countermanding orders. Incredibly we suddenly broke loose from the coral and drifted into deep water. When the storm cleared, one of the crew went overboard and found that although some of the copper sheathing had been torn, there was no serious damage.

We were able to resume our tour and we continued on to south-west Malekula the following day for the opening of a government-funded dispensary and a classroom. They had been constructed by a group of volunteers from Australia, arranged by the local Presbyterian missionary, Ian Taylor.

I was to find on my return to Lakatoro that ten volunteers had landed on our doorstep to await onward transport by plane. Not unexpectedly, the plane was delayed and Ida had to accommodate the visitors. They were young and easy to cope with and slept quite happily crowded in our little lounge. Nonetheless, they had to be fed. The next morning, Sallie woke up and seeing the prostate figures on the floor demanded in a loud voice, "What are all these people doing here?" Thankfully they got away by plane that day.

The new French Resident Commissioner had arrived the night before my return so Ida had to represent me at a dinner at Norsup. She found it pretty heavy going, the conversation all being in French. The following morning, the French Resident Commissioner visited the station and I was able to escort him around. I was surprised to find that his English was quite good and remarked that Ida had had difficulty. He said he felt more comfortable letting her struggle with French than he with English. I presented my staff to him, which now included two clerks, a police sergeant, and my mechanic.

I was finding my motorbike useful, particularly if the Land Rover was needed for other work, and one morning set forth to the north on it. All went well until my return when something went wrong with the steering and I had to push it home for the last five miles. I vowed that in future I would stick with the Land Rover.

On the station, progress was being made with prisoners still clearing back the bush, the tractor put to good use on improving our roads, and more thatched quarters being built. By mid-year, there were facilities to house six police in one quarter, prisoners in another, temporary quarters for Paul Binihi and Tinsley Lulu, my clerks, and a quite respectable bamboo and thatch building for my office. I had found that the tent was completely unsatisfactory—it was stifling hot and too dark.

Life here was so different to Santo, even more so for Ida. Although I was frequently on tour to visit the other islands and the inaccessible parts of

Malekula—dealing with the usual court cases, land disputes etc.—I was able to spend a little more time at base. Our first big social event was to be the Queen's Birthday celebrations.

Before this event, however, there was an opportunity to take my family on a 'get to know you' tour. The 'Euphrosyne' was allocated to me for a few days—we had been befriended by its Captain Kirkwood and he was always happy to call in on Oscar Newman at Tisman. This we did and Oscar, as usual, made us very welcome with a sumptuous lunch. Oscar regaled us with his customary fascinating stories of events in his life.

From Tisman, we went south to Aulua to meet up with the Presbyterian Reverend Kelvin Auld and family, and Heather Scott, a schoolteacher. From there we went on to Lamap where I had to make contact with the French agency. Monsieur Fabre had returned to France on leave without replacement and a French gendarme was in charge. He was not impressive; I must say that it reinforced my poor opinion of the French Gendarmerie in general.

The children loved being on the 'Euphrosyne'. The crew were incredibly kind and even Harry seemed to enjoy them. They fished overboard, swam when the opportunity offered, and it was an idyllic sea. Ida, now busier than ever at home with correspondence school for Karen and Simon and an increasing flow of British office staff from Vila to cope with, was able to put her feet up and read to her heart's content.

The visits from British office officials were nonetheless welcome. I could see that the more I could interest the various departments, particularly medical and education, the more likely it was that I could get their support for development in this very neglected district. This also applied to condominium officials responsible for agriculture and public works. It is no exaggeration to say that the agricultural offices had done absolutely nothing for the local population, concentrating in their rare visits solely upon the French plantations. So I bent over backwards to welcome official visitors and this meant that we were the only persons in a position to welcome and entertain them. Ida's social whirlwind in Santo had now been replaced by official duties. We were given a very modest allowance to assist with provisioning them. Visitors had to not only be fed but also housed when not touring, and the sooner we could get a rest house operating the better.

Queen's Birthday loomed, and I was determined with the very modest funds available to make at least something of this festival, the first of its kind for the district. After perfect weather, the Saturday dawned cloudy and showery but not enough to dampen the day. We had about 1000 visitors; the station staff had worked well, cooking sufficient rice and beef to feed the multitude. For the official guests who included the small European population, planters and missionaries, and neighbouring chiefs we gave a luncheon party. Prisoners had the night before gone out to fish for fresh prawns in the local streams and crayfish. Ida's curry looked bubbly (shades of Tanna) but we came to the conclusion that this was normal and no one suffered any after-effects. We had police to serve drinks and in the afternoon there were some sports in the limited space available. In the evening, I showed films with a projector borrowed from Vila and thereafter local musicians provided music for dancing which went on until daylight.

The next morning, I received a report from Pentecost that a launch with seven schoolgirls aboard had broken down the night before between Maewo and Pentecost. They were seen drifting off the Pentecost coast. Apparently a dingy went out from Pentecost to tow them but was unsuccessful and both vessels were last spotted being carried south. Gusty winds and seas were rising fast. I despatched the 'Bonite' to look for them, hoping that they would be successful, but the next morning found that the Gendarme at Lamap had countermanded my instructions and 'Bonite' had gone back to Lamap. I was still trying to get to the bottom of this but suspected that the French doctor at Norsup had intervened and had told the 'Bonite' captain to take him to Lamap. Anyway, I was furious and told everyone off at Lamap in my best French—rather difficult for me when I was so angry.

This meant no action was being taken to rescue the drifting vessels so I had to organise the 'Mangaru' from Santo and other trading vessels in the area to begin the search. I was also able to arrange a search by air. The expedition continued all afternoon with several false alarms. So having spent the whole day on Tuesday on the radio, I decided to recall the 'Mangaru' and go off myself. We travelled all night, arriving at dawn to find that both the missing launch and dinghy had been found. What had happened was that the dinghy had eventually overtaken the launch and towed it into land. As the weather had turned so nasty, they had sheltered in a creek all day, hence having been missed by the searching aircraft. They had no way of knowing about the search for them.

It was a pleasant surprise on my return that prisoner Jimmy Tasseri, my prisoner from Tanna still with a year to go, had arrived. The children greeted him with shrieks of delight and followed him around for the rest of the afternoon. He kept busy on odd jobs, fixing up the Land Rover, leaking taps etc.

That same evening, Yvonne Lenissa, the works foreman, cornered me at dusk. He was a great talker and spoke so fast in incomprehensible French, all I could do was say, "Oui oui" or "Non non" periodically and it usually seemed to work. But this time I could not get away and realised that he did have problems. I had got approval to build not only my own new quarters and the office but also two staff quarters. Yvonne was having problems with the construction of the foundations because of the lay of the land, rocks etc. I decided to hire the one and only bulldozer on the island from PRNH at Norsup and much to Simon's delight, it began work the next day. With prisoners, it would have taken weeks and weeks but with the bulldozer the two sites were ready within a couple of days. Yvonne was very pleased.

Earthquake 1965

Development on the station was progressing—the office walls were completed and with my own house, work was about to start on the roofing. Then came a catastrophe. On the 11th of August 1965, I was struggling in my office trying to catch up with my paperwork when at 3 pm we had a prolonged earth tremor. The whole earth rocked and it seemed like it was never going to end. Everyone automatically dashed outside and I followed. I raced over to the house and found Ida and the children sheltering under the table but not unduly worried. We all went back to work. That evening, we had another shorter one not long after we went to bed, gentle ones and nothing too disturbing.

A sudden jar or jolt, rather, woke us up at 4 am but we went off to sleep again, and there were several more light ones at breakfast time when I was in the office doing the usual chores. At 9.30, I was talking to Harry Kirkwood on the radio when we heard a loud rumbling and within seconds the very earth seemed to be in turmoil. Tinsley, Paul, and Sergeant Norman all thought the same thing as I did, and were all out of the office in a flash, me dropping the microphone and breaking the conversation with Harry in mid-sentence. As we ran, cupboards began to topple over. I dashed for the house. A most eerie feeling—trying to run with the earth rocking furiously under you, like trying to run on the deck of a ship in heavy seas. As I ran, I heard the sounds of glass and crockery coming down hard on cement floors. I got to the house and found Ida and Karen in tears outside on the lawn. Simon had started running over towards the office and was having trouble keeping his feet as well. The house was in a terrible mess. Even though it was over, you could hear it rumbling away in the distance.

I'd almost forgotten Sallie who had been with Sergeant Norman's family and was not unduly disturbed. I returned back to the office to finish my conversation with Harry. He said, "We've had a bit of a shake here, did you feel it?" I had, in fact, barely been able to get into my office. The building was still standing but every cupboard overturned, typewriters on their backs, papers everywhere. The radio miraculously was about the only thing in its proper place. I finished off the conversation quickly and went back to survey the damage.

The house looked a dreadful mess—no structural damage but both refrigerators (including the 11 cubic foot one) had danced a jig across the floor, spilling all their contents. The food cupboard, which had blocked Ida and children from getting out, was across the floor. The crockery cupboard was still upright but some doors had opened and everything inside had fallen out—glass, crockery, bottles broken right and left. All of our supplies on top of the cupboards like Shelltox, kerosene, and pressure lamps were all on the floor and all the contents of the refrigerator had mixed in with them. The bathroom medicine cabinet had capsized its contents onto the linen that had gone out first. In the lounge room, the bookshelves had toppled over, all the pictures had fallen down and so on.

I left Ida cleaning up with the house girls and went to survey the station. "Woe is me", the poor new house, with its walls just completed the day before. Most of the interior walls had collapsed completely and every wall was so badly cracked that it would have to be completely demolished down to the foundations. The office was not so bad. The exterior walls were okay but interior walls were all cracked and had to come out. The agricultural labourers' quarters down on the flats were flat as a pancake. Whilst doing the rounds and within minutes of the bad one, we started getting more shudders and shakes and with each, everyone would shout and rush out to open spaces, so my tour was interrupted now and again.

Meanwhile, the tide was running out fast, exposing enormous stretches of reef. Thousands of fish were left stranded on the reefs and we found dead fish for days. I sent out police north and south to tell the coastal villagers to watch out for tidal waves and posted them up on the hillside to keep watch; fortunately nothing eventuated. Very small cracks had appeared on the ground and some of the smaller islands took to their canoes and came to the mainland. I had got onto my motorbike and did a quick tour of the nearer villages. Most of the thatch houses stood up very well, though I heard the next day that some villages lost a lot of houses. No one was hurt which was the main thing.

For the rest of the day we kept getting tremors almost continuously, sometimes as often as every two or three minutes, none as severe as the one at 9.30 but sharp enough to make us feel a bit jittery. I spent the entire lunch hour on the radio calling the various mission stations on all the islands of the district and getting a good overall picture of the damage. Malekula evidently got hit the worst. Poor Ian Taylor said he had nothing unbroken in his house—concrete floors all cracked, crockery and glassware broken. At Aulua, Kelvin Auld who lived in a house sitting on piles about 3 feet high had an exciting time but the house had stood firm. At Tisman, everything in the store and house was broken. At Norsup, the solid concrete jetty—about 12 feet wide and 8 feet thick—had cracked in half and the electric street-light wires were all broken. A bridge broke farther up the coast. At Lakatoro, I found our little galvanised-iron-roofed dock down at the wharf had fallen flat and our stone wharf which had taken a lot of hard work to build was almost levelled.

In the afternoon, still with occasional tremors, some still sharp, I heard that Santo had been worst hit on the day before (the 3 pm one we had felt on Malekula). The big wharf there had been badly damaged; all the stores had lost a lot of merchandise and new buildings had cracked. The town was without water and light for two days.

The day just seemed to go, cleaning up and assessing damage and rushing outside every time there was a tremor. We all went to bed dog-tired. The children too were obviously worried. Sallie said, "I don't like all these earth snakes. I want to go back to Australia in the Polyneezie." To settle them, we put all their mattresses on the floor in our room and we all slept there together that night. They were fortunately too tired to hear anything but we were disturbed every few hours by tremors. The house literally rocked each time but we did not feel the need to leave our beds.

On Friday, we had a bad one at 5 am which woke us all and made us bundle up the children and dash for the door, but by the time we got there it was all over. It woke the whole station and we heard police and prisoners and clerks shouting as they tumbled out of bed and then went back to bed laughing and teasing one another. Friday was far more peaceful as far as tremors were concerned. Lenissa, the contractor, flew up at 9 o'clock to assess damage on the new house. He was horrified and, in Vila, had not realised how severe it had been. They had only felt the odd light tremor.

The public works director and the Assistant French Resident Commissioner had flown up to inspect the buildings with Lenissa as it would affect his contract. Work was put back about a month. All the walls in the new agency had to be demolished and started again. It was a pity as the work had only just been done and had not had time to set properly.

Friday night we still felt tired and after such a relatively peaceful day we felt we could all sleep in our own beds. Fortunately we did not rehang anything or replace ornaments and the like, for through the night we had constant and pretty heavy tremors, especially at 5 am, exactly the same time as the day before. This sent us scuttling again. Poor Karen had a restless night and several times I shot out thinking to move the children, only to find Karen sheltering in the doorway. At midnight I went into her bed and she went off into a deep sleep. From then on to about 2 am we had shakes every few minutes. Simon and Sallie slept right through and in the morning Simon woke very cheery to say, "No shakes last night!!" From then on things settled down with only an occasional one to remind us that we need not be too blasé.

When we went down to the coastline to check the reef and all the dead fish, the reef seemed to have lifted. This was apparent down the whole west coast where new reefs had been exposed. Radio Noumea said that the epicentre for the 7.2 magnitude earthquake was about 100 miles west of Malekula, so we did get the worst of it along with Santo. The day before, Santo had experienced a tidal wave, which had left several ships high and dry along the south coast, and a mission launch had capsized and sank in 20 feet of water. Fortunately, no one was on board.

A Wedding

Abel, marrying a girl from Litzlitz, had asked us to his wedding. It took place at the village. Ida had made the wedding cake and helped organise the bride's dress and cleaned her sandshoes for the occasion—sandshoes being the only white footwear available. The bridal party were almost hidden behind the most enormous sheaf of crotons (a coloured-leaf plant) you could ever imagine. The bride was dressed in a voluminous Mother Hubbard (a traditional missionary-inspired island dress) with a coronet of white paper roses, each blossom measuring about four inches across. The fact that the bride was expecting in about a month's time made no difference because of the billowing Mother Hubbard. In the parade, at funeral pace, to the tune of a mournful hymn, the bride had difficulty in keeping her sandshoes on. The *kaikai* however and the "danis casem daelaet' (dancing until dawn) was good fun.

The next day we were invited to Wala Island to take part in the celebration of the arrival of the palolo worm. This is a widespread occurrence in most of the Pacific Islands apparently and appears only once every year when the moon is full. You were expected to lunch and the family was well entertained. We were shown the worms swarming onto the beach and then being either roasted and fried or cooked in *laplap*. To make things worse, the palolo worm was locally referred to as a maggot. We did our best to taste it, but it really was the most revolting thing. I still felt squeamish that night.

Afterwards we were given a very tasty meal of beef and rice and the children ate like horses. Halfway through the afternoon, I had to return to Norsup to present the Resident Commissioner's Cup at the final of the local football competition. This was my first time to officiate at such a function and Mr Tanguy brought along a bottle of champagne with which to fill the cup. There was, however, a very embarrassing few moments when Tinsley Lulu, captain of the Lakatoro team, challenged the referee on some point and with his team, walked off the field. After a lot of unsuccessful negotiation, I went over to investigate the trouble and found that Tinsley was making allegations of favouritism towards the Norsup team. I could have kicked him in the teeth but after very controlled and patient discussion, Tinsley agreed to go back and finish the game, which Lakatoro won. When I presented him with the cup filled with champagne, he refused to drink from it and passed it on to his team. I felt embarrassed that Mr Tanguy's esprit sportif had been rejected.

The following week, Doug Williams, the new District Education Officer, and I set out with backpacks for the Big Nambas settlement in Amok, in the mountains of central-north Malekula. My arrangement for accommodation on the track had fallen through and by the time we had reached Amok, night had fallen. We were glad to sleep in the little rest hut that Chief Virhambath had built for me. We were also glad of our blankets that we brought.

The following day we spent almost all of it discussing the possibility of establishing a small primary school there. It was always my hope that the last of the Big Nambas tribes would remain there rather than be tempted down to the coast. The Big Nambas plateau, fairly level, had beautiful soil and tremendous potential for rural development. The proposal was discussed for some hours during which time we had a little siesta. The end result was not very satisfactory because they did not want a school there at all, but would send their children to the mission schools on the coast. It was apparent that they did not want to have their traditional way of life disturbed, which was understandable.

During the discussions that afternoon I was trying to ascertain why they were not combining with the neighbouring village to Amok if they were to move to the coast. Apparently Amok and its neighbours had been traditional enemies and were frequently fighting. This discussion led onto a discussion about cannibalism. Most of them had eaten their neighbours and told me it tasted like turtle. The one man I was talking to, however, said he had never tasted human meat and when I asked why, he said, "Oh my mother came from that village." The point being that one was apparently not allowed to eat one's relatives. It was incredible to think that this was still going on in the fifties.

French High Commissioner's Visit

The new French High Commissioner visited in September 1965. My French colleague Monsieur Boileau had planned a joint guard of honour at 7 am. My detachment of five policemen under Sergeant Norman turned out to join their French Colleagues at Norsup. I was very proud of my little detachment—they looked really smart and showed up well against their French colleagues. After an inspection of the French hospital at Norsup, it was soon time for an aperitif followed soon after by a "dejeuner intime" which revealed itself as a seven-course meal beginning at noon and ending at 3.30 pm. Ida, as the senior and incidentally only lady present, sat on the High Commissioner's right and had to struggle away in French. In fact, she did extremely well. The following morning, the High Commissioner inspected my station and did so with interest. He remarked that he felt my colleague was in the wrong place down at Port Sandwich. My heart sank because I felt this was a pretty good indication that he would be moving north in due course.

At Lakatoro, development continued, my agency being roofed and the office almost ready for occupation with its two flagpoles already in place. Wilben, my all-rounder mechanic, was using the tractor with its ancillary equipment with great skill, corralling access roads and clearing a site for a tennis court for which I thought there was justification for some expenditure of public funds.

I had quite early in the establishment realised that I was sitting on a small goldmine of copra which was to be made from the Gaby's plantation as it was cleared. I was able to dispose of it through Oscar Newman who happily bought any copra my prisoners could produce, paying cash which went into my rapidly growing goat bag.

District Summary

By the end of 1965, I was able to reflect on our station with some satisfaction and pride. Wilben with his tractor, slasher, and front-end loader now had the road leading up to the office white coralled and edged with large white coral rocks. Most of the flat areas were slashed, being covered in buffalo lawn, and a football field with goal posts had been installed. The football field had necessitated the removal of a large number of coconuts using a gadget, which I borrowed from Norsup plantation. It used a pulley system to pull out the coconut trees, roots and all. I felt rather sorry to be losing a lucrative crop for my goat bag from the loss of copra production, but a playing field was essential for the station, and besides, my cows now could find good grazing there.

The prisoners had constructed quite a nice little jetty with rocks and coral, and carpenter Atis Aviu had concreted the seaward end to make a convenient landing. Atis, an innovative builder, had supervised construction of a temporary quarter for Meli, temporary quarters for the prisoners, and a temporary New Hebridean rest house. Permanent buildings were slowly taking shape, my office almost ready for occupation and Yvonne promised that my house would be completed by the end of March, 1966, which augured well for the future.

Peter

In June 1966, Ida announced to our families in Australia the impending arrival of our fourth child in December. She had had problems with Sallie's birth and was concerned about the next one. After consultation with the specialist in Sydney and Dr Bill Rees in Vila, it was decided that it would be safe for the baby to be born at PMH (Paton Memorial Hospital) in Vila. She was advised to go to Vila in November and took Simon with her to supervise his schooling which required more attention than Karen's. Karen was by this time doing well and only needed occasional supervision from me and Sallie aged four was looked after by Elsie, our housegirl.

Ida and Simon were housed at the Vila rest house until she was admitted to PMH when the Allens (Resident Commissioner at the time, Colin Allen and family) cared for Simon. I had curtailed my touring at the beginning of December and awaited news. Finally, on the 11th of December, Peter arrived. I had been listening all day on and off on the radio and had arranged for regular contact to continue at night. At 11 o'clock, Betty Allen confirmed that Peter had arrived safely and I walked back through the trees to the house bubbling over with excitement but with no one to share it with until the next day.

When finally some ten days later it was arranged for Ida to return with the new baby, the Norsup airfield was closed after torrential rains and the plan was she would fly into Lamap. I set off at dawn with Tinsley in my Land Rover, having arranged for the 'Bonite' meet me at Bushman's Bay. Here we waited and then received a message from Sergeant Norman in the long wheelbase Land Rover that the 'Bonite' had broken down with engine problems. So we drove on to the end of the road near the Pankumu River. I thought if I could get to Tisman, Oscar Newman would be able to help with shipping. I walked on to the mouth of the Pankumu thinking if I could not cross upstream I might be able to swim across.

On arrival, I found the Pankumu a 400-yard-wide raging torrent flooding from the heavy torrential rain from the night before. Whilst I stood there contemplating, a large shark was washed up onto a shoal midstream flapping vigorously. Oscar, however, no doubt listening to the radio, guessed the predicament and whilst I stood by the river the 'Lakaleo' appeared around the point. I boarded and we went at 'Lakaleo's' top speed, which was very slow, down to Port Sandwich. The gendarme had a Land Rover waiting for me and I hurried into Lamap to find Ida, Simon, and baby Peter waiting at his house. They had arrived an hour or so previously.

The new babe was happily bedded in a Solomon Island basket sound asleep. To my delight, he had red hair. We returned to the jetty, boarded the Lakaleo, and set off for Bushman's Bay. Tinsely had waited patiently for us in my Land Rover. Bushman's Bay provided an accessible passage to land. By this time, Peter was obviously hungry and Ida fed him in the shelter of an old copra bed. We then drove on and arrived at our house to find Sallie and Karen sitting on the steps awaiting us. It was just about dark. The excitement of the reunion cannot be described. It was Christmas Eve.

Schooling

Our children loved life on Malekula but as Ida said, she wondered whether they were getting all the opportunities they needed at this stage of their lives. They climbed mango trees, would knock off all kinds of fruits and nuts with bamboo poles, they roasted crabs down on the reef, roasted yam in open fires, danced custom style, played guitars, and spoke fluently in pidgin.

Later, of course, Karen and Simon went off to boarding school, detesting every moment of it. Sallie and then Peter came under Ida's tuition at correspondence from Blackfriars Correspondence School based in Sydney. Then came the day when Sallie joined Karen at boarding school. Peter continued as an islander until my retirement.

Lakatoro Life

On Pentecost, a problem arose when the senior geologist from Vila working on the island met with local opposition. He was conducting a geological survey of the island for potential minerals. The locals rightly were suspicious and fearful for the loss of their land. I spent a week on the island holding meetings in the various villages, assuring them that there was no intention of immediate exploitation and if there was it would be discussed before the island leaders before any action was taken.

The priest at Melsissi, on the west coast of Pentecost, had asked me to look into a case of witchcraft in one of the villages in his area. I was rather flattered because it would have been more usual for the French-speaking priest to turn to my French colleague rather than me. So on my next tour of Pentecost, I made a point of calling there and spent most of the morning looking into vague allegations about unexplained illnesses etc. As usual with this sort of report, it was very difficult to obtain any concrete evidence to prosecute and I had to give it away. During the discussions, I heard another amazing story of an outbreak of cargo cult in the bush villages in the mountains behind Melsissi and went up to investigate. Two children—one about six and one around 12—started to relate their dreams, one finding a 1 dollar coin in the creek and saying that he found 2 shillings the next day. From then on, they seemed to become oracles, telling first their father and then the village and finally the surrounding villages what they should do to obtain hidden monies. They said that the villagers should dig out rocks from the earth, break them up, and inside they would find money, guns, scissors, tinned meat, which was everything that people wanted. The boys said that the villagers should build separate houses where cooking would be done. Everyone turned to it and began building. They also dug enormous holes to get out rock and break it up. The two boys supervised the smashing of the rock and their father was shrewd enough to make a business out of it, charging 5 shillings a head for people to see the process. All without result of course. After about a year, most people were sensible enough to start demanding some return. Nothing was forthcoming, arguments developed, and this was where they called on me to adjudicate. By now the arguments had blown over and people had seen the humorous side and laughed at themselves for being so gullible. I warned the father and the boys if they tried such a stunt again, I would take action. There was provision, incidentally, in the Native Criminal Code to deal with witchcraft in all its forms, but I always had difficulty in finding sufficient evidence to prosecute, even though the practice I think was widespread.

The Native Criminal Code also included provision for action against a villager who refused to build a pit latrine, known in pidgin as "closet". I was fully aware that in a lot of villages people were still going into the nearby bush to defecate. Marauding pigs would then provide for the incubation of intestinal worms, thereby providing a vicious circle of disease. In my touring, I would as a matter of routine make an inspection with the village chief or elder to see that the legislation was being followed. Not a very envious task and more often than not, closets, even if built, were not being used. On Vao Island for example with its large Roman Catholic mission dominating the island, there were practically no village latrines. It always astonished me that the mission appeared to have no influence over their congregation's health. My early French colleagues Fabre, then Lecuyer would certainly not have involved themselves in such necessary action but Boileau threw himself into the public health issue with gusto.

The British Medical Officer, Dr Ramm, an Australian, proved to be invaluable, energetic, and enthusiastic. I did my utmost to encourage him to tour the district. He was amused but very approving of my efforts to encourage the locals to build and use latrines. He was very supportive in the setting up of dispensaries for which funds had to be allocated. This was a slow process because it had to await estimates submitted to Vila and then London for approval.

Yet another French naval vessel, a frigate, the 'Protect' arrived at Norsup in March 1966, and once again there were the formalities of calls, station inspections, cocktail parties, etc. I was rather flattered on this occasion at the cocktail party to be piped on board and piped again on departure. It appealed to my naval training and was good for the ego.

On the station, house and agency were nearing completion and new furniture was arriving. With the office, there were last minute delays; no doorknobs, no lights. We had incidentally by now received a second bigger generator that was installed alongside the smaller one. The smaller one was to be used for my agency and at the turn of a switch would operate anytime, night or day. In the early days, Karen even at the age of eight would happily go over to the workshop where the generator was housed to turn off the power nightly at ten; she had no fear whatsoever of the dark.

Yet another World Health Organisation (WHO) campaign began in 1966. This was the eradication of tuberculosis and comprised a small team headed by Sister Peg Agave. They were fortunately completely self-contained but Sister Agave would call in occasionally for a chat and to update me on progress.

Carpenter Atis had at last begun work on the rest house using goat bag funds. We were desperate to have more accommodation because the stream of visitors seemed never-ending. A new condominium agricultural officer (French) was appointed to the district and housed in Norsup. I never really was able to find out what he was doing. Apparently he devoted his time to the French plantations and so I never really made much use of him.

The year had seen some important visitors for us, including the Secretary of State for the Colonies himself, Mr Fred Lee, and I was proud to find that the Resident Commissioners had decided to show him my station. He came for lunch, accompanied by both British and French REs and entourage. For Ida it was quite an exercise, particularly deciding on who should sit where but she apparently made no faux pas. The lunch went off very successfully. Mr Lee seemed to be very impressed. He was an easy guest.

In Vila, the Resident Commissioners had a more exacting task in receiving General De Gaulle in a short 4-hour visit. Apparently he said all the right things with the usual platitudes. He inspected a guard of honour to which I had contributed my little detachment. Fortunately, the especially long bed for the general which had been brought in from New Caledonia in case there was a delay somewhere was not used.

There were rumours at this time throughout the group that Britain as part of its austerity campaign was going to withdraw from New Hebrides, thus handing over to the French. The French were beginning to clap their hands with glee. Both Mr Lee and General De Gaulle dismissed these rumours.

The most tragic event of the past year was the crash of New Hebrides Airways 'Rapide' on Tanna with the loss of Paul Burton, pilot, and all eight passengers. It cast a shadow over the whole group because most of the expatriate population knew most of the passengers who had been killed. My sympathies were especially with Guy Wallington, BDA Tanna, who on the third day after the crashed aircraft was located, had to try to identify and retrieve what few remains were to be found.

Fourteen

1967 Lakatoro

Routine Administration

In 1967, the WHO tuberculosis team completed its mission, and the New Hebrides census was also completed this year.

The changeover in currency from pounds sterling and French francs to a national decimal currency of dollars was slowly taking place in the district. After some publicity, I set out with about $5,000 in cash to tour the districts, making provision for a changeover. This was an incredibly intriguing job. I would set up in a village overnight and allow people the opportunity to change their money with privacy. An extraordinary array of money was brought forth, sometimes wrapped in a dirty old cloth or a tobacco tin or just in leaves. It would include coins mainly from English sovereigns and half sovereigns and Maria Theresa silver dollars. These latter coins, often very worn, were beautiful solid silver. It was during this time there was an amusing mix-up in regards to the safekeeping of the cash. A new shipment of money had arrived on a flight from Vila and was picked up by staff and carefully packed away in my safe. On the same flight, a box of paint arrived which was duly stored in the paint room. At some point we took the cash out of the safe, only to find four tins of white paint. Luckily the money was still stored safely in the paint room. It could have been an embarrassing thing to explain if it had gone missing, but it didn't.

We had, climate-wise, a reasonably quiet year, although in March, the official end of the hurricane season, we were threatened by three successive depressions heading straight for us. On each occasion, luckily for us they veered off leaving a lot of debris behind them. There were occasional minor tremors and on Ambrym on several occasions the volcano threw a red glow into the sky—a lovely view from our verandah.

An interesting visitor was Austin Coates, son of the well-known English composer Eric Coates. He had been commissioned by the Colonial Office to visit and write about the territories of the Western Pacific. Like so many other odd characters, he was shipped up to me to entertain. He joined us, Dr Greenough, and Doug Williams on the 'Euphrosyne' and we collected my colleague Monsieur Boileau to tour Pentecost. This was a routine joint tour during which we heard numerous land disputes, one or two serious assault cases, and the like. We called on the Smiths at the Church of Christ mission at Ranwadi and were, as usual, sumptuously entertained by the Thevenins at their plantation. Austin Coates enjoyed listening to Boileau and I bickering, disagreeing over different matters but ending up in the evening reasonably amicable.

When we got back to Lakatoro, I had to leave him with Ida whom he obviously thoroughly enjoyed. He visited the French at Norsup and enjoyed the company of station staff, particularly George Kalkoa. Paul Binihi at Austen's request took him to a local village *nakamal* to drink kava. I was pleased when later we received a complimentary copy of his book on the Western Pacific. Ida was given a very warm write up.

Dr Tabankai at the French Norsup Hospital slipped away unheralded mid-year. I was always sorry that he had departed without any expressions of appreciation on the public's behalf. Dr Tabankai was trained in the very early days in Fiji and was the best qualified of any New Hebridean medical officer at that time. He was always helpful with us, extremely patient with our children, and at all times concerned about Ida, particularly when she became pregnant with Peter.

This Queen's Birthday, I was determined to set a fixed pattern and perhaps a more imposing one for future years. Even with the modest police detachment of six under Sergeant Norman, we followed the precedent set in Vila of at least a little parade. They turned out in their immaculate best and, driven by Kilman, I arrived in my Land Rover in full Colonial Service uniform. I had the full regalia with brass buttons, pith helmet, and sword. I inspected the guard and Sergeant Norman called for three cheers for Her Majesty the Queen.

I had organised Paul Binihi to cope with food and Sergeant Norman to deal with the sports. In the evening, we had a small group for cocktails. Paul had had two teams cooking all night the usual 12 bags of rice and two 44 gallon drums of stew, mounds of vegetables, bananas, *laplap,* etc. About 2000 people were well fed. The sports, with prizes for winners, were well organised with one rather alarming moment which was the timing of the coconut tree competition. The first to knock off a coconut and get back down to the ground again would be the winner. On this occasion, one climber on the way down, seeing he was going to lose the race, jumped a much greater distance than he had evidently anticipated. He fell with a thump but fortunately although winded, suffered no serious damage.

As in the previous year, there was the ever popular show of cowboy films and dancing "go go kasem delaet". The next day I unofficially proclaimed a holiday but prisoners were turned out to gather up the many empty beer cans.

A minor triumph was the completion and opening of the air terminal at Norsup. Scraping together, quite legally, condominium funds, some cash from the goat bag, and prisoner labour, we were able to have built, under VSO (Voluntary Service Overseas) Alan Hardiman's direction, a terminal with waiting room, toilet block, and bar at which coffee was served. Peter Wright—

the Fijian working at Norsup—and his wife took over the running of the bar. This meant that our visitors could fend for themselves on arrival and departure and it was a tremendous asset.

In June, we at last moved into our new district agency—luxury indeed to have space and a guest room. Evacuation of our previous quarters meant that there was now housing available for a long projected Assistant District Agent and George Kalkoa (later, as George Sokomanu, to become the first President of independent Vanuatu) arrived to take up his post. He was a valuable staff member and considerably reduced my workload.

A few months before, I had been approached by the Assistant Resident Commissioner about the possibility of being awarded an MBE (a Member of the Order of the British Empire). Would I accept it? Of course, I said yes and that was that. On the Queen's Birthday, I did not receive the usual telegram which promulgated birthday honours and I forgot about the matter. The next day, I began to receive telegrams congratulating me, evidently my MBE had appeared but Vila had omitted to send me the usual telegram. It was all very exciting and I was particularly appreciative because indirectly it reflected the tremendous backing I had from Ida.

Two days later, there was a deputation of my staff inviting us to a party that night. Organised by Paul Binihi, the entire station had got together and gave me a tremendous feast in the little temporary classroom behind the workshops. It was a wonderful evening and I felt very moved by the enthusiasm which they had put into the party.

We were thankfully in the new house when Ida's mother arrived after a pretty tortuous trip through Noumea, to spend several months with us. She was a tremendous help to Ida, especially with the sewing of curtains for the new house. On one occasion, I had received a deputation from the Big Nambas at Amok to discuss a land dispute and I couldn't resist the temptation to invite them up to my house. They were led by Chief Virhambath adorned with a pig's tusk bracelet, a bone threw his nose, and dressed in the traditional, very large, red woven penis wrapper, which extended from the base of the penis and swept up into the bark belt. I introduced them to Ida and her mother. They sat around the room, with Ida's mother in true Victorian style sitting erect and smiling graciously, quite unperturbed.

With Christmas 1967 upon us, we decided that it would be just a family affair for us and for the station although we did have a Christmas Eve party just for the station children. I bedecked myself in a Father Christmas outfit and appeared from the bush from the NE of the house with the traditional bag of goodies. Afterwards, Sallie said with uncertainty in her voice, "You were Father Christmas, weren't you, Dad?" By this time, Peter was really a model baby and wriggled in delight when anyone looked at him. He was always a prized exhibit for our visitors.

Local Councils

In the early days, Jacques Fabre was reasonably interested in local council promotion and development, and we took quite a lot of meetings jointly. Fabre's successors were much less interested and it became obvious as the years went by that the French administration generally were opposed to the local councils, which had been introduced at British instigation and based on the British East-African system. I viewed the introduction of local government as the cornerstone for independence and pushed the issue with all the energy and enthusiasm that I could muster, beginning with the local councils on north Pentecost and north Malekula.

Later, with very little French assistance—in fact in many cases, opposition—I was able to establish councils on central and south Pentecost, south Malekula, and south-east, west, and north Ambrym, and Paama. I had always hoped that we could have island councils but this was strongly opposed and would never have been agreed to by my colleague or by the French residency in Vila.

The councils had to depend on raising their own revenue, in some cases, getting dollar for dollar grants from the condominium government. Head tax then was the principal means of revenue and the annual amount was usually something between $4.00 and $5.00. Not a great amount even for those days and with the copra prices varying between $100-$150 per tonne, it should not have been difficult to meet that tax.

But in practice it became extremely difficult and it was one of the things that I pursued vigorously, supporting the local council secretaries in their endeavours to collect tax. Even falling back on the legislation, which empowered me as a magistrate of the Native Melanesian Court to prosecute and if necessary, imprison. I avoided imprisonment as much as possible because I feared it would turn people against councils. Usually it was a question of constant pressuring to get the taxes paid.

I might add that my French colleagues gave me no support whatsoever with the secretaries and their tax-collecting endeavours. My preaching about local government was very basic. Local government was a means of training the indigenous local people to govern for themselves. By paying taxes, people were contributing to the running of their own country and learning not to be dependent upon grants from the British and French governments.

I talked about independence from the 1960s onwards. As I have said, it was usually met with scepticism, particularly when I said it would only be a matter of a few years and a New Hebridean would be taking my job. It was not long after, in the late 1960s, that the National Party, or subsequently, the Vanuaku Party and the Nagriamel movement began themselves talking about independence. And from then on the move to independence snowballed, reaching its climax with complete independence in 1980.

Fifteen

1968 Lakatoro

My station continued to expand. Our greatest joy was, of course, the new house with ample space and new furnishings, but alas with our family of six no spare room. The domestic quarters behind us were temporarily used as a guest quarter whilst we urged carpenter Atis on with the building of the permanent rest house using the goat bag. It was well-sited like our own quarters, looking out over Port Stanley to Uripiv and the small islands. When it was finally completed, the rest house comprised of two bedrooms, bathroom and kitchenette, and front verandah. It made a tremendous difference to our lives, particularly Ida's because she always made herself responsible for our increasing flow of visitors. Usually rest house visitors continued to eat with us. However we now had a much better organised domestic staff—Meli, first of all, who was a goldmine but who subsequently became pregnant to Paul Binihi. We hoped they would marry but Paul was reluctant to undertake responsibility, and much to the children's regret, she went home to her home island of Paama. At a later date, after his return from a course in Australia to learn English, Paul returned and he and Meli were married at Lakatoro.

Elsi from Litzlitz was always a favourite of the children but from time to time she would like to "spell",(take time off). Finally we decided to look for someone, and through Captain Filimone found a wonderful Fijian woman Anna Draka, who became our housekeeper/cook. She was a staunch and reliable friend for some years. Of course she adored Peter, calling him "nicey littley boy".

At last the tennis court was completed with a hitting wall made from the old agency materials at Bushman's Bay. This became quite a social centre for the station and for the French expatriate population at Norsup. It helped to unify all of us. Tinsley Lulu, a born sportsman, became quite a proficient player.

The 'swimming pool' official water supply reserve was taking shape again with the help of the goat bag. The original piping from the spring water three quarters of a mile up from the station had been replaced with a bigger diameter pipe and provided a much better flow. The prisoners were now also constructing a small non-denominational chapel.

Metemet Club

On Tanna, I had put forward the idea of a sort of social club where people could meet in the evening to talk, play games, etc., but after much discussion with the local big men the answer was "I gud be mi fella no wantem". At Lakatoro, the idea, which I put forward in 1965, was welcomed both by my own staff and the local villagers. Atis, who was never daunted by anything set to work. Together with Wilben, they combed the local forests and helped by prison labour, cut and dragged down to the station six enormous natora posts about 24 inches in diameter. Our idea was to build a *nakamal* big enough to hold a large crowd for dances and concerts.

The finished building was finally about 10 metres by 25 metres. It was clad in natangura thatch which ensured much more permanency than the more common pandanus. Initially we were given access to natangura locally but supplies were soon diminished and thereafter every time I visited Pentecost with a government vessel, I would buy and bring back as much natangura as the captain would accept. The exception to this was Captain Kirkwood in the 'Euphrosyne' who refused adamantly to transport it. The building was finally completed towards the end of 1966 and our first dance there was well attended by station and village people. In subsequent years, I was able to add to one side a supper room, kitchen, and small library, and on the other side, a toilet block. The men's urinal (sourced from Australia) gave rise to a lot of mirth in the early days with the less-sophisticated visitors.

Touring continued unabated. I would recall Sir Edward Twining's dictum that every administrative officer should spend a minimum of 14 days on safari. Within my own district agency region, people had access to my office and when I was in my office there would always be a queue of people with their problems and requiring action; land disputes, bride price, and minor criminal matters such as assault. The outer islands, however, including north and south of Malekula were only accessible by sea and necessitated regular touring to make contact. I remember when I first took over the district, visiting the small village of Laravat on the west coast of Malekula, where I dealt with several minor matters. One such matter was an application for a gun licence which I said I would deal with when I returned. I could see the scepticism on their face when I said this. When I returned a month later, I issued the gun licence and saw the surprised looks of the villagers concerned.

On my return from tours, I would be greeted with a host of people waiting to see me at my office and the usual array of visitors from Vila. I had by this time a sub-accountant, Oliver Tevi, who was quite competent in dealing with financial matters and payroll for all staff. However the chief accountant from Vila arrived one day to inspect our books and found, horror of horrors, $58 missing. We spent a whole day looking for it, and my suggestion that I refund the $58 and forget about it was not well received. As it happened, Oliver found it somewhere in the books a few days later.

My motorbike had been useful for short visits but I was not an accomplished rider. On a visit to the north, I capsized in heavy sand and burnt my leg. I patched it up but later it turned septic and I was disabled for about a month, hobbling around with a stick and feeling like a Masai herdsman. Thereafter, I left the motorbike in the capable hands of younger staff.

In July, we were provided with a leave replacement. David Dale, came from Vila to take my place. He arrived the day before we were due to depart, so we sat up the whole night while I handed over to him. I was astonished that he was able to consume almost a carton of beer without turning a hair. The station had given us a wonderful farewell party at the little schoolhouse the week before. The next day we headed for Suva and Australia, with the assurance that we would come back in January to Lakatoro, which we duly did.

George and Leitak Kalkoa (Sokomanu) and sons moved on. He was an invaluable assistant, had a responsible approach and was well liked on the station. On his departure, the station turned out in force to give him a farewell party at the Metemet club, and at the same time to welcome his replacement, John Naupa and his wife Anne. Anne was already known to us from her short visits in the past and she became a good friend to the family and most helpful support for Ida in coping with the visitor flow.

Our visitors now included regular visits from Archdeacon Rawcliffe, head of the Anglican mission on Ambae. The majority of the station people had been Presbyterian but now we were getting more Anglicans, for example Anne, Inspector Keith Wekas, and others.

The Presbyterian Assembly again had its annual get together on Uripiv, thus resulting in a flow of visitors coming and returning to other parts of the group and needing hospitality while awaiting aircraft. Tom Lang, in charge of the development of cooperative societies, was a regular visitor as more and more cooperatives became established throughout the district. The concept of cooperatives was well received and it gave more and more opportunities for villagers to reap some benefit.

One day, Wilben came to me with a complaint that prisoners had interfered with his tractor. On investigation I found that sugar had been poured into the petrol tank. Wilben suspected the prisoners, who had complained about lack of rice for one particular meal. I took firm action, and put all the prisoners on a mainly manioc diet and water and locked them in, which was not normally done. Sure enough, that afternoon a young prisoner came to me with the story. His job was to wash and polish the tractor each day. He had decided this particular morning to make himself a lemon drink and the cup of sugar which he brought out to sweeten his drink had capsized into the open petrol tank. Wilben cleaned out the tank. The tractor restarted without damage and the prisoners went back to normal rations. Perhaps I was very gullible but the solution was satisfactory.

The swimming pool was now completed and became a hive of activity for everyone after office hours, and tennis continued pretty regularly with people from Norsup enthusiastically taking part. Using the last of the old British Agency materials from Bushman's Bay, Atis constructed a neat little classroom behind our house for Ida to supervise the children's correspondence school education. On Sundays, I would take my precious yam spade and plant out cuttings of hibiscus, frangipani, and bougainvillea along the roadsides and wherever there was a suitable space. Slowly the station appearance improved.

I had, perhaps in a very dictatorial fashion, instituted a monthly inspection of all housing both inside and out. This was the only way to ensure that the station was kept in a respectable condition. Household rubbish was a constant problem. I also ordered that no washing be displayed during visits of VIPs. Finally I awarded a prize at the end of each year to the best-tended household garden.

Inevitably this was won by mechanic Wilben, an entrepreneur in his own way. He had just bought a new vehicle and paid a driver to act as the first taxi on Malekula. My rigorous inspections (which the senior cadet administrative officer—now John Naupa—would carry out in my absence) were possibly a bit tough, but they had the effect of keeping a station looking attractive and after all, were a teaching process.

Patrick Bulu had taken up appointment at Lakatoro as public health inspector and I was thankful to be able to hand over to him the job of checking village latrines.

We continued to have occasional visits from Dr Couch, senior British Medical Officer in Vila. Like so many Vila-ites, he was not accustomed to rugged touring. On one occasion, we toured in the 'Pankanu', not exactly a luxury liner, and camped in the villages. One night we were late in arriving to our destination and the path we followed was littered by very large land crabs, some as big as a bread-and-butter plate. He was not very happy about this, and on his return to Lakatoro, I took him in my Land Rover, together with Peter in the back, to Norsup.

Whilst we were both occupied briefly, we left Peter in the back of the truck. When we got back, Peter had found and opened a bulk supply of Phenergan and he was playing with the tablets. I raced across to get Dr Bonnin, not knowing whether Peter had consumed any tablets or not. Dr Bonnin looked extremely worried and said to watch the child for the next few hours. It was a worrying time but Peter showed no reaction and all was well.

A tragedy had been averted, but Oscar Newman the following week had a more harrowing experience. He was on his way to Santo with one of his wives and baby in arms. It was an extremely calm sea and mother and child slept on a mat on the stern. Without warning, they were hit either by a freak wave or even bumped by a whale. Mother and child were thrown overboard. The coxswain was slow to react and put the wheel hard over but without result. Apparently the steering mechanism had failed and only by some juggling was Oscar able to get it operating. When they turned back, the mother was still afloat but the baby had disappeared. They searched diligently for several hours and then gave up. Poor Oscar, he was devastated and very distressed when I met him a few days later.

We seemed to have a large number of interesting visitors during 1969; Sir John Fletcher Cook stepped off the plane with enormous Bombay bloomer shorts and safari jacket, the caricature of a pukka colonialist. He had come to the Western Pacific to advise the British Government on the state of affairs generally in that remote part of the world. He proved to be the most charming and interesting man. We had John Naupa and Anne join us for a lunch of lobsters and lemon meringue pie and a good French wine. Sir John said it was the most enjoyable meal of his Pacific tour and we felt that he meant it. I took him around the station and neighbourhood and he just wanted to talk and ask questions of everyone he met. His French was fluent and at night we had the usual cocktail party.

He was a great admirer and friend of Julius Nyerere, first President of independent Tanzania. He was friends with people like Sir Edward Twining and Dag Hammarskjöld, head of the United Nations. He had written a book which I had read of his account as a prisoner of war. He had that incredible knack of talking to people of all ranks, making them at ease and getting what information he needed out of them.

The most illustrious visitors that year were the Duke and Duchess of Kent. Being my first royal visit, I was astonished at the detail of preparation required, not only timing but dress, brief biographies of people being presented, order of presentation, and the like. I had always felt that preparing for High Commissioners was difficult enough, but the royal visitor's programme with minute detail had to be submitted to Buckingham Palace in advance for vetting. The royal couple, having visited Vila where the Resident Commissioner Colin Allan had vacated his house for them, flew up to Santo the following day. I was thankful that here they were hosted by Chris Turner BDA Santo and his wife.

We led the VIP list at the airfield to be presented and attended the luncheon party at the agency for 12. It was a buffet self-serve meal that made it much less formal. The Duchess was particularly charming and we found her easier to chat with than the Duke. He was fluent in French but the Duchess not so. Ida was able to take in the Duchess's dress. I quote from her letter: "She wore sapphires, diamonds and pearls—a pearl and sapphire bracelet (which I noticed as being very old), a necklace of three strands of pearls, and single-pearl earrings. She also wore a long-sleeved dress, like a coat with pleats and covered buttons down the front, belted with high neck. It was white with a deep blue flower pattern all over. Her little hat sat back low on her head with her hair tucked neatly underneath. It was made of a material and had dainty flowers similar to those in her dress stitched over it. She looked so lovely and cool and slender."

After lunch we set off in a motorcade to the airfield, waving to a large crowd that included my own children. At the airfield, the royal red aircraft awaited them and after formal farewells from Chris and I and our wives, they departed. We went back to Chris's for a cup of tea and to discuss the visit that had gone off so well.

At Lakatoro, the little chapel, all in local materials except for the concrete floor and approach steps, was now completed. I invited representatives from the various missions to attend the opening that I had asked Kelvin Auld, the Senior Presbyterian on Malekula, to open. They all turned up—Archdeacon Rawcliffe, Father Soucy from the Catholic mission, Pastor Giles SDA, and pastors representing the Church of Christ and Melanesian Mission. A large crowd attended and the church was beautifully and tastefully decorated under Anna Draka's direction. All denominations took part in the service, after which we adjourned to our house for coffee. I was glad that the church representatives all appeared to welcome the idea of a non-denominational church.

Not long after the chapel opening, I received members of the breakaway Presbyterian Church led by Graham Kerr. They came to ask my advice on where they should set up a new base. They had in mind the Big Nambas coast. I had to say that I was not enthusiastic about the idea because the local people had already been proselytised and divided by Presbyterian and Catholic interests. In the event, they disregarded my advice to look for new fields and settled between Brenwe (Roman Catholic) and Leviamp (Presbyterian). Poor Big Nambas, already confused, this must have just added to their confusion.

Lakatoro, although I say it myself, had now developed quite a reputation as the jewel of the archipelago. As a result, we paid a penalty in the continuing and ever-increasing flow of VIPs and lesser mortals. Perhaps the most important event to take place in district administration was the arrival of the 'Ida' (named after my wife). This meant that I had a reasonably comfortable vessel with a crew well trained under Captain Kirkwood to maintain it always at my disposal. She was 34 feet long, cruising at ten knots, a cabin aft with two bunks, which folded down to make a small saloon, a refrigerator and gas cooker. She was initially crewed under Captain Martin Ligo from Pentecost in whom I had complete confidence.

Mid-year, Ida and I were invited to Santo to take part in the Fijian Independence celebrations. The Fijian Independence Committee insisted on paying our airfares and accommodation in Santo. Under Filimone Bwataweti's direction the celebrations were impressive with traditional dancing and kava drinking. At the end of the ceremony, I was asked to propose a toast to the new Dominion of Fiji. The year saw the usual host of

VIPs led by Miss Emery, head of the Pacific and Indian Ocean Department of the Commonwealth Office. Other visitors included Dr Comorrsky, a Mallocologist; Dr Lee planning arrangements for the forthcoming visit of the Royal Geographical Society; Dr Tryon, specialising in Melanesian languages, and a Mr Carrol who had directed the biannual arts festival in Australia and was now researching a proposed arts festival for the rest of the Pacific. He was keen for me to find an exceptionally spectacular group of custom dancers and said that whoever was chosen would have their fares paid to Fiji and back. I decided to approach the Small Nambas at Southwest Bay about this, and later they agreed.

The new Lakatoro Agency

Lakatoro Church

Lakatoro Court House

Island Court

Darvall and Peter at Lakatoro football stadium

Lakatoro station BBQ

Early Lakatoro station BBQ

Kids Christmas party Lakatoro agency

Wilkins kids travelling by canoe at the Maskelyn Islands

The Metemet Club and community hall

Tautu Council house opening

Darvall with Chief Virhambath of the Big Nambas

Island Court

Family at the old Norsup airport

Lakatoro Queen's Birthday, Darvall and Ati George Sokomanu officiating at the Queens Birthday 1966

Ida and Darvall at the Queen's Birthday at Lakatoro

Lakatoro Queen's Birthday sports

Queen's Birthday Lakatoro police parade led by Inspector George Kaltoi Kalsakau

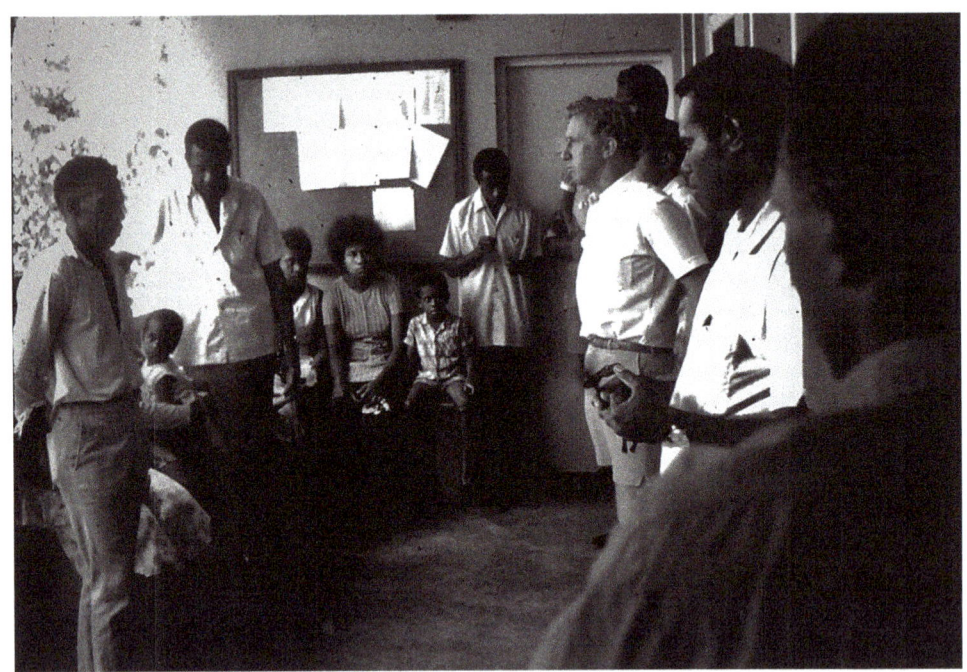

Lakatoro staff meeting, identified are Chief Rion, Tom Bakeo, George Palmer, Darvall, John Naupa

Darvall and the Duke of Edinburgh

Darvall and the Duke at Lakatoro

Queen's Birthday Lakatoro, Darvall and FDA Monsieur et Madame Lecuyer

Darvall officiating at the Duke of Edinburgh's Stone ceremony

Darvall outside the fake Lakatoro building at Aop beach, a practical joke

George Hart's farewell, a practical joke

Lakatoro office

Unboxing the Rolls Royce in Port Vila, 'spesel car'

David Attenborough drops in to Lakatoro

The Ida

Darvall and group at the new Norsup Airport Terminal

Darvall officiating in court

Darvall on SE Ambrym with the Talo family

British volunteers at Queen's Birthday celebrations

Home Sweet Home, the volunteers' accommodation at Lakatoro

Lakatoro 'water reservoir'

Jerry Marston, Henry Wright, Val Marston, and John Bent in the Metemet club bar at Lakatoro

Comedy night at the Metemet Club

The original Man Ples stone and inscription outside Lakatoro office

Lakatoro, road leading down to the Metemet club and what is now Wilkins Stadium

1974 Royal visit

The Queen's visit to Pentecost, Darvall with Queen Elizabeth, Prince Phillip, Princess Anne, Mark Phillips and Lord Louis Mountbatten. Ida in the background

Queen Elizabeth and Darvall during the Pentecost visit

Darvall and Ida joining the Royal Party to board the Royal Yacht Britannia to travel to Santo from Pentecost

Family just before leaving for Australia

Darvall's farewell tour begins

Ida at a Malekula farewell

Paul Binihi, Tinsley Lulu, Darvall, Sgt. Norman Kalangai, original Lakatoro founders farewelling the family in 1977

Darvall's last view of Lakatoro station upon leaving in 1977

Sixteen

Vignette – Notable Maritime Visits
HMAS Supply 1965

A more imposing naval visit was that of 'HMAS Supply' in September 1965, a vessel of 26,000 tons and a crew of more than 200. Surprisingly, she had no trouble finding an anchorage in Port Stanley and I went aboard to discuss the programme with the captain. On the way out to the ship, the old man coxswaining my vessel told me that his father had regaled him with a story of a big vessel coming into this very harbour to open fire at the nearest villages because they had apparently murdered a white trader. I was able to pass this story onto the captain.

Both captain and crew were most cooperative and after coffee with the captain, I took him ashore to see our establishment. I had arranged three separate groups of 20 to visit different villages where they would provide a traditional feast and dancing. This they did extremely well, greeting the visitors with coconut drinks and tropical fruits. The sailors thoroughly enjoyed it all.

At 11.30, we had 12 of the officers and local guests including the French Europeans from Norsup plantation, my senior clerk, now Richard Tarileo, Dr Tabanki, the medical officer from the French Hospital, and other New Hebridean representatives. I had organised a group of prisoners to play their guitars under our mango tree during the lunch and they did so bedecked in hibiscus flowers. Ida produced a sumptuous repast (Tahitian salad, fish, and lobster). The officers were charming and did their best to chat with the French ladies. I think they would happily have stayed on for the afternoon but had arranged a visit to the Norsup plantation; Mr Tanguy served them with champagne after which, with three borrowed vessels, I ferried them back to the ship.

The captain had told me I could bring up to 50 guests to the cocktail party aboard, so I was able to let my head go and invite French, Tahitian, Gilbertese and Wallace Islanders, Fijians, and Malekulan representatives. From the station I had asked the clerks, Sergeant Norman and his wife and Wilben and his wife, and Meli our house girl. No doubt the navy entertained well and everyone thoroughly enjoyed the evening. The captain had been so delighted by my prison band that he asked if they could come aboard to play, which they did.

We all felt quite sorry to see them sail the next morning. Their visit had certainly impressed Malekula and I chuckled to myself as it rather flattened the frequent French warship visits. One should not have been nationalistic but nonetheless, it was a very cheering visit.

'HMS Dampier' 1967

On one occasion, the British warship 'HMS Dampier' visited Port Stanley on a routine, show-the-flag visit and we were able to turn on a reception for them at Lakatoro. I remember that Peter Wright, who was a staunch supporter of the British Government, and his friends organised a kava drink for the visitors. They walked up to the agency because we did not have sufficient transport, and they were served kava under the big mango tree just to the right of our house.

The one snag of that visit was that the Royal Navy's launch stuck on a reef during the evening when some of the crew members were being taken back to the ship. The next morning, waking up, I could see the launch slightly lopsided, stuck on the reef, waiting for the high tide and the warship anchored farther out towards Uripiv. She spent several months based in Port Stanley doing hydrographic work and captain and crew became old friends. Simon especially loved visits to the ship.

Craigstar 1969

The 'Craigstar', a vessel of about 20,000 tonnes, arrived with a team aboard to carry out a geological survey of Malekula and other islands. They remained anchored in Port Stanley for several weeks and were no imposition upon us. They carried a helicopter and occasionally landed on our oval. It was certainly the first time for Malekula and drew many onlookers. Again, Simon was a particular spectator and would rush out from his classroom and sit gazing until the helicopter took off.

'HMS Decoy' 1969

'HMS Decoy', a large destroyer with a complement of 300 men arrived mid-morning from Singapore and I went aboard to discuss the 24-hour stay with the captain. He offered us cocktails for lunch for 15, so I was able to take selected members of the staff on board. In the afternoon, 100 men were landed on our passage to meet our local soccer teams and in the evening we had the usual traditional feast prepared by everyone on the station, and inevitably tins and tins of Foster's lager. The sailors didn't make much headway with the *laplap,* but they did with the Foster's. Meanwhile, we had opened our house to commander and officers and as usual, Ida had loads of food. They were all scheduled to return to their ship at 10.30. It was a pitch-dark night and the ship's coxswains were not accustomed to finding their way into coral-infested passages. Inevitably, one of the larger ship's boats went aground on a reef well off course and there it stuck. The weather blew up and the situation looked pretty grim. I organised the 'Ida' to go to the rescue and the crew from the ship's boat were taken aboard in lifeboats. I was astonished to find that many of them could not swim. With the captain of the 'Decoy' on the bows, we got a rope to the stricken boat and hauled it off. It was badly holed and it was touch and go getting it back to the ship's hoists. I thought the captain would be extremely angry but he was cool, calm, and collected in the good Royal Navy tradition. Although the boat was full of water and just about ready to sink, they managed to get it aboard. The 'Decoy' sailed the next morning for New Zealand and we had subsequently very heart-warming letters from captain and officers. The captain called it "an exciting night".

Seventeen

1970 Lakatoro

Barry Weightman

In mid 1970, there were new arrivals in our lives. Little did we know what impact they would have on us all. Barry and Lesley Weightman, Barry being the first British condominium qualified agricultural officer, and George Hart, the first permanently based education officer for the district. Both men were enthusiastic and diligent; they were a great asset to the station. George was unfailing in his touring regularly to pay monthly salaries of an increasing number of teachers trained at the Kawenu Teachers Training College in Vila. Prior to George's arrival, this was my responsibility but it was not always easy to be in a position to pay teachers on time.

Barry Weightman had wide experience in west and east Africa in agriculture and was in fact the first agricultural officer in the condominium service to look further than the French plantations. He began encouraging the production of better quality copra, the planting of coffee and cocoa, and impressed the whole group with his introduction of anti-rat control by tacking aluminium strips to coconut palms at head level to prevent rats climbing up the tree and destroying coconuts. Both men had a wonderful sense of humour and we were constantly kept amused by their off-duty antics.

George's quarters were finally completed and he moved into a new house, leaving the rest house free and thus reducing some of Ida's responsibility for housing guests. He was no gardener and was delighted when one Sunday soon after he had moved into his house, I took an army of prisoners and laid out his garden and planted it all in an afternoon.

Another newcomer was Mike Sackett, a fully qualified horticulturalist VSO and under Barry's direction, he established a section of the Lakatoro land beyond the football field as a nursery and base for experimentation of plants.

Medically we still awaited a permanent qualified medical officer to supervise the district's health service, but meanwhile Patrick Butu, trained in Fiji, and a European Sister Beverley Brighouse routinely checked the island dispensaries and ran a small bush-constructed dispensary at Lakatoro.

1971 began with the news that the Duke of Edinburgh would visit us during his Western Pacific tour, and for the next two months I was heavily engaged in detailed preparations. He would fly his own aircraft into Norsup in the morning and continue his tour onto the Solomons by ship that evening.

More on that later …

Routine administration continued and I found the little 'Ida' a tremendous asset. Initially there was panic on her first tour when she lost her rudder. This was on a short trip and I was not on board but spent an anxious day on the radio frantically searching for the nearest vessel to come to her rescue. There were, as usual, pretty heavy seas and she was drifting onto the Malekula south coast. I was finally successful in contacting the 'Navaka', which was able to take her in tow before she reached the danger zone.

Perhaps my most memorable tour in the many years of touring ahead was one where I set out for Ambrym in incredibly glass-like seas. Halfway between Port Stanley and North Ambrym, we suddenly found ourselves in the middle of a pod of whales. Presumably as they moved south, they had decided to take a break because they just appeared around us lazing in the sun. I counted 25 and there must have been more. There was nothing we could do but continue, and one of them brushed up gently against the 'Ida's' side giving us a nudge. It dwarfed our little ship. We were reluctant to sail on, being fascinated by the sight, but decided that it would be wiser to leave them alone.

We continued onto Ambrym and quite suddenly the wind and seas blew up and the barometer began to drop. I had urgent matters to attend to on Ambrym and had to decide whether to abandon the tour and seek shelter or try to get ashore. When we arrived at Nebul on north Ambrym, the captain was reluctant to lower the dingy and so I decided to swim ashore. For the next three days, I depended on the cooperative store locally for a toothbrush and towel, pen and paper. The 'Ida' headed straight for Lamap, the closest safe anchorage, and waited there till the very nasty storm had passed over. She returned two days later to collect me.

On my return, I was met with another problem—a message from Chief Virhambath from the Big Nambas region. There had been a mysterious death and he wanted me to come. This meant a two-day sojourn, and on arrival I found the body of a girl trussed up against a small tree with a vine around her neck. Talks began with the men and went on all night. I slept intermittently in the *nakamal* while discussion went on in their language. The night was cold and I huddled over a tiny fire with some of my constituents, naked but for their nambas, sound asleep on taro leaves. Quite clearly the supposed suicide had been rigged and she had in fact been murdered. The difficulty was in attaining evidence for a prosecution. And finally, after hours and hours of discussion, it was agreed by the family of the deceased that they would accept a fully tusked pig worth about $200, and I would take back the suspected murderer in the hope that he would confess. In fact, he never did and I had to release him. However, the matter was settled from the point of view of the families concerned and the possibility of even a tribal war was averted. I arrived home that night very weary indeed.

Public Works

Another momentous time for Malekula was the arrival of the condominium public works team together with a bulldozer, heavy grader, trucks, and other equipment. Initially they were housed at Norsup until accommodation was provided at Lakatoro. Contracts had been arranged for the erection of housing and workshop. Construction of a road northward to replace the existing rough track began immediately. The alignment of this road proved to be a source of disagreement between my French colleague and myself. He favoured a completely new road farther inland. I preferred following the existing track along as much as possible. We reached an impasse and in order to proceed with the work, I gave way to him.

The arrival this year of an expatriate administrative officer (Assistant British District Agent or ABDA) made a tremendous difference. He was 25 years old and an honours graduate in social science at Birmingham, with obviously no experience in native administration. His name was David Stephens. I should say again that my local cadet administrators, George Kalkoa and John Naupa, had both been extremely helpful and keen but because of their lack of education and experience, they were not able to cope with all aspects of the job. Housing inevitably was still a problem and as a temporary measure, David was housed in the rest house, much to Ida's regret. This meant that more pressure fell on Ida to accommodate visitors in our 'spare room'. In addition to the ABDA's house which was a British National Service responsibility, contracts were signed for a fully self-contained guest wing to be added onto our agency and for a large office to be added to the existing office block for my own use.

Around this time, the National Geographic Society from the UK, led by Dr Lee and Lord Medway, appeared on my horizon. This consisted of a team of 27 scientists ranging from entomologists to horticulturalists. Fortunately, they were fully equipped to sustain themselves, but transport was required to move them as far as possible to different parts of the island. Thus my two Land Rovers and the 'Ida' were put to good use. They stayed about three weeks and were constantly popping in for cups of coffee and meals—poor Ida. They were a likeable crowd, appreciating our help and we were quite sorry to see them leave by air and sea.

During this time, I had another 'rescue operation incident' with Peter, now aged four. I took him down to the wharf to pick up some luggage. He was standing on the side of the wharf as I backed my Land Rover past him when he suddenly panicked and disappeared over the side. I jammed on the brakes, jumped out and over the side to meet Peter, spluttering and rising to the surface, 'a la Meg's pool'! At age 2 he'd fallen into the pool on the farm Dulla Dulla. I had to make a running rescue dive and grabbed him from the bottom of the pool. He seemed pleased to meet me, all well and very proud of the fact that he was trying to swim. We both came home to change, dripping.

Eighteen

Vignette – The Duke of Edinburgh Visit

In 1971, the Duke of Edinburgh visited us on an official tour. What follows is a discourse of the visit and subsequent event.

The day after the visit, I was up early at six, bleary-eyed from the previous night's dance. There were some Small Nambas dancers sitting patiently on my verandah steps to present me with some of the regalia from the dance, but I had to get moving to organise sea, air, and land transport for our overnight guests. I got dressed and jumped in the Land Rover and drove down to the sports field, the scene of so much activity the night before, to find the last of the dancers moving off and the field littered with papers, tins, and burnt-out bamboo torches, but most of the big slit gongs still in position. One of the senior primary school boys was beating the Wala gong when I drove down and it resounded from the hills. The day after was in some way a summary of the complexities and variety of challenges that accompanies such an event. Prince Philip's signed photograph on my sideboard is a constant reminder of what preparations had to be made before his arrival. I found myself with time to reflect over the preceding week and this is how it unfolded.

The last week prior to the Duke's visit was the culmination of some careful planning for my work gang; the prisoners had been cleaning up, cutting grass, trimming around shrubs and trees, repairing roads, painting rooves etc. And by Thursday, the time His Royal Highness (HRH) landed from Britannia at Vila, the station looked as trim and lovely as it had ever done, but the weather was against us from the start.

At the weekend, Ida arrived back from Australia in bright sunshine and it was a hot but superb weekend. By the Monday, it had begun to rain and we thought that was fine, it would clear up again by Friday. It was not to be. On Thursday, it was hot and showery still and this was our day for rehearsals; it was too expensive an exercise to bring in 600 school children more than once, and things began to go wrong.

Joe—who was in charge of feeding an estimated 4000 visitors with 25 bags of rice, two bullocks, and three pigs—instead of being on the job with his army of volunteer cooks, had decided to celebrate early and was more interested in beer than cooking. I blasted him until he sobered up and went back to work looking rather sorry for himself. Then the wind began to blow and the barometer dropped; by midday there was a heavy northerly sea coming into the usually sheltered Port Stanley where Britannia was due to disembark HRH at 6 pm the next day; the tusked pig for presentation to HRH had not arrived and John Naupa went to search for it 25 miles up the north coast; the chiefs had not all come in for their rehearsal of what was still a pretty vague sort of ceremony to me; and the school children were late. We got started about midday when our first visitors began to arrive.

We found the English-speaking school children sang the "Marseillaise" much faster than their French-speaking counterparts; the French children on the other hand, sang "God Save the Queen" much slower than our children. So we decided that they would each sing their own anthem. The pig arrived, it was in fact a beauty, a big boar with its tusks doing a complete circle and turning back into its flesh again on the lower jaw. The chiefs began to drift in, each with a different idea about the correct custom procedure. After three hours of talking and rehearsal, we got it into a set procedure and cut it down from an hour to the seven-minute ceremony I had planned for.

The chiefs began constructing the pen for the tusked pig and erecting a miniature Stonehenge on which HRH would stand to symbolically kill the pig. I dashed into Norsup to see the special team who had just arrived to supervise the Air Melanesian royal flight. Although the airstrip was already well ploughed up and the wind 25 to 40 knots, they seemed to feel that it would be okay tomorrow. The sky was now inky black and as I drove back, the heavens opened. It poured and I drove the whole way back in a lake of water.

At Lakatoro, it was even heavier, and a stream of water a hundred yards wide was racing across the oval—the sand and coral placed that day by the tractor for HRH's approach was almost already back onto the beach again. It was almost dark when it stopped and I heard the last special Air Melanesian flight overhead and wondered whether the plane would be able to get down. I was about to race back into Norsup again thinking that they would need all the headlights they could muster for a night landing, when the plane droned off again in the direction of Vila. Then the station generator suddenly failed and the whole station was plunged into darkness. Ida, in the throes of preparing food for tomorrow's lunch, was trying to work by lantern, the VSOs finishing off a temporary shelter outside the house where the reception was to be held. I organised a search of wires to find out where the short had occurred as it was certainly fallen branches which had caused the trouble, then found that both tractors taking children back from their rehearsals had got bogged in the mud—so I had to send out the remaining tractors to look for them.

The wind was still roaring overhead and I was beginning to worry for all my little fleet of ships bringing in dancers and guests from Pentecost, Ambrym, and Paama. There was nothing I could do but hope that they would be okay and in fact they were. The 'Envoie' arrived with the Aulua Mission families, the 'Ida' from Paama and Ambrym with Sister Todd, the local council presidents, and the leading chiefs. I could see the dance teams from Pentecost and Ambrym sheltering in boats off Uripiv Island opposite, waiting to get ashore to their allocated accommodation. George Hart was in charge of this and of allocating people to various houses for meals the next day, because everyone had to be fed. It was still pouring down and the prisoners began erecting more temporary shelters for the dancers.

At home, Ida was setting the table with our best silver, which I had been polishing for the three nights prior to this for the private lunch with HRH, his private secretary and police officer, the British and French Resident Commissioners, the Turners (who had arrived from Santo just before dark after a hair-raising landing through a sea of water that almost obliterated the plane as it ploughed its way to a halt), the Weightmans, George Hart, and ourselves. Lesley Weightman had done superb place names for everyone in fancy writing with traditional motifs on the back of each card.

For Prince Phillip, she had put HRH Lokorinmal Bunten Vanu (the traditional name meaning Great Chief of all their lands) to be given to him during the pig-killing ceremony. Ida had planned to serve local freshwater prawns as a fish cocktail to guests where they were sitting, then to ask HRH to serve himself for a cold sideboard of Tahitian salad (a marlin which we got from Palekula and which Peter Wright, the Fijian at Norsup, had prepared for us), cold roast turkey, ham and lamb, millionaire salad, and tossed lettuce garnished with tomatoes.

The Turners, Weightmans, and Ron Sankey, who arrived also at dusk with his Santo detachment of police to reinforce my meagre detachment, all came out to see if they could help and to look at the preparations about which they were most enthusiastic. We decided where HRH would sit when he arrived to have the best view of the room, and admire the newly painted guest wing in Wedgwood blue. Also, my pictures of the Duke of York and telegram from Sir Admiral Frazer when he notified the Admiralty that he had signed the surrender with Japan on behalf of the British government—these were intended as talking points if they caught the Duke's eye as he had served on 'HM Whelp', which at one time escorted 'HM Duke of York' during the Pacific War.

Meanwhile we had got the lights going and more people were coming in and finding somewhere sheltered to sleep. The wind still howled over us from the north and the seas pounded. The poor old cooks, cutting up the bullocks and cooking rice in the rain, looked very dejected. The barometer was still low and I felt most discouraged. Finally we fell into bed and slept at about midnight.

We woke to the alarm clock at the first sign of light to hear rain! And even worse, wind! At 6 o'clock, I went down to my office to contact Vila on the radio and found that the radio would not work. We fiddled with it and finally got it working again about 7 to hear the Met report from the radio station set up at the airfield; to my astonishment they still thought that the aircraft could get in. At 7.30 I got onto the British Office. Mike Townsend was then on the phone to Lt. Cdr Willet, HRH's private secretary, and they were discussing the weather reports. The weather in Vila was just as bad and at 7.45 a cyclone warning red was issued from the Met station at Vila. At 8 I got directly onto Mike—the special flight with HRH was off. I felt relieved more than disappointed because it would have been dangerous and I said that it would have been my decision if I'd had to make it. Mike said we would revert to the alternative programme—HRH coming in the 'Britannia', arriving during the afternoon and following the programme as originally planned but putting it back six hours. The royal yacht would anchor in Port Stanley, and HRH would disembark at my jetty at 5.30 pm and depart from the jetty at 10.30 pm. He would therefore have dinner and not lunch.

My first phone call was to Ida to let her know the change of plan; then a meeting with my staff most directly concerned—George, Barry, Ron, Chris, Tom Bakeo, and Gordon Haynes who had flown in at 7 that morning. The later programme meant that we needed lighting for the HRH to watch the dancing; bamboo flares seemed more attractive and appropriate than headlights and pressure lights, and John Wilson who had come up to photograph took that job on with the prisoners to cut 100 flares and set them up. We went down to the jetty to find that landing there was out of the question; there were waves five feet high crashing into the passage; then to Litzlitz village where HRH was to have disembarked from after inspecting the village there; a fleet of ships were riding out the seas, their anchor chains stretched taut and slowly moving up the bay.

I was to give Mike, on board the 'Britannia', an amended programme by 10 am but got no answer for some time. Finally, I was able to convey it to him—HRH would disembark at 5.30 pm at Goode Beach, just above Port Stanley—this was the only shelter in the bay with the northerly winds—drive straight to the sports field, attend the national anthems and pig-killing ceremony. Then on to Litzlitz village for a special display of traditional cooking, copra making, a special market set-up, and then proceed to George Hart's for cocktails. Finally, to our agency for dinner, re-embarking at 10.30. The private secretary was fine with the arrangements.

The next move was to build a temporary bridge across the river at Aop between Goode Bay and Lakatoro. Now that HRH was arriving at high tide, the Land Rover would not be able to traverse the river. Chris Turner went off to muster the bulldozers and tractors at Norsup to start on it. To be on the safe side, I got the 'Ida' to put her dingy up there too so that we could row across if necessary, though I hoped not.

Meanwhile the rain had eased, but the wind had not, and the barometer was still ominous. People were pouring in, mostly by foot. The 'Neptune' arrived from Santo with the Aoba dancers and ice for the reception. The VSOs were busy organising the drinks. All the European guests who had been housed on the station overnight were busy on the savouries. The cooks had all cheered up with daylight and abating rain, despite being wet and up all night cooking.

Some two to three thousand had eaten their fill on the sports field, the dancers had painted up their bodies, the flares were in position, the reception guests were being taken care of—everyone was happily occupied. We had notified all the invited guests of the different arrangements for the reception.

At 3 o'clock, I spoke to the 'Britannia' again. Mike came on and apologised but he had just received a message from the Solomons of the deteriorating weather there and a further depression near the Banks Islands, and that HRH would have to return on board by eight—the dinner would have to be omitted. It was time to dress anyway so I went up to the house instead of ringing to tell Ida that the dinner was off. I think she felt more like tears than anything else but didn't show her disappointment. We dressed, I into white shorts and long socks thinking this was the most appropriate to HRH's naval garb he was going to wear, and Ida in her new dress she had planned to meet the plane in that morning.

The Land Rover-cade, which had been drilled and redrilled as the programme had changed throughout the day, set off. I had the royal pennant in the glove box. The bulldozers had just finished the bridge and we sneaked across, thus avoiding a long detour over an appalling road. As we got down to the beach at Goode Bay, we could see the 'Britannia' moving slowly in the heavy seas into view between Port Stanley headland and Uripiv Island. She looked majestic and high against a sombre sky of grey clouds. We lined up the Land Rovers in position and waited. I checked the seating in the various vehicles again and redrilled my police orderly on the procedure for opening and closing the Duke's door. Gordon Haynes who had been with him the day before said he hated having to sit and wait, and once in his vehicle liked to move off quickly. I noted that.

The 'Britannia' seemed as though she would never anchor, but finally she did and they lost no time in getting down the royal barge. The barge, with the Duke's special pennant streaming, came shooting in. HRH cut a tall figure at the little bridge with Mike and the French Resident Commissioner beside him. They gave me heart failure by heading for my jetty. I had visions of them not having understood my instructions but when we blinked our headlights, they turned and headed for us where my carpenter had earlier in the day erected temporary leading marks. One hundred and fifty yards from shore, they transferred from the barge to the Gemini landing craft which I had asked them to use for landing on the beach, and Ida and I moved down to greet HRH. Which side of Ida should I stand? Whilst we were deciding, HRH jumped agilely ashore and Mike was presenting us.

Ida forgot to say 'Your Royal Highness' and said, "How do you do, sir" but it did not seem to worry him. HRH apologised for the necessary changes to the programme but the admiral was a bit jittery with all the weather as it was, and we felt immediately at ease. We got into our Land Rover—Kilman had remembered to unfurl the Duke's pennant—and off we went; HRH in front with me driving, Ida with the private secretary, Jim Balmain, behind. Mindful of not keeping the Duke sitting in his car, we moved off and left the others to follow. HRH asked plenty of questions on the drive to Lakatoro; I was thankful to get across the narrow bridge and be able to give more attention to answering him, mostly about the plantations we were passing through, where the labour came from for the plantations, native grown cash crops, etc. At a bend we found a tractor just about to turn back onto the road in front of us and the Duke remarked that he was glad he changed his mind when he did.

The police lead vehicle was well ahead because HRH made it clear that he did not want to see it. We travelled along the new road completed that morning through native land then on through the hibiscus drive up to the station. I pointed out the VSO-constructed dispensary, the new office and the courthouse, and the old office. HRH said he hoped we would not pull down the buildings made of local materials and I assured him we would not. We drove past the VSO quarters and down towards the sports field to hear the beat of the slit gongs, and the dancers chanting and shouting.

I briefed HRH as quickly as possible on the procedure on arrival. As we halted, the dancers suddenly and dramatically subsided and a crowd of about 2500 people were silent.

Sergeant Berry opened the door and HRH set foot on the oval. His pennant went up and the Union Jack came down. So far, according to plan.

We walked across to face the royal standard and the French tricolours and took up a position in front of the miniature Stonehenge. The children sang "God Save the Queen" as HRH came to the salute and sang with great vigour. I forgot to remind him about the "Marseillaise" and he came down from the salute and up again as the "Marseillaise" began. He then began asking questions about the pig-killing ceremony until five men blowing conch shells (bubus) announced the beginning of the ceremony and denoting the grade of the pig (the size of the tusks) to the audience. As the plaintive and eerie notes of the bubus faded away, four chiefs—Virhambath's heir, Nisai, paramount chief of the Big Nambas, resplendent in only a red penis wrapper and a mass of pig's tusk bracelets on either arm and on his chest—and two other custom chiefs dressed in nambas, pulled the tusked pig forward from its hiding place to reveal it to the audience. It came forward reluctantly, grunting and squealing and I noticed that the French TV team recorded the sounds on a soundtrack. Then the Mae Bethel villagers sang a song of praise to the great chief who had arrived in their midst, then shuffled forward as they did so, plumes of feathers warbling in the wind (which had begun to drop as evening approached). Finally Virhambath, himself in nambas, and a European-clad chief brought forward the peculiar-looking hat which HRH donned before killing the pig. HRH handed his naval cap to me (and I subsequently forgot to hand it back to him until he politely asked for it) put on the hat with a remark aside to the fact that he always seemed to get involved in ceremonies to do with hats, and stood up on Stonehenge where Chief Ati handed him an enormous pig-killing stick, a carved club.

Meanwhile the pig tethered nearby was objecting, and HRH said, "How hard do you want me to hit it?" I said, "Oh just gently will do." But he gave it a fairly firm tap. As he did so, Chief Ati stood forward and shouted out in traditional fashion the great chief's new name, "Lokoinmal Bwaten Venu". As he did so, there was a tremendous and spontaneous shout from the audience. The tamtams throbbed and the dancers began to pound the earth with their feet, the seed pods around their ankles clattering like a mass of machine guns firing off. The din was tremendous.

I then presented to HRH the District Agent Northern District and my staff. He had an easy word with each of them and then we moved across to three groups of school children. Each group greeted him in turn in dialect, pidgin then English and French, saying, "Welcome, our Royal Highness." Each group also sang a song in the appropriate language. A pidgin song of welcome was especially composed for the visit and appeared to amuse Prince Phillip. He talked to each of the teachers above the vigorous and very tuneful singing. We had been worried that the children would be too nervous to sing but that was certainly not the case. They sang with tremendous enthusiasm and HRH was very impressed by it. Then we moved on towards the ten groups of custom dance teams. They came forward quickly as we made our way over to each group.

I planned to move HRH fairly quickly around as I had continually to bear in mind his schedule for departure at 8 pm. But HRH was more interested in talking to the crowd. Melanesians are normally shy and retiring people and difficult to bring out, but HRH had a crowd about him and had people chatting within seconds. To one father he admired the tiny baby he was holding and asked where its mother was. He apparently replied that he didn't know, and HRH called out, "Has anyone seen this man's wife?" The crowd thought that was a great joke. HRH stopped continually, bringing 10 or 15 people into the conversation, trying out his pidgin to the amusement of the crowd and turning to me for translation when he or the audience was stuck. He was interested in where they came from and how far they had come and so on. People had no fear of him and answered more readily than I had ever seen, their eyes shining with pleasure at being spoken to. Out of the corner of my eye I could see people angling to get into position in the hope that he would stop.

Meanwhile Barry Weightman, George Hart, and Tom Bakeo had gone ahead and were grouping leading personalities near each dance group for presentation informally as we passed, and this worked very well indeed. Some 100 dressers, teachers, chiefs, assessors, and women's group leaders were introduced to HRH, and this will certainly have gone down as a memorable day in their lives. HRH was fascinated by the dancing, which was magnificent. All ten groups continued dancing with tremendous vigour and enthusiasm as we walked around. And as darkness fell, the scene was even more impressive; the dark figures gaudily painted, the spectacular headdresses, the naked bodies glistening in the flickering light of the bamboo torches, the tremendous noise of song and bare feet thumping on the wet earth, the clack of the anklets of seed pods—the whole noise surging to a crescendo as we approached each particular group.

Above the tumult, Michael Ala was presented in a traditional costume of penis wrapper, war paint, and a superb headdress of the spines of the coconut leaf, each tipped with coloured feathers. He bowed to HRH, almost knocking off HRH's peaked cap as he did so, much to HRH's feigned horror. After an excellent speech in language and English, presented HRH with a traditional *malimalo* loin mat. Then the Big Nambas, and after them the north Pentecost team led by Silas Ngari, John Keo, President of the North Pentecost local council, and Mr and Mrs Laone, had a short chat with HRH before he moved on to the north Ambrym dancers. Here I presented Tofor to him and he remembered the slit gong, which had been presented to the Queen. Tofor gifted him with a pig's tusk (although I noticed at the time that the tusk was not a very good one) and assessor Willy Bongmatur presented him with a walking stick plated with human hair, which gives the owner of the stick great power over others.

Probably most magnificent of all were the Small Nambas, their bodies a mass of colour—enormous peaked hats with feathers reaching 3 and 4 feet above their heads, bows and arrows decorated with miniature faces worked in mud and cobweb decorating each end of the bow, and displaying tremendous movement as they dashed to and fro in a mock war; the Uripiv islanders with their bodies completely painted one side in yellow and the other side with cerise, and the Wala Rano group in feathered hats and feathered bodies with two enormous slit gongs being beaten sufficiently to awaken the dead.

Between the groups of dancers, HRH kept pausing to talk to the crowds. He insisted on putting the smaller presents in his pockets, the larger gifts he gave to Sergent Berry who with the private secretary, a very large man, were always at his side. I was completely blinded from time to time by the flashlights from the cameras but it did not seem to worry HRH at all.

Finally we made it back to the club, somewhat dazed by the noise and the excitement. I found later that Ida had been right behind us with the private secretary (whose vehicle had trouble crossing the bridge and had been delayed) and I did not even see her. The private secretary in a letter, which he later was directed to write by the Duke, thanked me for the visit and described it as a "dramatic and splendid evening".

At the club verandah brilliantly lit by electric light, a contrast to the bamboo flares, HRH was greeted by Tom Bakeo as president of the Metemet Club and his wife Naomi. I was afraid that the reception guests, some of whom had been sitting on the verandah, would distract HRH's attention as time was running out, but fortunately they did not. HRH gave them a cheery wave as he went by. The club looked lovely with its floral and coconut leaf decorations, put up by the school children under Lesley Weightman's expert direction; some of her paintings and various artefacts also decorated the walls.

In the club where members of my staff directly concerned with the visit were waiting and ostensibly having a drink, I presented each one of them in turn; Sister Ponninghouse who did a very neat little curtsy and chatted easily with HRH, the VSOs whom he baited about modern materials being inferior to traditional ones. On the way into the club, HRH had remarked to me that this was the sort of building he enjoyed. The sports VSO told HRH he was mainly occupied in instructing in physical training, to which the Duke replied, "It hardly seems necessary to give PT when you see people doing the physical jerks (he had just witnessed outside)." The agricultural assistants, who he asked whether they were practising what they preached and turned to me for confirmation when they seemed a little nonplussed. Mike Sackett brought HRH a beer and offered to relieve him of his walking stick, HRH said, "Then you won't be able to drink one—my policeman will look after it for me." And carpenter Atis, whom HRH questioned about local materials and so on. It was a very enjoyable ten or 15 minutes and afforded great pleasure to all those who met HRH there.

After a wave of farewell, we went back to the Land Rovers. On the way up, I said to HRH, "I am taking you up to our house first and then we will go down to the reception at Mr Hart's house," not knowing that Ida had already asked the private secretary if there would be time to do this and the PS had said very firmly, "No." On the way up to the house, the Duke remarked that the station looked like one huge garden, which of course in my eyes, it was. We passed the three Auld children standing in the lights of the car and I slowed down whilst the Duke called out to them and waved. They were thrilled of course. At the agency, I had no door opener but by the time I had got round to open it, the Duke was already out and striding up the path. I had completely forgotten to arrange for lights for the path, but fortunately the verandah light was on and Ida had to forge ahead with apologies to turn on lights whilst HRH tried to get some of the mud off his boots on the doormat.

Here with only the police officer (we had lost the PS again, who I found afterwards was in a bit of flap because he did not know where we had gone), HRH was completely informal. He had a good look around the lounge, and after using the guest wing especially prepared for him, came and talked to us for a few minutes, asking us how we liked the life. Did we enjoy our house, which he thought looked attractive and so on. We too felt completely at ease. Ida asked him if he would sign our visitor's book, which he said certainly he would. Ida gave him his place name 'HRH Lokorhimal' and he again apologised for having to cancel the dinner, and remarked that he would far rather have cut out the morning programme at Vila to have more time watching the dancers whom he had found fascinating.

Then we drove down to George's house to take a position on the verandah.

Thank goodness it was still fine. Barry meanwhile had organised the guests into groups so that they did not come too thick and fast. There were 70 of them and this gave me time to give a little biography of each one as they arrived. Again HRH had a few words after greeting them. Towards the end, they began to struggle and he called out, "Come along. Don't be frightened." Inside, the VSOs dressed in Tahitian shirts and white shorts were doing a sterling job as drink waiters. I asked the PS if he thought I should steer HRH around. He laughed and said don't worry about that, watch him. I did then and noticed that he moved around with complete ease from group to group systematically; I found afterwards that despite the short time, he had chatted with practically everyone inside the room and each and every one was thrilled pink about it. HRH even found time to pop into the kitchen where the VSOs were working and remark what a hell of a mess it was.

My enjoyment of the reception was shattered when I was told that the temporary bridge had washed away. I then set to organise a Land Rover to confirm that the boat and crew were still standing by; this unfortunately upset the transport arrangements to a minor degree because I had insufficient Land Rovers to be able to afford an advance one. I asked the PS if he thought HRH must adhere to the departure time and he thought they could not be too late.

Shortly afterwards, he asked Mike and Mr Langois, Jim Balmain who had organised the royal visit, and Ida and I to sit on the verandah, and soon after that we were asked into George's bedroom whilst HRH made a private farewell. He presented us with a signed photograph of himself and said he had thoroughly enjoyed the evening and wished it had been longer. I said that in the 13 years I had worked in the New Hebrides, I had never seen such enthusiasm over a visitor and that we were deeply grateful and honoured that he had come, particularly in view of the appalling weather. He seemed very pleased and again apologised to Ida for not being able to have dinner with us. Then we were ushered out by the PS, and Mike and the French Resident Commissioner went in.

After personally thanking George Hart for the use of his house for the reception, HRH said a general farewell and we loaded into the Land Rovers and moved off. As we did, the six VSOs gathered together and loudly sang "Rule Britannia". The Duke put his head out the window and waved and laughed. He seemed to thoroughly enjoy the VSOs. On the way to the river, we passed no less than three oncoming taxis that were reluctant to move aside until they saw the royal pennant. I got the impression that HRH was not used to oncoming traffic.

During our drive, Mike remarked that Harry Kirkwood who was staying at Tisman had not come and HRH commented that he had heard that Captain Kirkwood was staying out here at the moment. In fact, Harry and Oscar had set out after telling me the day before that they would not come and had turned back because of the bad seas after losing their dingy from the stern of the Tisman.

When we arrived at the river, I was relieved to see car headlights flooding the area. The boat crew were standing by and bulldozers were still trying to rebuild the bridge. The Duke said, "Good heavens, what tremendous activity." He seemed to enjoy his little crossing and suggested that we walk on.

Soon afterwards, the police Land Rover arrived and we all clambered into that and drove on down to the beach where the Gemini was waiting, the royal barge just a little farther out, and the 'Britannia' magnificently lit was still anchored between Uripiv and Tautu.

We waited for a few moments for the rest of the party to arrive and talked generally. By this time the sky had cleared and the wind dropped and it was a lovely night, though still clearly heavy seas running. When the others arrived, HRH said goodbye to each of us and thanked me again for a fascinating evening, leaped aboard, and wasted no time in getting underway as we all called goodnight. In a few moments, the 'Britannia' was moving rapidly out to sea; the royal barge was apparently winched on board with HRH and all passengers remaining in the barge, hence the quick getaway; all gangways would already be hoisted.

We drove back to the party and shortly afterwards, everyone, about 50 people, moved up to our house where Stephanie and Sister Ponninghouse and other willing helpers had set out the dinner for 12 and healthy reinforcements for a buffet dinner. Ida and I changed from the clothes we had worn to meet HRH into our finery planned for the reception. HRH had remained throughout in naval bush jacket with his admiral's shoulder insignia. No doubt he was a fine-looking man, though a little older than I had imagined; I noticed that he wore his hair a little longer and in the modern trend of the time.

Our guests, British, French, and New Hebrideans, seemed genuinely thrilled by the visit. Finally the last of them moved off at about 2.30 in the morning, after which Ida dropped gratefully into bed and Mike and I drove down to the oval to see how the dance progressed there. Over a thousand people were dancing very happily to ukulele and guitar bands in the club and some were doing custom dances outside in the open. A few flares were still burning. The party continued on until dawn. We returned finally and gratefully to bed at 4.

Saturday was a busy day getting people fed and away; four plane trips to Santo, some going by sea and thankfully the seas had abated. I took the last of the reception guests to Litzlitz village about midday after Ida had packed them lunch to eat on board; then we had to clean up the house, and what a mess it was in. Mike and Jim who had stayed overnight with us I saw off about 9 am. Poor Jim had some strife with his bag. I had made special arrangements for HRH's bag to be placed in the guest room in case he wanted to change and to be returned aboard, but the VSOs after singing "Rule Britannia" were dying for a chance to see the 'Britannia'. One of them admirably thought of HRH's bag and came dashing up and asked Stephanie about it. Stephanie saw "a bag" and gave it to them. The bag was hoisted on board the 'Britannia' and departed, along with all Jim's personal effects. Poor Jim after two long and trying days was quite upset. Fortunately they were flown back from the Solomons on Tuesday.

Saturday afternoon we were too tired to sleep and we asked in the

Weightmans, George Hart, and the VSOs and Sister Ponninghouse who had been a tremendous help to Ida in preparing the food, to talk over the visit and we heard and exchanged titbits. I think Barry and Lesley were the most disappointed; they had postponed their leave and worked so hard, Barry especially with the agricultural station. HRH had had a few words with them but Barry had been looking forward to talking to him when showing him around the agricultural station. We exchanged notes on how the day had gone and commiserated with ourselves on what a day it would have been had it not been for the weather. Sunday we suffered a recovery but by Monday we were back to normal routine again.

Despite the terrible bad luck with the weather (the irony was that the following week was superb) we really felt that the visit had all been well worthwhile. I was particularly pleased to be sincerely complimented by the French Resident Commissioner and all of the Norsup French contingent who seemed to genuinely enjoy the visit. I had a very nice letter from Mike and Lt. Cdr Willet. The New Hebridean population were tremendously enthusiastic and those who could not come because of the bad seas, and there were many, were deeply disappointed.

Ida and I were filled with admiration for Prince Phillip—his impressive personality, easy manner and dignity, and I felt that British prestige had reached an all-time peak in the surrounding islands.

Lakatoro Life Continues

My colleague Boileau departed on leave in mid-1971 and was replaced by Monsieur Teppe. I had to admit that Boileau was a good administrator and his energies kept me on my toes, but he was not always easy to get along with. I was told by the British Office in Vila that Monsieur Teppe was a veteran of the North Africa campaign during the war, that he was not very robust, but intelligent and not to be underestimated.

On his first visit to Lakatoro, I held a cocktail party for him to introduce him to my staff and the Norsup fraternity. I felt obliged to attend his first wave-the-flag celebration at Lamap for the 14th of July celebrations. Ida and I went down in the 'Ida' in time for the formalities starting at 8 o'clock and a very extravagant lunch party, after which we felt we could nip away. Over the past 18 months, there were regular visits by the French over proposals to move their agency at Lamap to Lakatoro, and before Teppe's arrival, I had chosen sites somewhat reluctantly for my French colleague's base. I knew, however, Teppe obviously felt the same way. Within a month or so of his arrival, an agency was under construction at Norsup.

In September 1971, the Presbyterian mission announced that it was handing over all its educational facilities, classrooms and the like, to the British government. In my district this amounted to a considerable amount of work and responsibility. Fortunately the new District Education Officer, George Hart, was on hand to cope with it.

Medically we were making progress—new dispensaries, in addition to those already built by the VSOs with goat bag funds assisted by local offerings, had been built at Lakatoro and Bushman's Bay.

Sister Ponninghouse, responsible for rural health, moved into her new quarters completed by Mr Alan Hardiman, one of our UK VSOs. She too was an asset to the station. Apart from her medical work supervising dressers (doctor's assistants,) throughout the district, she was a tremendous help with our continuous flow of visitors.

In November, Santo received the brunt of a pretty savage earth tremor, force 7 on the Richter scale. In Luganville there was widespread damage, buildings were toppled and the American-Army-built Sarakata Bridge was moved a metre but undamaged. We tumbled out of our beds at Lakatoro to the clatter of broken crockery and the like. By the time we had taken shelter with the children under a doorway, the shake had passed. Fortunately for us it had not done any serious damage to buildings but left a trail of broken household effects. This time we were lucky.

Nineteen

1972 Lakatoro

Barry Weightman's 1972 New Year fancy dress party at Norsup was a great success. We all dressed up, Barry and Lesley had some wonderful ideas both for dress and antics, which carried on throughout the night, finishing at dawn. At midnight, balloons were released and we all joined in the usual hullabaloo. At the toilet window they had painted and positioned a man's face with a wicked leer looking through the window. All the children except Peter, who caved in at midnight, danced on till dawn. We returned in the open Land Rover, because luckily it had been a fine night, singing lustily, and were happy to hit our beds. I was awakened at about 8 o'clock with raucous singing. At out front door were about 50 visitors from Tautu, heartily singing "Happy New Year" and greeting us with bunches of flowers. I noticed that the flowers had been picked from my own garden! Traditionally I should have invited them in for food and drink but I confess I was too tired to do so and left them to wander on their happy way.

We returned from leave in February 1973 to a very warm welcoming party by all the staff in the Metemet Club. The new FDA, M Lecuyer, a short stocky man, seemed on first impressions very amenable. He had as his aide Maxime Carlot and there was a much more extensive expatriate French group at Norsup, mostly teachers. However I soon noticed that there was something of a rift between the French community and us. They seemed to be satisfied to go their own way and Lecuyer obviously was not interested in joint touring. Anne Naupa, who had valiantly carried on English lessons for the French community, had now only one Frenchman in her class, and this was indicative of the growing separation.

My own staff now went on strike for the first time, taking the lead from their Vila colleagues, over an effort by the colonial administration to equate all salaries in the different Pacific Territories—a fairly difficult task and finally it was abandoned.

In April 1973, we received a visit from the 'Lindblad Explorer', an imposing vessel carrying some 50 American tourists around the Pacific, and we took the opportunity to lay on a number of elaborate series of hoaxes. Every effort was made to welcome them and I mustered all the vehicles in the north of the island, a whole ten of them, to bring them firstly to my station where I talked to them briefly about the historical background of the New Hebrides, then they set off southward.

Coming round a corner after leaving Litzlitz village, they were met by a ni-Vanuatu in US Army dress guarding a barrier with a sign 'US Army Missile Testing Base – No Entry'. The guard obligingly raised the barrier and they continued on—satisfaction being expressed that the mighty USA had its influence everywhere. A couple of miles down the road, there was another barrier with a Russian guard and a sign 'Missile Detection Base – No Entry'. (Lesley had gone to great lengths to ensure the correctness of the Russian uniform). The tourists apparently met this with some disapproval.

Further on, there was a sign 'Elephants crossing' and large round balls of dung spread across the road. Remarks like "Didn't know there were elephants out here" were overheard. Another few miles, and there was a sign 'Cock and Bull' hanging from what had been an old copra shed and was now painted very appropriately in black and white Elizabethan-style colours. Three expatriates sat at a pub table quaffing beer from pewter mugs. Ida, dressed in a long frock and straw hat, fluffed about with a butterfly net trying to catch butterflies, and Lesley similarly dressed was flitting to and fro. As the cavalcade passed by, VSO Alan Hardiman in a suit and top hat wobbled his way on a bicycle, raising his hat politely as he did so.

Finally the cavalcade passed a large cast-iron cauldron (used for breaking down whale blubber) in which sat George, with my uniformed policeman and a prisoner stacking firewood at the base in preparation to setting it alight. By this time our guests were realising that it was all a joke. They continued to custom dancing and were offered *laplap* to taste. On the way home, all signs of the practical joke had been removed. They thoroughly enjoyed the day and that night we were invited on board for cocktails before they sailed at midnight.

My children were all home for school holidays with the exception of Simon who was in Scotland with the Scots Pipe Band to attend the The Royal Edinburgh Military Tattoo. This was the first Australian pipe band to take part in the famous event, and as reported in the local newspaper "for 6 weeks Simon was billeted in Edinburgh castle and fed on army rations". He had a wonderful time and still plays the bagpipes to this day.

Karen was now thoroughly enjoying every dance at the club, which seemed to be every weekend, either celebrating someone's arrival or fundraising for a school or the club itself. Sallie renewed her friendship with the station population and enjoyed her meals with them very frequently. On one occasion she brought us a clam *laplap* to try. I thought it was revolting but Peter said it was really good.

From time to time, the children were now bringing friends from school to stay with them and we sometimes had as many as two or three over the holidays.

The Queen's Birthday followed the usual pattern and this new Lecuyer evidently wanted to set up a rival celebration for the 14th of July. There was a parade at which the French police contingent had not had sufficient practice because on presenting arms, several got confused and put their rifles on the wrong shoulder, thus bumping their neighbour's rifles with a clang. I could hear Lecuyer saying "merde, merde" under his breath. At night there were fireworks and a dance which we all attended. This was fun, the first time we had gotten together as a community, and the celebrations finished at dawn.

Lesley and Barry Weightman decided to throw a medieval party and went to great lengths to decorate the Metemet Club and to encourage guests to dress accordingly. Some did, much to the wonder of the New Hebridean guests.

This year we were as usual besieged with visitors, including a farewell visit by Sir Michael Gass, the High Commissioner. Ida and I had a small luncheon party and the inevitable cocktail party at night. Sir Michael was very relaxed in contrast to his visit to Tanna many years before when as number two to the then High Commissioner, we almost came to blows over whether the 'Coral Queen' should serve one or two eggs for breakfast.

Among the many visitors, there were a series of specialists—the Colonial Office Labour Commissioner, a senior scout's commissioner, UNICEF representatives examining the need for development funds, and medical specialists from Sydney who carried out various operations on patients organised by our own medical superintendent Dr Dorney. Another interesting visitor was Lady Cannon, the wife of a leading unionist in the UK whose book *Road from Wigan Pier* was apparently well known. She was interesting and a great talker so took up most of my day.

I had friends from Sydney, three doctors and Rudy Korman, a famous Australian art gallery owner, who I took on a tour of Ambrym and Pentecost. The doctors were able to deal with several patients during their visit. We went on to Paama where we met the acting Resident Commissioner from Vila on the 'Euphrosyne' for the presentation of an MBE for Sister Alison Todd. There my guests were able to see some traditional custom dancing and the usual village feasts.

On the station, buildings were going on at a pace. We now had a house for the District Medical Officer, my new office extension was complete, and the guest wing to my house, which would be completely self-contained, was nearing completion. This would also reduce Ida's workload as she was heavily engaged with women's club, kindergarten, and library and sewing lessons at the Lakatoro School in addition to her constant duties as hostess.

I had been impeded by back problems and despite plenty of medical advice, eventually took to my bed, staying there for three weeks. Most of the advice was rest but this was not easy trying to combine it with running a district. In the last week, I began hearing court cases and dealing with the ever-mounting village problems, land disputes, etc., from my bed. Later I went to Vila to seek further advice and treatment, but with very little improvement. I was thus very hampered in my work and it was not until I went to Australia and sought treatment from a chiropractor that I gradually found complete relief.

The station depended on itself for amusement on weekends and George

Hart decided on an evening at the opera. This was an outdoor event in his garden and we listened to a recording of *The Beggars Opera*. Guests wore long frocks and black tie, and two VSOs dressed appropriately acted as ushers and served champagne at interval and after the performance. On another occasion, as a true Scotsman, George held a Robert Burns night at which the haggis dinner was served on my best silver salver to the tones of Simon's bagpipes. Barry Weightman slashed the haggis open for serving after a dramatic speech. During the slashing, he scratched my good salver, which bears the mark to this day. Incidentally, in Barry I found a 'confrère' in his interest in sterling silver, and from time to time we would pore over Sotheby's silver catalogues and put in bids for certain items. Occasionally we were successful and there would be great excitement when a parcel of silver arrived.

Around this time, the British Resident Commissioner Colin Allen was posted to the Seychelles as governor, and I was sorry to see him go. He had not only been a good friend but a constant supporter in the opening of Lakatoro and the development of the district. A Foreign Office appointee, Mr Roger Du Boulay, who had previously worked in the embassy at Paris and been responsible for the Queen's visit there the previous year, replaced him.

On his first visit to Lakatoro, we gave him a small luncheon party to meet senior officers and a cocktail party at night to which my colleague and the entire French contingent at Norsup were invited. He spoke fluent French and got on well with them. He was a very suave operator and had obviously been appointed to enforce the 'entente cordiale' (cooperation between the administrations). Whilst I could see that there was perhaps need for this, it was not going to work unless there was cooperation from both sides. There were already indications of more friction, with the French exerting all efforts to expand their educational service and I was already at loggerheads with my own colleague over a French school which had been set at Lalinda, south-west Ambrym. It was adjacent to an existing British school. It was inevitable that children from the British school, amongst others, would succumb to pressure with a French school and equipment and no school fees required by the French government. On our side, we were following the tradition established by the English-speaking missions, particularly the Presbyterians, in insisting that a small school fee be charged. This was only a beginning and the Nagriamel movement, which had started in Santo over quite justifiable complaints of land alienation, was now being used as a political weapon. It was strongly supported by the French administration. I felt equally strongly that the entente cordiale policy was just not going to work.

We returned to Lakatoro from the Fiji Festival to true hurricane weather. Firstly there was Hurricane Carlotta bearing down from the north-west. She introduced herself with pouring rain and high winds which continued for some days. We took all precautions possible, erecting shutters where we had them and closing up any openings. The house soon became very stuffy. After the third day, the wind strength increased to about 80 knots and then appeared to pass over. I had been trying to monitor the situation on the radio and a second depression developed very quickly from the west, Hurricane Wendy. Again we were lucky. High winds and pouring rain continued for days and finally the weather cleared and I was able to survey the damage. Worst hit had been Santo, Aoba, and Pentecost where buildings had been demolished or de-roofed. We were fortunate. The only serious damage was the fall of trees, branches, and vegetation. My wharf was smashed by the heavy seas and was almost a write-off.

Funnily enough, from Vila came the seasoned engineer from Wilton Bell, the engineering company contracted to build the new wharf for tourist liners in Vila, to advise me on its reconstruction. I think he was a bit taken aback because there was nothing practical that he could suggest that I did not already know, but he was a nice guy and prisoners began rebuilding with the aid of the tractor and front-end loader.

The Queen's Birthday—yet again with the usual performance of parades, sports, *kaikai,* and cocktail party; this time I was able to announce Sister Alison Todd's MBE. We opened some champagne to toast Alison's health. She was, in fact, an incredibly efficient nurse, often coping with situations which would normally be dealt with by a qualified doctor or surgeon. As part of the celebrations, Barry had organised a concert for which Atis had constructed an impressive stage with rice-bag curtains. The performers involved only the European members of my staff and I, and the slapstick comedies that followed gave the large New Hebridean population a lot of laughs. It was very successful.

On the station, the VSOs—now eight—contributed to the social life. On average they mixed well with the New Hebridean community. Some, of course, were more useful than others, but most of them had some sort of qualification which could be put to good use. It was odd that the other districts did not seem interested in VSOs, so that most of those available came to me and 'Home Sweet Home' developed quite a reputation. Ida mothered them and there were very frequent afternoon teas on her verandah with her speciality: coconut and or banana cake. VSO Alan Hardiman was exceptionally versatile and understanding. It was he who had built Sister Ponninghouse's little house, and he had organised regular cinema evenings starting at a set hour and stopping for interval when the women's committee would have coffee and cakes available at a charge, which went to their organisation.

My children all loved the life. Karen and Simon were still at boarding school in Sydney but counted the days until they were able to fly back home. Sallie was at the Lakatoro Junior School, loving every minute of it and speaking both Bislama and the local language from Litzlitz. Her dog, Patch, provided offspring regularly which became treasured pups for the local community. At our first agricultural show, which we had combined in the first year with the Queen's Birthday celebrations, Patch, well groomed, won first prize for the best dog. She was the only entrant but Sallie was proud and delighted when Ida presented her with the prize. From time to time, the family suffered bouts of malaria, but overall, provided one took additional precautions, these were kept in abeyance.

I had procured a large flat-bottomed barge and 60 horsepower outboard motor to use for unloading building materials, furniture, etc. I found this most useful for taking virtually the whole station out to shop on the Konanda (the local ship-based corner store), which was now calling regularly each month and providing a much wider range of household goods, which everyone needed.

I also used the barge for picnics at weekends when the station population would join together to go and picnic at the small island of Suaru. This with a secondary island, Tetika, were initially owned by the Gidley family and in the early days, Mr Gidley would whisper into my ear that these two islands belonged to them.

With the emerging independence movements, these claims were soon disregarded, and as a family they abandoned their house at Bushman's Bay and made their headquarters in Sydney. Mrs Gidley also had property on Norfolk Island. She was the daughter of Mr Ewen Corlette who was a highly respected Australian planter at Bushman's Bay. The story went that as a young man he had married a "princess" from Aoba. I remember her as a tiny little figure who kept a shawl over her head, winter and summer. Her daughter, Madeline, was the only offspring and they also took under their wing four or five children from the neighbouring villages of Lingarak and Hatbol. Kilman, my driver, was one of these, another was Benni whom I employed as a tractor driver at Lakatoro. Both Kilman and Benni were valuable, reliable employees. Both tended to drink to excess at weekends but even then could be relied upon if necessity arose. Benni fell from grace later in a drunken brawl at the Metemet Club when he bit off a public works employee's finger.

I had had a series of ABDAs, Kalpakor Kalsakau (who had done exceedingly well but after a short time was sent to England on a course); David Stephens whose life was made a misery because of his reaction to mosquito bites and only stayed a few months; David Browning who had replaced me whilst on leave and made a good job of it, and finally Jerry Marston who arrived in October 1973. The selection board in UK reported him as a stocky plump and jovial lad whom they felt would do well.

Their assessment was accurate. Within a month, he was speaking fluent Bislama and took to the work like a duck to water. I was very keen for him to take on board the imperative to tour the district, so in his second week I had Martin take him in the 'Ida' down to Aulua and unbeknownst to Jerry, drop him ashore and leave him to his own devices for a couple of days. It seemed to work, and after several tours jointly, I felt he was capable enough to tour on his own. He was enthusiastic and capable, and reduced my workload considerably. He had an honours degree from Cambridge in French and Spanish and was 22 years old.

Twenty

Vignette - South Pacific Festival in Fiji 1973

I had no preparation for the South Pacific Festival at Fiji and made several visits to Southwest Bay to discuss plans with the team of custom dancers who had agreed to perform at the festival. In May, we flew off together direct to Suva. I was delighted that the organisers accepted wives of the team leaders and we left the children in the capable hands of Anna. We were met on arrival with a bus for the team, and for us there was a car and driver and a personal aide who was at our beck and call. Throughout the ten-day visit I was astonished at how well the dance group accepted everything that was completely new to them; the flight, electric light, running water, traffic, etc. Ida and I were accommodated at the Grand Pacific Hotel. During our entire stay we were given VIP treatment. Each day I checked in with my dance team who performed in accordance with the programme. They were thoroughly enjoying themselves.

Ratu Sir Kamisese Mara and Lady Lala invited us to a party at the Prime Minister's lodge at which all the visiting territory delegates were present. We sat around in a magnificent bure and were entertained by dancers and musicians. Then each of the delegates was invited to provide a small performance of their own and one by one, this was done around those seated. As it grew closer to us, we grew more panicky, desperately trying to think of something suitable which would represent the Anglo-French condominium. However the day was saved because when it became our turn we were invited to partake of a sumptuous repast. This included two pigs on a spit and delicious island food. I met and talked to Sir Edward Cacobau, an Oxford graduate and paramount chief of Fiji. It was his predecessor who had ceded Fiji to Queen Victoria.

On another occasion, we attended a reception given by the Indian High Commissioner who we had met at a cocktail party the night before. We saw some superb Indian dancing and drumming. After checking my dance team again, we returned to the hotel for an ecumenical service attended by the Governor General Sir Robert Foster and other dignitaries. In the evening, a reception was given by the President of the Republic of Nauru, Hammer DeRoburt. Here we had a good chat with Lady Lala Mara amongst others.

Finally, we went to a concert conducted by John Antill with the New Zealand

Philharmonic Orchestra and Choir. I was busy each day organising dancers to be on time at rehearsals (not always easy), checking their requirements (food, pocket money, sightseeing, etc.) and organising the New Hebrides artefacts section at the exhibition of The University of the South Pacific.

I was asked to open the fine arts exhibition at the university in front of a fairly formidable audience and felt I should speak partly in French as, after all, I was representing the condominium, but it seemed to go down well. We were then served sherry and taken around the exhibition. As we were the condominium official representatives, we were asked to all the many social functions. Ida remarked that she changed her frocks more often in two weeks than she had done in the past 12 months.

At the Prime Minister's cocktail party, we saw Sir Robert and Lady Foster whom we had met before in the New Hebrides. They had a chat with us and recalled their visit to Lakatoro. The next day, Lady Foster asked Ida to coffee at Government House.

We watched some superb dancing, especially from the Cook Islands and the Solomon Islands. My team were well received and at one performance, Sir Robert Joel, who had flown up for a few days, said how impressed he was with the Southwest Bay dancers. He said that he would keep them in mind for the forthcoming Opera House opening in Sydney.

One evening, we were asked to a drink with the Fosters at Government House and they showed us over the house and garden. The house was truly magnificent with enormous rooms and balconies, and beautifully furnished. We stayed on until 7.45 and then went directly to the theatre to see the Old Tate production of *The Legend of King O'Malley*.

On our final evening, the Governor General held a dinner party for all the representatives in the Government House building. At the dinner, I sat next to Lady Tu'ipelehake, wife of the Tongan Prime Minister. She had been schooled at Ravenswood and when I said that I had been born in Dubbo, she asked if by any chance I knew Shirley Brice, who was a school friend of hers. Shirley was an old school friend of mine and in my class at Dubbo High School!

Next was a grand parade of all the performers involved and attended by Fiji's dignitaries and the heads of performing teams. Ida and I sat directly behind Prince Tu'ipelehake and his wife. The chair arms had been removed to allow more space and we found that we had to lean hard over left or right for a view of the oval where the dancers paraded. I have never in my life seen such large human beings. The closing ceremony was magnificent—20 different teams, one after the other, picked up by spotlight and led by Fiji's Military band in red jackets and white sulus. They marched out of the darkness into the centre of the arena, all the dancers massing around them. The Prime Minister Sir Ratu addressed the gathering, giving a farewell speech and everyone joined in singing the "Isa Lei". It was a tremendous performance.

My group did extremely well; I was relieved to see them appear out of the darkness right on time. I felt I should have been there with them to make sure they took their cue but we had rehearsed three times and they looked magnificent.

That was our last night and at five in the morning, my driver, Mr Rajeng Khan, called us. He had one evening taken us to eat a traditional Indian curry that he and his wife had prepared. It was delicious, but I found eating with just fingers a bit messy.

The team were taken by bus to the airport and we flew directly to Vila. On this flight I was able to talk my way out of completing 31 immigration cards, telling the girls concerned that I was an immigration officer for the New Hebrides and I would authorise that action to be dispensed with. It worked. Mr Khan, had presented us with parcels of curry, and chapatis, which smelt delicious on our way over on the plane so we had those for lunch. The dance team returned to Southwest Bay by ship. They had been able to sell all their regalia and were delighted with their visit, all of which they took as a matter of course. For Ida and I, treated as VIPs with all expenses paid, it was a wonderful experience.

Twenty-One

1974 Lakatoro

Queen's Proposed Visit

I had been advised by code of the proposed Queen's visit in March, but was not able to release the information publicly until January 1974, and thereafter I seemed to be very fully occupied with preparations for the visit. This necessitated regular visits to south Pentecost to consult with people to obtain their agreement to performing the 'gol' jump (land diving). After much discussion, this was agreed, and a suitable site on the slopes of the south-east coast was found. One of my biggest concerns was the weather and the direction of the wind, because in a high wind the east coast could sometimes receive a heavy swell and landing from the royal barge could well prove difficult, if not impossible. A site was found about 400 metres inland, rising up to a height of about 200 metres, and thus with a sandy beach would make a comfortable approach.

Work began on the tower and later a suitable and reasonably comfortable dais, from which the royal party would view proceedings. The BRC Mr Du Boulay came up to view the site and talked amusingly and at length about his experiences when he was responsible for the Queen's banquet for Monsieur Pompidou the previous year. He said that a tonne of gold plate was brought in from London for the occasion and 30 seconds before they sat down to dine, he received an urgent message by phone saying that a bomb had been placed under the table and would explode immediately. There was nothing he could do but grit his teeth. It was in fact a hoax but it gave him a nasty few seconds. I felt reasonably confident that I would not have to face such problems for Her Majesty's visit.

The visit was in the hands of Tony Worner (Information Officer) and I was regularly in touch with him about proceedings and was given detailed instructions about the formalities. Ida and I would be presented on the beach when HM and party arrived. I would then proceed on her left, not as I would have thought on her right. I would then present 12 of Pentecost's senior chiefs, doing so in a loud voice for the benefit of the whole entourage and avoiding further presentations.

I was also involved in organising gifts for the visit. This included an eight foot slit gong from Ambrym for a presentation on arrival in Vila and for the Duke of Edinburgh, the tusks from the pig he had ceremoniously killed at Lakatoro in 1971.

Station Life

Despite all this, routine life went on. There were now growing political movements throughout the group, predominantly the Vanuaku Party led by Father Walter Lini from Pentecost, the Nagriamel under Jimmy Stevens, and several lesser groups with French affiliations. The Nagriamel was especially becoming difficult and in my region, I had opposition from them for various government supported operations.

I was called to north Ambrym to negotiate with the Nagriamel leaders there who had prevented the construction of a transmission booster tower. My French colleague Monsieur Lecuyer needed to be involved and as usual did so reluctantly, arriving separately in his own vessel the 'Acquitaine'. As he was never able to master Bislama, I had to interpret into French for him. We talked for five hours, and while I stressed the importance of this tower for the whole archipelago, the outcome was inevitably 'no'. As it happened, there was an alternative siting on the east coast of Malekula and we proceeded immediately back to the Malekula coast where, as I knew it would be, approval for the tower was readily given.

One Sunday afternoon, Barry and I decided to investigate possible sites for the future expansion of the station, which by this time it was beginning to need. We had little difficulty climbing up and finding a possible road route with some flat land above and immediately behind the station which would be admirable for further development. By this time the light was starting to close in on us and we decided to return home. This we found was easier said than done, and without torches, in no time we were completely bushed. We could hear the usual sounds of the station, but found the way blocked by fallen *kassis* so dense that it was a nightmare trying to step over and through it. In complete darkness trying to bear towards the station, we kept meeting deeper and steeper inclinations and we began to think seriously of the need to camp where we were because there was every danger of slipping over a minor cliff. We reminded ourselves of the presence of wild dogs and decided we should persevere. Barry was extremely worried about Lesley, who was a very nervous and highly-strung person who had already experienced several tragedies in her life, so on we went trying to keep the sounds of the station as our direction— slipping, sliding, and struggling over *kassis* as we slowly descended. By this time, we knew that the police with torches would be out looking for us but we could see no sign of them. Then quite suddenly, about 10 o'clock, we pushed our way through a strip of level land and found ourselves on the Norsup-Lakatoro road. We could not believe our eyes.

I had hoped after the royal visit that Queen's Birthday in 1974 need not be too extensive, but inevitably it grew. And under Jerry Marston's direction, there was the usual programme, with the addition of a custom ceremony to move the site of the Duke of Edinburgh's ceremonial pig killing, because of the need for the land where it was located. Incorporating this move was the erection of a plaque to commemorate the Duke's visit.

The flag-raising ceremony proceeded very well with my colleague also dressed in full uniform and a reasonable number of French from Norsup attending. We had discussed whether my colleague should follow me down to the flagpoles or not but someone remarked that if we left him standing alone on the dais it would be as though he was about to be executed by a firing squad. After the parade, we went onto the "*Nawud*" ("Stonehenge" as the VSOs called it). There the Duke's plaque was draped in the joint national flags.

Mme Lecuyer and Shirley Morrison acting for Ida met my colleague and me and we walked down to the *Nawud* where Shirley cut the ropes holding the flags. I then had to mount the *Nawud* and was handed a pig-hammer with which to symbolically kill a tusked pig tethered nearby. Having done so, Chief Artie from Wala Island, who had named the Duke, then announced my new name, "Meltek Talinvanu" (meaning a graded chief who has brought peace and improvement to the island). Chief Sukon then explained the significance of the *Namangi* (custom ceremony), that the Duke's Nawud had had to be moved to make way for the football field, and that I as a chief of Lakatoro had to kill a tusked pig to do so, which at the same time entitled me to my new name. The pig was subsequently slaughtered and given out to the various neighbouring villages and cooked in *laplap*. After my name had been announced, there was a special word of acclamation, which everyone shouted out and which sounded like "*Laos*". This completed proceedings, and sports and feasting began followed by the usual cocktail party at night and "*danis kasim daelaet*". I recall this being the first of many subsequent appearances of Jerry as the band's singer, alongside the seasoned usuals which included Avok and Atis, usually in various degrees of inebriation.

The French administration made more of an effort this year for the 14th of July celebrations and, although the parade was pretty chaotic, the fete and dance at night that continued on till daylight was very enjoyable.

About this time we were concerned to hear of the loss of the 'Trudy'. She was a little vessel owned by the Cook brothers, which I had chartered from time to time whilst on Tanna. Bob Paul whose eldest son acted as captain for charters etc., had subsequently bought her. On this occasion he had been absent and the vessel was on its way from Vila to Tanna when it disappeared without a trace, except for later, the recovery of part of the canopy of the ship. There were nine people on board. They had struck heavy seas and presumably the vessel had broken up.

Around this time, I was very concerned about Ida who had returned to Australia for medical treatment and an initial operation which subsequently led to a further operation after which she developed malaria and pneumonia. This resulted in a long stay and rest in Sydney and I was glad to be able to persuade her not to return in time for the national celebrations.

Towards the end of 1974, we were sad at George Hart and Barry Weightman leaving, both of whom had served two-year tours. They had worked diligently, putting every effort into their jobs and contributed wonderfully to station life. For George's farewell, we met up at the airport to see him off and, disregarding his objections, dressed him in magnificent cardinal's robes, which Lesley with her usual skill had prepared down to the last detail. George looked resplendent, a tall lanky figure with his cardinal's hat. He was told the Roman Catholic hierarchy in Vila under the bishop would be turning out to greet him on arrival in Vila. He was bundled into the aircraft saying, "What about my clothes?" and was told the next plane would send them onto him. In fact, they were put on board at the last moment and no doubt he was relieved to be able to change before arrival in Vila.

Practical Jokes

With Barry Weightman as the ringleader, ably supported on his arrival by Jerry Marston and a range of willing volunteers, the station became notorious for staging sometimes very elaborate practical jokes.

One involved the arrival of VSO Mike Sackett's fiancée Eileen. In advance of her flying in, the tin shacks at Aop were converted to look like a very shabby Lakatoro. As she arrived from the airstrip, Eileen was confronted with the station in full action; George Hart was teaching highland dancing, dressed in a mini-kilt; prisoners were mock chained together working on the road; Ida was cooking a pretty evil-looking concoction on the roadside; and I was in full uniform and in the throes of sentencing an unfortunate defendant to 'death by hanging'. Despite Mike's upbeat commentary, Eileen was clearly shocked, and even more so when the convicted man was dragged screaming and kicking (behind a large tree where he was swapped for a life-sized dummy) and summarily hanged from a low-hanging branch. Unfortunately, the body came away from the head which was the cue for us to 'call it' and relieve the poor girl of her growing alarm.

Our absence during annual leave was also an opportunity for the practical jokers to work on projects, and while in Australia, Barry and Jerry worked on a couple of schemes. The first was to make a recording of pigs grunting and snorting, then install a speaker high up in the tree adjacent to our bedroom, connected to the wiring of the antiquated telephone system that criss-crossed the station. Wild pigs from the surrounding bush were occasional marauders on the station, causing damage to gardens and fences. On our return from leave, the two of them camped out just below the house in the middle of the night playing these recordings. Unfortunately for them we slept through what they later said was an authentic sound booming out in the quiet of the night, which could be heard across the station. It wasn't until the third night that I came out with my torch, and after a moment or two announced to Ida, "I think there's a pig at the top of this tree!"

Another deceit they hatched up played on my love of trees. As I've mentioned, the house was set in beautiful landscaped gardens enjoying the benefits of a number of magnificent trees through which one could enjoy the spectacular views over Port Stanley and Uripiv Island. Visitors to our verandah would often tease me that there was hardly a view because of the ever-growing trees, but I held firm to my philosophy and kept trimming to a minimum. I returned from leave and noticed the garden looked well, if a bit overgrown. I was astonished to see three enormous Namatal trees growing conspicuously in the garden and almost completely blocking our view of the sea. I made a mental note to get the prisoner to cut them out next morning, and when I told him to do so he and Leikari burst into shrieks of laughter and explained that Jerry and Barry had been up early prior to my arrival to plant them. Jerry had had hard work controlling himself the previous night when I had remarked on the tremendous growth of the Namatal trees which must have "shot up" while I was away!

For Barry's departure, we wracked our brains for something both startling and original for which to farewell Barry who had contributed so much to our fun time on the station. The plan we came up with was that he would be arrested at his house, taken to the airfield, and summarily tried and convicted for a number of spurious offences and then publicly guillotined on the strip. As always, Barry played along by furiously resisting arrest and having to be forcibly held down on the mock guillotine after the guilty verdict, and the guillotine had been successfully 'tested' by dramatically cleaving a watermelon in two. With a growing sense of unease on his part and a roll of the drums, the surreptitiously replaced polystyrene blade drifted slowly down and caressed his neck, to huge applause and his obvious relief.

Barry incidentally had had other ideas, which he had to abandon, because he needed to get to Vila for a connecting flight that day. With the pilot's cooperation, he'd planned to be let out at the end of the strip after the plane had taxied down the runway slope and out of sight, jump into his truck, and shoot down to Aop beach where the pilot would circle and a dummy would be seen to leap from the plane into the bay. He would then appear dripping from the sea as we the onlookers rushed down to the bay to rescue him.

Station Life

We were saddened by the death of Peter Wright from Norsup. Peter had been a stalwart supporter of us all and was tragically killed when his vehicle collided with a tree on his way back to Norsup from Lakatoro. His brother Henry continued to do a sterling job at the Metemet Club, providing excellent meals when we required them, especially for visitors.

We were faced with more problems from the Nagriamel movement. It had assumed a preference for the French administration, and was now encouraging the establishment of French schools in place of British ones. On Pentecost, at Wijumwel, the Nagriamel people there wanted to replace the existing Anglican mission-established school with a French one and it was difficult to counteract this move. The French would provide a permanent building, uniforms and school materials, and instruction free of charge whereas the Anglican mission (now sponsored by the British government) asked for the payment of these necessities. At Lalinda in west Ambrym, I found that the villagers there under Nagriamel encouragement were asking for the establishment of a French school right alongside the British one.

I decided to take this up directly with the powers that be in Vila as it was contrary to all existing practice between the two governments and was certainly contrary to Mr Du Boulay's instructions about cooperative education. It was becoming very apparent that the French were making a concerted effort in the education field to counteract the influence of the Presbyterian and allied English-speaking missions, which had been widespread in their initial teaching of the English language. With the increasing interest in the independence movement, it was obviously in the interests of the French to try and catch up with the English-educated elite.

David Attenborough

Our next most interesting visitor was David Attenborough who came to produce a film on native custom to be called *Tribal Eye*. The six-man team arrived by chartered aircraft and I was able to accommodate them in John Bent's house as he was away on a protracted tour. By this time, Ida was back on deck and her usual capable self. We found the team all very charming and had them and some members of the station around on the night of their arrival.

David Attenborough had a fund of amusing stories and kept us fascinated with them. One story I recall was about him as a young man producing a television show on unusual London occupations. These were live shows, unrehearsed, and David said he had to emphasise that on this particular show, the interviewee who was a rat-catcher should be respectful of RSPCA regulation. The rat-catcher appeared with a cage full of the most awful-looking rats you could ever wish to see. The rat-catcher went into some details about his job of removing rats from the city, but mindful of David's warning about the RSPCA, he said, "I do it gently, mind ya, not hurtin them" and proceeded to extract a large rat by the tail. As soon as he withdrew the rat, he began spinning it vigorously round and round holding it by the tail and getting faster and faster all the time. "It's not hurtin it, mind ya." "But," said David, "why are you spinning it?" "Because," said the rat-catcher, "I if don't keep him busy, the bugger will bite me."

In the course of the evening, one of the VSOs Tony Thompson, emboldened by a few beers, came up to David and told him he thought he was "Brilliant in *Brighton Rock*". After a moment of shocked silence in the room, David politely advised him that this was, in fact, his brother Dickie, but he would pass the compliment on next time he saw him. Much laughter followed.

The next day was occupied with plans for their trek up to the traditional Small Nambas settlement on the south-west of Malekula, and answering their queries about such things as mosquitoes, snakes, and so on. I said that mosquito nets were the best protection for all these vermin and these they had with them. I took four of them, leaving two at the camp to set off following the river. They returned four days later footsore and weary. David said they had crossed the river some 25 times going upstream, and coming down he just lost track. Kirk Hoffman, a young anthropologist from Cambridge University, was included in the team and quite rightly said that it was shorter to approach the Small Nambas villages this way than from Ahamb. It was certainly a more direct approach but harder work following the river's course.

On their return, Colin March, the sound recorder for the team, remarked that he could not recall a minute of the last three hours walking as his legs were giving way under him. On the day of their return, the 'Hydra', a Royal Navy survey ship based on the west coast of Malekula had sent its helicopter to Norsup to collect mail, and I prevailed on them to take the film crew on a flight over the Small Nambas to film. Kirk went with them again and they remarked that it was a much easier way than accessing by foot. The 'Hydra' aircraft promised to land the film crew at my football field, and I hastened down to the nearby villagers to tell them about it. Quite a large crowd had gathered by the time the helicopter landed on the field. When it disgorged the crew, there was a great cheer and a lot of clapping. Moments later, it rose up into the sky and spectators were astonished as it flew back across the island to rejoin the 'Hydra'. Under Mike Macintyre, the film producer's direction, the team and my family went across to Uripiv to film the making of a slit gong and a custom dance.

Excerpts from this filming would be used in their final production. The following day the team planned to carry on to the Solomons but their departure was delayed by torrential rain and it looked as though they would not get away. But just before dark the rain eased and their chartered aircraft departed. We were all genuinely sorry to see them go. They had been such a friendly and entertaining crowd.

David Attenborough was a keen collector of both silver and artefacts and so we had much in common. I promised to send him, and later did, some Small Nambas artefacts including a large *rambarat* figure. He extended me a warm invitation to stay when in London. Later when Jerry Marston organised a reunion of volunteers in the UK to his house in Swindon, he also invited David Attenborough, but unfortunately he was otherwise occupied but sent us a warm telegram of greetings.

That week we dealt with a sad occasion when Tetti, a young mechanic trainee under Wilben, was returning from Sydney where I had arranged his hospitalisation to treat kidney failure through my old friend Dr Elliot. As Tatti returned, he died in the aircraft just before arrival at Norsup. He had been a bright and intelligent lad, a keen sportsman, and the whole station felt his loss.

Twenty-Two

Vignette - The Royal Visit

The royal visit to Pentecost, Santo – 15 and 16th February 1974. As this would be my swansong, as far as royal tours were concerned, I recorded it in great detail for my family. These were the notes I sent to family and friends.

On the Tuesday prior to the royal visit, I went to Pentecost. It was as well I did as so many problems arose which needed my attention. The biggest one was mud—it was a foot deep! The weather was lovely but marred by torrential downpours. The jump site was on the side of a steep slope, about 200 feet up, so you can imagine how slippery it was. We had to cut a ten-foot-wide pathway with steps all the way up, and then coral it, the villagers carrying the coral by hand in baskets and rice bags; they finished the job at 9 o'clock on Friday evening, with me driving them. I had visions of the royal visitors slipping over on the mud, breaking limbs, etc., so it was a great relief when it was finalised.

The other major problem was a dais, perched on the hillside, secure enough to satisfy the security people in attendance. It needed to be showerproof, yet still giving a view from the foot of the tower to the top of the tower, 75 feet above us, so the thatched roof had to be about 25-foot high in front. This was a constructional feat without ladders or nails, but in the end, it looked most attractive. The seats were made with palm-tree slats, and it was decorated with red ginger and a magnificent Pentecost mat, finely woven and dyed in cerise traditional patterns. One of the chiefs, very thoughtfully, put this over the Queen's seat at the last moment. Incidentally, I have been given the mat as a souvenir. Then there was the problem of getting the people of the lesser ranks to their seats without tripping over HM, necessitating side paths, places for the royal household (16), the press (24), and so on.

Ida, the children, and the Weightmans arrived on Thursday night, and it was fun that night, setting up the tent for Barry Weightman and eating communally on board 'Navaka'. Captain was very good and fed us all whenever we needed it. The children all looked sunburnt when they arrived, they slept ashore, and Ida, Peter, and I slept in reasonable comfort aboard. Friday just flew away, with me ploughing up and down that hill a hundred times, the sun fiercely hot, beating fairly and squarely over the hillside, and in the afternoon, it seemed to get more steamy and sticky. I got burnt and in fact my lips took a long time to recover.

We had a last-minute panic decorating the 300-yard-long path from the beach to the foot of the hillside, again with red ginger and croton leaves. I had difficulty in finding someone agile enough to get up the slippery trunks of the coconut palms alongside the path to remove dried nuts and leaves, visualising newspaper headlines, 'Royal head crowned by falling coconut' etc. I then rehearsed the presentees-12 chiefs, assessors and council presidents and drilled the police on their final duties.

Finally we all ate together in the little rest house before Ida, Peter, and I went back to 'Navaka' to sleep again. There had been the usual downpour at dark, but after that it cleared and promised to be a fine night at least. It was after midnight when we got to bed as we had to pack a suitcase for 'Britannia' and the rest of our clothes to go back to Lakatoro, and we were determined to be highly organised as far as clothes went next morning.

Simon had a battery loudhailer ashore, and we'd organised for him to give time signals at 5, and 7 am so that everyone would be on the move in good time. I had also asked the captain to call me at 5 am, and at 4 I heard him knocking—he'd mistaken the time! I did not sleep again, but watched the weather until 5, when I heard Simon's signal. Though it was still dark, there was plenty of activity ashore as people moved down the road from farther north, towards the jump site. I could hear the jumpers singing in their little camps just above the tower. In fact, they had been there singing and dancing most of the night. It was heavily overcast as dawn broke, and sure enough down came the rain in buckets!

After a heavy splash to make it more slippery than ever, Ida and I went ashore—Ida to see the children were organised and food, etc., packed, and I to get people moving on the jump site as we wanted them well underway before the Queen arrived. People were already moving along the path and around the tower.

Barry, who had been helping supervise the previous day, had organised an excellent site for the press—a press box as it were—and we had cut somewhat hazardous steps up the hillside to their position so they could get there without walking along the royal way. I was determined to keep all traffic off that so it would be in good order for the visitors—the mud, a foot deep, would soon have come up through the coral.

The next hour just vanished. I had to get the police quickly into position and Barry, in charge of the jumps, got the jumpers marshalled. I called the 'Britannia' on a brand new and very powerful walkie-talkie at 7.30, and was able to have a very easy last-minute chat with Tony Worner on board about some minor details over seating and departure procedure. In the meantime, 'Aquitane' (French) had gone off with my speed boat to bring down three planeloads of press and the French Resident Commissioner (FRC) from the airfield. Soon after 7.30, Ida and I went aboard 'Navaka' to change, and we could just see 'Britannia' on the horizon through a rain squall. There was another heavy shower—I saw Karen and Gali absolutely soaked just before I left the beach. After that the weather miraculously cleared and the sun shone as the Queen stepped ashore.

We dressed and were back on the landing beach at 8.15, just as 'Aquitane' returned with her passengers, and 'Britannia' with her escort, 'HMAS Torrens' (a frigate), came steaming in straight towards us. I was astonished to see how close both ships anchored, not more than 400 yards from the beach. They looked magnificent, particularly 'Britannia' in her navy blue duco, the enormous royal standard, and the Lord High Admiral's flags flying at the masthead. As she dropped anchor, the flags the ship was dressed with literally sprang into position from forecastle to stern. Within minutes, the royal barge and a flat-bottomed 25 knot job called a Sea Truck were down. Mr Du Boulay, Tony Worner, Gordon Haynes (security), and some of the crew were ashore in good time, so we were able to discuss protocol, where to stand etc. I had my 12 chiefs all lined up—some in immaculate shirts and trousers, others in the traditional mats bedecked with pig's tusks and *nulla nullas*—they looked tremendous!

Firstly, the royal barge came alongside the starboard after gangway, then it moved out and the Sea Truck came alongside to embark Her Majesty and all the royal household. The sea was flat-calm. The Sea Truck swept in, dropped its flap front, and there was Her Majesty stepping ashore with the Duke, Princess Anne, Captain Mark Phillips, Lord Mountbatten, and 16 of the royal household behind her. Mr Du Boulay, the FRC, and their wives met them first. Then they introduced me, Ida, the acting French District Agent and his wife, Tom Bakeo, ABDA, and his wife Naomi, who looked very smart in a new frock bought especially for the occasion.

The Duke said, "So you look after Pentecost as well as Malekula then?" and gave me a keen searching look. He gives you a very direct look when he speaks, and he obviously remembered and had of course likely been briefed on the fact that he had met us at Lakatoro. As soon as I had greeted Lord Mountbatten, who was far more active than we'd thought he'd be—the Queen calls him Dickie—I nipped around to come up on HM's left and asked, "May I present representatives of the people of Pentecost, Ma'am?" We had said 'Your Majesty' on first meeting, 'Your Royal Highness' to the Duke and Princess Anne, and 'Sir' to Captain Mark Phillips and Lord Mountbatten.

My introductions went without a hitch. I did not forget or have a blackout of any names as I had thought I might. When we walked up the path towards the jump site, HM talked quite easily about the crowds, the colours, the rich vegetation, and kept the questions up so that I felt quite at ease immediately. The Duke and FDA came immediately behind, then the Resident Commissioners, with the rest of the royal family and Ida leading the royal household.

Just prior to the royal family's arrival at the jump site, there was a panic over the press who had started on their track up the hill. Despite my many warnings to the contrary, they had all come smartly turned out in suede shoes etc., and returned very peeved to say they could not possibly get up that hill with all that mud; needless to say, I told them I had been up and down at least 100 times during the last two days.

Eventually, I had to agree that they follow the royal path, but, after we had gone ahead. I did not notice, but Ida said they shouldered their way through the entourage and were a jolly nuisance. They simply ignored the police when told to wait and, of course, my police were too reticent to do anything about it.

The walk up was simply superb, with the white coral path gleaming in the sunlight, the bright coloured dresses of the girls and shirts of the men, the rich green of the grass and the undergrowth, and this enormous 75-foot tower—a mass of pieces of wood, something like 3000 pieces, was bound together with rope. Not a single nail anywhere. As we arrived, the jumps were in full swing, with the dancers at the foot of the tower, stomping up and down in the mud, the women whistling through their teeth in high, short, sharp whistles as they traditionally do. Barry was doing an excellent job, and several jumps took place as we made our way up the steps to the dais.

I was relieved to see the mat covering the seats as I'd completely forgotten to remind anyone to do so, and they would have been wet with the rain blowing in. When we got to the dais, there was some confusion—not for HM or the Duke. I went slightly ahead and indicated where to sit, but Princess Anne, Mark Phillips, and Lord Mountbatten were right behind us and sat on the next row of seats; then, while Mr Du Boulay was quick enough to see that he could not, or should not, cross immediately in front of them and went behind, M and Mme Langlois, to whom I'd gone to great lengths to explain the procedure, squeezed in front, past Princess Anne and her party—she obviously did not approve!

It was hot and sticky, and I kicked myself for not having organised local fans as HM, who like the others was in slacks and a long-sleeved blouse, was obviously hot. She had to borrow Phillip's handkerchief to mop her brow—I would have liked to offer her mine, but thought that perhaps it wasn't done! Then Anne sitting right behind me lent forward and said, "Mamma, may I borrow your handkerchief?" "Mamma" then explained that she had to borrow "Papa's"!

The jumping went on, with Phillip asking questions galore and the Queen holding her breath, almost giving a shriek as each man in turn headed off into space and the ground. It was an incredible and exhilarating sight I thought, and certainly all the royal family seemed to think so. Anne was madly photographing with an enormous telephoto lens, and Barry, who was standing right above us and occasionally giving me a broad wink, remarked that she looked as though she were photographing my right ear all the time!

I had thought time might drag for me doing all the talking, but it certainly did not. The Duke occasionally asked the FDA a question in French, but mostly talked to me. And he and HM talked away, Phillip constantly leaning back saying, "Did you see that, Anne. Did you see that?" Lord Mountbatten, too, kept leaning forward to ask me questions, but Mark Phillips hardly said a word. I had arranged with Barry at a given signal to get the smallest jumper—a boy of ten who had jumped first from about 30 feet—and a teacher who'd jumped for the first time to be brought down for me to present them at suitable intervals, which he did. The little boy was petrified, but his headmaster came with him and answered questions. He was still muddy from his jump, but the Queen shook his hand, asked him how old he was, etc. The teacher, whom I presented later, spoke very well indeed, and very naturally, and both HM and the Duke were obviously pleased.

I had to keep reminding myself of the barrage of press cameras. Every time I looked up there was an enormous telephoto lens focused straight at me, really at the Queen of course, but I was in the way.

The most dramatic moment, was when the poor fellow jumping from about 65 feet plunged headlong into the mud. He lay there, buried to his chest, obviously hurt. He was pulled out, and with the womenfolk wailing, water was poured over to revive him and he was carried away. It was a moment, but I made light of it, assuring HM as I had been assured time and time again that there had never been a serious accident and that he would be alright.

When the next jump took place one stage higher, the man did a perfect landing, and stood up to bow and wave to tremendous ovation. Her Majesty said, "I am sure he is the bravest man I have ever seen."

Meanwhile, I had received a report that the accident victim had recovered consciousness and was okay (as they apparently thought at that time), so it was a relief to be able to tell HM this. The poor Queen had been visibly shaken, but she said later that accidents were something one had to get used to, and that she had seen plenty at race meetings etc., and that she was not unduly perturbed.

He was attended by Dr Dorney and after our departure, flown to Vila Central Hospital where he later died. His back was broken in three places. It was a tragedy for this sad event to have happened at that particular time, and of course the press made the most of it. It inevitably gave everyone a shock, and temporarily depressed the proceedings.

We had to leave the jump site at 10.10. I was watching the time but the aides, hovering in the background, gave the Duke a signal. I did not hear what Phillip called the Queen, but she certainly called him Phillip in a perfectly normal way. As we stood up, Phillip gave his wave and turned to the Queen, saying, "We are going now," obviously reminding her to wave, but she was trying to put her, or Phillip's, handkerchief into her pocket. He said again, "We are going now. What are you doing?" She answered quite crossly, "I have my hand stuck in my pocket and cannot get it out!"

I could see the children as we went off down the steps, and Sallie caught a nice smile from the Queen. I was sorry afterwards that I had not asked the children to group together near the path as I'm sure HM would have stopped to talk to them. I felt she was a bit diffident about talking to the New Hebrideans who, not unnaturally, tended just to stare. The Duke called to an American planter, "I hope you got some good photos." And Joel answered, "Yes, I'll send you some if they are any good." The Queen said, "Thank you very much indeed."

On the way down, we talked about Aneityum where they had had an unscheduled stop. They had a swim there and a picnic the day before they arrived at Vila. HM was very amused with Artie Kraft who lives there and met them. She said he kept lapsing into pidgin which she found very hard to follow, not surprising either. Probably he was so nervous that he thought they were French!

At the beach, the Sea Truck was waiting. I caught Ida's eye as she went aboard, and was about to follow when I realised my arrangements for Tom Bakeo to escort HM as she was receiving gifts from the chiefs had fallen through. Tom was probably diffident about coming forward too. So I stayed on to explain the significance of the pig tusks, *laplap*, and mat. I suddenly realised everyone else was on board—following naval procedure, the highest-ranking officer goes on board last. As HM was flying the Lord High Admiral's flag, there was no doubt about who was the highest! HM said as I went, "I will see you later." Simon, who was standing by the Sea Truck, noticed my predicament. The Sea Truck was crowded, and I found myself next to Lord Mountbatten who started firing questions again but with a twinkle in his eye! The sailors had to give the truck a shove to get it moving, and we were off.

We went alongside the royal gangway—I thought we would move along to another, but we all trooped up behind the royal party who went straight to their state rooms. Ida and I were shown to the wardroom, where we were given a most welcome cup of coffee and were able to relax—our duties done, our responsibilities over.

Mr Du Boulay was delighted with the arrangements and said so repeatedly. No doubt the whole event had made a tremendous impression and was evidently something they would never forget. It really was a magnificent sight to see these men taking off into the air with the vines attached to their ankles, to hurtle to the ground and then, except for the one poor man, leap to their feet.

The commander gave Ida and I his cabin in which to shower and change and then had a delicious lunch in the wardroom. Gosh! She was a beautiful ship, and so impeccably kept; the decks were all teak and spotlessly white, with polished wood everywhere. There were some beautiful pieces of silver which had been given to the ship.

After lunch, we were asked if we'd like to go out on the bridge, which we did, and watched the ship being brought into Santo. It was a superb day, and one would not know one was at sea—of course she was well stabilised, but even so, there was not so much as a suggestion of vibration.

We were at Santo at 3.30, right on time, and we went ashore immediately after we anchored in one of the three magnificent royal barges with Tony Worner and the Du Boulays. We swept alongside the jetty where about 4000 people were waiting. They obviously thought we were the royal party as cameras clicked etc. Afterwards, one of the New Hebrideans from Malekula told Ida they thought she was the Queen, and had raised the camera about to take a photo, when his wife said, "Missus belong Gavman no more!"

It was now Dick Baker's turn as BDA Santo, so we were able to relax. He had provided a car for us to join the royal cortège, so we did this, waving to the crowds like royalty. We did not see much of them until we reached the hospital. It was all very typical and humdrum—the presentation of councillors, planting a tree, visit a school, etc. At the French hospital, the Duke kept wandering off on his own, as did Mark Phillips and Lord Mountbatten. The latter, at one stage, asked Ida if she would help him find a piece of sensitive weed, which he wanted to show admiral Sir Peter Ashmore (Master of the Household). So there were Ida and Lord Mountbatten scratching around on the lawn, looking for sensitive weed!

We tagged along with Connie Baker and Mark Phillips who was obviously just learning the job and having great difficulty in thinking up the right questions etc. No doubt the Duke was a past master at it, so Mark had a good instructor in his father-in-law. The Duke had a constant flow of sensible questions and comments. He seemed so keenly interested in everything and everyone and just radiated charm as of course does the Queen, though in a less dynamic way.

We went back to the wharf to watch custom dancing—not a patch on the dancing at Lakatoro for the Duke!

Then the royal party returned to 'Britannia' by barge and the Du Boulays and ourselves went to the British paddock to rest for an hour.

Tony Worner and ourselves went to the Stobers' house, had a rest, then organised ourselves for the dinner; all our clothes were already there. These arrangements worked like clockwork. Our 'Britannia' suitcase had gone forward by the first boat to Pentecost and awaited us when we went on board. Judy Stober had unpacked and hung our evening clothes up ready for us at their place. We allowed ourselves plenty of time to dress and were on the wharf with M and Mme Langlois, the Du Boulays, Bakers, and M and Mme Scemama, FDA Santo, and Tony Worner, who was also invited to dinner.

The French ladies were in their Parisian models, Mrs Du Boulay in a black gown with red and green spots, and Connie and Ida in their homemade—and they looked just as good or even prettier than the models. Mr Du Boulay said the next day that he thought the British ladies had outshone the French with their dresses. I thought that Ida's frock looked perfect and with the water sapphire necklet and earrings, it was ideal for that auspicious occasion.

We sped out to 'Britannia', now all floodlit. Gosh, the power in those royal barges was fantastic! She was anchored in the canal. We went up the gangway and were met by the commander. From there we went to the foyer of the royal apartment where we were met by Sir Peter Ashmore, Master of the Household, and where all the staff, who of course we'd been with earlier in the day, were assembled—men in Red Sea rig, ladies-in-waiting in long frocks.

They were all so nice, greeting us like old friends. We were served drinks from silver salvers (I would have liked to look at the hallmarks) by liveried stewards, and all the conversation was about the Pentecost jump, which had fascinated all, even if it had horrified or exhilarated others.

Then there was a whisper, "Princess Anne." We all moved aside to form a horseshoe-shaped group, and Princess Anne in a pale blue frock with a magnificent antique pearl and diamond necklace and matching earrings—I was going to say swept, but that was not the right way to describe it—moved forward as the ladies curtsied and the men bowed. She stood with Mark behind her, smiling and I must say radiant, then she came forward and began chatting to one group after another. Lord Mountbatten must have been just behind her. Then the Queen—this was just as one visualises—made a really regal entrance. She also was in blue with the most superb diamond and emerald necklace I had ever seen. The emeralds were at least half an inch in diameter. She too stood for a few seconds while we all bowed and curtsied. It looked and felt terrific! Then she moved forward with Prince Phillip behind her. Her Majesty went straight over to Ida, who was talking to Lady Mary Morrison, one of the ladies-in-waiting, and they had a long talk.

In the meantime, Lord Louis came over to me and said, "I believe you were on 'Duke of York'?" So I was able to remind him that at Colombo, as Commander.-in-Chief Indian Ocean, he had come aboard ten minutes before the scheduled time to catch out our Commander, Commander Hodges. He had a great old chuckle over that and was evidently pleased to be reminded about it. He called over Admiral Trowbridge, flag officer of the royal yacht, and told him about it. Then we got onto 'Duke of York' personnel, Captain Nichols etc., and finally onto 'Duke of York' in the Pacific—when it transpired that Admiral Trowbridge had been first officer on 'Wager' and Prince Phillip, of course, First Lieutenant on 'Whelp', our two escorting destroyers. Lord Louis then called out to Prince Phillip, "Phillip, come over here," which he obediently did, with Princess Anne joining us. Lord Louis said, "Do you realise that you and Trowbridge were escorts to this man"—pointing at me—"in the Pacific?" They all had a laugh over that, and Prince Phillip started talking about the day Admiral Nimitz was made a Knight Grand Cross of the Order of the Bath (CKMG) on board the 'Duke of York' when he was invited to the investiture. I remembered that, of course, and we talked about the surrender and the takeover in Hong Kong.

Then we moved into dinner. The dining saloon was magnificent with a long centre table, the Queen and the Duke sitting opposite each other, and the 11 guests interspersed with the 22 members of the royal household.

Dick and Connie Baker, as hosts at Santo, rightly had the places beside Her Majesty and the Duke. Ida was between Mr Du Boulay and Mr Heseltine, the Queen's assistant private secretary, and I sat between Lady Mary Morrison who was very nice, and Admiral Trowbridge. They both talked well and asked so many questions, that I always seemed to be the last to finish, and would look down and see the Queen finished and I would have to leave the rest of a delectable dish untouched!

The table was magnificently appointed—individual salt, pepper, and butter, a Rockingham dinner service (I think), and of course all solid silver dishes. The centre table pieces were about two feet high in solid gold!! Actually, I thought they were monstrous, but obviously very valuable. There seemed to be a steward to every guest, and we had a delicious meal with an orchestra playing dinner music in the foyer. We had chilled soup, fish (sole I think), roast chicken with zucchinis, roast potato etc., and individual salads. Then a bombe Alaska filled with grated chocolate and an array of fruit, with finger bowls, fruit knives, etc. There were four wines—sherry, white wine, burgundy, and port, and biscuits. The difficulty was keeping up a running conversation and taking everything in. The meal seemed to be eaten at a great rate! Ida said she had some difficulty in keeping up.

Dick Baker said he had a good yarn to the Queen, mostly about the condominium agriculture!! Then we adjourned for coffee together, the ladies not retiring, and coffee was served from superb silver coffee pots, which would sell at Sotheby's for about $2000 apiece!!

I was again with Lord Louis when Mr Heseltine came over and said, "You speak good French. Would you go and help the Queen out with Madame Langlois and Madame Scemama?" So, with some diffidence, I did. Her Majesty seemed quite pleased to have some help, and the four of us talked about the Pentecost jump—Her Majesty and I doing most of the talking, as Madame S. seemed petrified, and Madame L. was no conversationalist at any time. I was able to help HM out with a few words she got stuck on. She couldn't remember the word for mud or for chest, but of course she was very fluent. A perfect accent, they said afterwards. I made one faux pas in addressing HM during the conversation as Madame instead of Votre Majeste. It just slipped out, but I am sure it did not worry her.

At this juncture, a lady-in-waiting caught Her Majesty's eye, and she said to me in French, "Our guests are about to arrive. I must go and put my—what do you call it—my chapeau." Meaning, of course, tiara. This story vastly amused Madame Langlois. So, off she went to return in a few minutes in white gloves and her diamond tiara—the one which Queen Mary gave her. HM told the Du Boulays that she was rummaging in a box one day and found the other half of it—apparently Queen Mary did not like it!!

Her Majesty looked her part, and everyone was thrilled to see the tiara. She, with Prince Phillip and the royal family, then lined up at the entrance to the foyer and greeted some 250 guests.

In the meantime, the dining saloon had been cleared, thus giving two enormous reception rooms. I would dearly have liked to have taken a day off to study the artefacts, silver, furniture, paintings etc., in these saloons! There were some magnificent pieces, including the Archbishop of Canterbury's mace, dated 1620. The artefacts are apparently changed according to the region in which they are travelling. We saw the pig hammer which Prince Phillip had used to symbolically kill the pig at Lakatoro two years ago.

During the reception, I did not get into conversation with any of the royal family who of course were involved with their new guests and circulated systematically. I talked some more with the royal household instead and saw a lot of people from Santo and elsewhere who had come in especially for the reception. I joined in a conversation with Mark Phillips for a few moments—he seemed very shy and overwhelmed with it all I'd say.

The reception went on for two hours, during which time HM seemed to have talked to all groups, and everyone was saying, "Oh, the Queen said this, and I said that etc." Everyone was terribly thrilled, and the French community most of all.

Halfway through I was called down to the private secretary's office for a conference with Sir Martin Charteris, private secretary to the Queen, Mr Du Boulay, and Mr Heseltine as we had just received word that the man who was hurt at Pentecost was not expected to live. There was concern that the press might make too much of it, or that it might in some way reflect discredit on HM. It was decided to play it down, but if the unfortunate man died, as sadly he subsequently did, I was to go at once to Pentecost to convey HM's condolences. I was to do all I could to see that no liability was foisted on us, the Government, and what was necessary to relieve any hardship which might be brought about as a result of the man's death.

When we got back into circulation, it was about time for the guests to move. The royal family had just retired, and the guests moved off rapidly. Ida and I, with the Du Boulays, Dick and Connie, FRC and FDA, and Tony Worner were ushered into a small lounge to await being called to say goodbye to the royal family.

Lord Louis came in and sat down to talk while we waited. First Dick was ushered into another large room. I followed to where HM and Prince Phillip were with Princess Anne and Mark beside them, and I think Sir Martin Charteris in the background.

Her Majesty said, "I'd like you to have these as a little memento of our visit," and gave me a very elegant pair of gold cufflinks with EIIR on them. She said how much they appreciated all the effort I had put into the preparation for their visit. I said how honoured the district, particularly the people of Pentecost, were to have had Her Majesty land on their shores, and that I had been asked by the chiefs to say that they hoped one day Her Majesty would return. That little piece said, Princess Anne said how disturbed she was by the news which she had heard over Radio Australia earlier in the evening—they said the royal family had watched a man plummet into the ground and seriously injure himself during a Pentecost land dive that morning. She said she felt that the accident had only happened because of their visit. She seemed genuinely disturbed. I was able to reassure her that people jumped for the love of it, and not just because there was a royal visit. I then bowed, shaking hands with HM and Prince Phillip and, I think, backed out!

Prince Phillip handed me a photograph of HM and himself, signed by both and nicely framed. As I went out, Sir Peter Ashmore gave me a very nice letter from Bill Heseltine—"The Queen has commanded me to write and express her thanks for the arrangements which you made to enable her and other members of her family to witness the famous Pentecost jump this morning. She was delighted to have had the chance to see the spectacle, unique in the world, and as exciting as it is unusual. Her Majesty knows how much preliminary work was necessary before the jump could be mounted in her honour, and thought that all the arrangements had been beautifully made in the face of extraordinary difficulty. She and the other members of her family have asked me to repeat their thanks to you for arranging the jump and send you their best wishes for the future."

Oh, one other small thing I did not mention. As we went into dinner, the Queen turned to me and said, "What an interesting career you have had, starting off in the navy and finishing up in this fascinating part of the world." Evidently Ida had been talking to her about what we had done and she had taken it all in!

Well, we all sped back to the wharf comparing notes and gifts. Tony was given an MVO (Member of the Royal Victorian Order) for his part in the visit, and we still do not know what the Du Boulays were given! M Langlois was given a CVC (Commander of the Royal Victorian Order) which pleased him greatly. He was trembling with excitement when he came down the gangway.

We all felt dog-tired as we saw 'Britannia' steam out on her way to the Solomons. Poor things. They would have a few days break before beginning the next round. Princess Anne had talked about a concert being arranged on board in which she was to dance a hula, Lord Louis a Fijian war dance, and everyone was to take part except HM and Prince Phillip!

There is no doubt the Queen radiates charm. She was looking older than photos suggest, but after all, she was in her late forties. She had a lovely speaking voice, and certainly a royal presence in the true sense of the word.

I think she found the heat very trying, in fact she said so. I was so sorry she got so hot going up the steps to the jump, and of course, with slacks and long sleeves, that would make it so much hotter. They will feel it even more in the Solomons and New Guinea.

Next day, Sunday, we had a well-deserved sleep-in, gathered our things, clambered aboard the 'Ida', which had done noble service helping to run guests to and from 'Britannia' the previous evening, and headed for home. Good seas and we slept most of the way, arriving at 5 pm to find the family all safely home. They had not got home themselves until Sunday. We were thankful for another early night and exchanged reminiscences of the jump and THE VISIT!

Monday we were back into the humdrum of routine, and the family were madly packing for Australia and me to go to Pentecost at Her Majesty's command, to look into the tragedy that had occurred on the day.

And so ended my swansong as far as royal tours are concerned.

Twenty-Three

1975 Lakatoro

Our next staff appointee was a health inspector, John Taffe and his wife Chinchoo, a Chinese Malay fully qualified nurse and midwife. John was from Ireland and completely new to colonial service but well qualified. We decided that as they were arriving on a Sunday, we would turn on a "Barry Weightman special Aop Bay greeting".

The volunteers, always keen for a prank, raised the two flags on bamboo poles in front of an old copra dock. Medical assistants Luke and Pierre set up a dispensary and clinic inside. Nurse Dora stood by at a delivery table, whilst Ian (a New Zealander fourth-year medical student) appeared ready with forceps dripping tomato sauce. I was in my usual uniform—pith helmet etc.—industriously dictating to my clerk Esther, gin bottle on the desk beside me. David, a VSO, had his Ag office set up, and nearby were police headquarters in a canvas tent. Jerry's wife, Val, conducted a small class under a tree and Ida sat on a comfortable chair under a parasol with an eccentric 17-year-old Stuart playing in the sand at her feet. The Taffes were met at the airfield by the resident doctor, John Mills, and taken on tour of the 'station'. It apparently all looked so realistic that John Taffe said that he really thought that he had come to some old colonial diehard with an eccentric wife who was running the administrative centre. They were completely fooled. That night we had a welcoming party for them.

The most confronting event of the year was the closing of the airport at Norsup on the instruction of the condominium civil authority. There was some justification for this because it was too short for the bigger aircraft now being used, and the surface was unstable in wet weather. A new alignment was designated, running almost parallel to the existing field and extending into the Norsup PRNH plantation to the north and the Tautu land to the south. My own feeling was that the French administration had precipitated the closure to hasten a decision on the field. Whatever the case, it certainly stirred up feelings.

Pressure came from the north led by the MANH Party and by Nagriamel, all of whom were French-speaking Catholics. There was also pressure activated by Father Soucy in charge of the Catholic mission at Wala. The outcome was an extensive and hostile demonstration on the airfield in November 1975. Some 2000 people arrived armed with machetes and sticks demanding the presence of my colleague and myself to solve the problem. It was certainly the most antagonistic and difficult situation I had had to encounter in the New Hebrides. It was made more difficult by my French colleague, who had little to say.

Discussions took place throughout the day, and at one stage I decided that my police establishment should stand by in case of an outbreak of violence. I had been reluctant to do this but it seemed to calm the situation. My colleague and I attended the very heated discussion but no progress was made towards a settlement. Argument went on all day and it was not until evening that the crowds dispersed. I was relieved that there was no bloodshed. It was finally agreed that we would refer the matter immediately to the Resident Commissioners in Vila for their action. I spent the next day mostly on the radio with the residencies.

Soon after, the Resident Commissioners jointly visited and decided that a representative assembly committee would be asked to adjudicate. This was led by Bob Paul from Tanna and John Ratard from Aore. They were admirably patient and listened to the views of the Norsup plantation led by Monsieur Thevenin and the Tautu villagers. They were unable to find a solution, not unexpectedly, and returned to Vila where it was decided that if necessary, force would need to be used to allow work to proceed on the new airfield.

Meanwhile a second demonstration had been organised by the north and appeared to be more hostile than ever. Again we turned out our police to control the situation, which they did well. They broke up the meeting. At this stage, M Thevenin verbally attacked me for deliberately supporting the Tautu people against the extension of the strip. This I hotly denied and a very unpleasant argument ensued. Relations between the two camps remained very cold. Finally there was a directive from Vila that work should proceed on the airfield with, if necessary, the support of police detachments from French and British to ensure that works went ahead unhindered.

My colleague and I met with firstly the Norsup management and then the Tautu villagers to advise them of the Resident Commissioners' decision. At Tautu, on delivering the message, we were met with cold hostility, and they were warned that the reinforced police detachments would be standing by. The next day, the public works began on the airstrip and proceeded without incident. Nonetheless because there was so much hostility from both the north and from Tautu, it was decided to retain the extra police for another week or so to be on the safe side. With no further friction, work proceeded and a month or so later the new existing airfield was opened.

It was thankfully agreed that the residencies would send a deputation of advisory councillors elected the previous year by the local people, and the delegation arrived the following day. I had arranged for representatives from PRNH and Tautu (the warring party) and representatives from the demonstrator's group to meet. And again at the end of a long harangue, the Norsup Company and the Tautu native landowners gave way. It was agreed that the French company land concerned would be given free to the condominium and that the Tautu people would be given certain rights over the airfield, including its management and the right to set up and control the ticket office and amenities. Thus the kiosk previously run by Peter Wright (and after his death by a Tahitian lady, Titine) would now be run by the Tautu villagers.

Early in December, I encouraged my colleague to take part in a tour attending all the district local councils for their budget meetings. My colleague attended in his own acquired vessel, but it was a satisfactory end to the year to at least obtain his nominal support in an organisation like the local council. Overall the French administration had never really accepted our enthusiasm for such councils. They were, after all, a stepping stone on the road to independence and in my view the most important administrative effort that we could put into our work.

Independence was now a much discussed issue. I well remember the time in 1963 when I had my first big meeting with the people of the Maskelynes and talked about independence and the time when my own job would be taken on by a ni-Vanuatu. This remark was taken with much scepticism, but by 1980 this had come to pass.

In February 1975, the District Agents were invited to attend a meeting in Vila with the French and British Ministers of State, Monsieur Stirn and Miss Joan Lester, for discussions on the future of the New Hebrides. As a result of these meetings, it was agreed that a representative assembly elected by universal suffrage would be established, hopefully within the year. In addition there would be an election of four custom chief representatives, one from each district, who would be chosen from a committee of island chiefs. At this stage of events, I proceeded on leave, returning in July and was replaced by Gordon Norris.

On leave I was heavily involved in the construction of two units immediately behind our existing home in Tamworth Street, Dubbo. My mother would be moved into the closer of the units and we would move into the original homestead on my retirement. When I returned, Ida stayed on for some time to give her a further break from duties on the station.

At Vila, I had the added excitement of receiving a car, which for over a year I had been negotiating for and this was a 1939 Rolls Royce Wraith. Reece Discombe, a friend and well-known Vila identity, was kind enough to house the vehicle for me, which on arrival was securely boxed. It was an exciting moment opening up the crate to reveal such a beautiful car. In my few drives around Vila town it caused quite a stir, and whenever I stopped I would be surrounded by an admiring crowd—rather embarrassing.

People would call out "spesel car". It was to remain housed in Reece Discombe's dock until we departed on final leave in 1977.

On my return to Lakatoro, following our annual leave, I was given the usual warm welcome and made a quick tour of the station to find all well except that there was more rubbish about than usual. It always amazed me that senior staff were unaware of the need to set an example and appeared to be oblivious of untidiness. It did not take long to get the prisoners cleaning up and the station back in good state.

The major task for the rest of the year was the preparation for the election of representatives to the Representative Assembly. This entailed the drawing up of an electoral listing, detailed instructions on the voting procedure, the establishment of polling teams and polling booths. For the district this meant that we had 47 polling teams and 51 polling stations. The next step was to instruct people individually on the procedure for voting and this was a mammoth task involving all of us.

In addition a chief was to be elected from each district and this was the first action taken. A committee of 12 chiefs was decided upon after discussion with the various islands concerned. These chiefs were brought to Malekula for the actual election of one of their members. It was decided that the election take place at Aop which was presumably on neutral ground between Norsup and Lakatoro. There was inevitably strong feeling between my colleague and I over the chief's election and although it was pretty clear that there was sufficient English-speaking chiefs to carry the day, my colleague Datchary was sceptical of the outcome and after some heated discussion walked out of the meeting. The result was the appointment of Chief Willie Bongmatur from Nebul on North Ambrym. Willie was an outstanding chief, a born leader, and although he had no formal education, was a very intelligent man. Following independence, Willie was to head Vanuatu's Chief's Council, which would act as an advisory body to the independent government.

For the next few months, both my colleague and I and our respective staff were fully involved in touring and explaining the electoral procedures. As election day approached it was necessary to arrange transport for the polling teams to travel from booth to booth, and this occupied all our resources. Fortunately on polling day we had clement weather and surprisingly enough, the elections proceeded in almost every case without a hitch. In Lakatoro and Norsup, my colleague and I sat at our radios to cope with any problems which should arise and await the return of the ballot boxes. We had tossed for decision of the site where the counting would take place, and this was at my colleague's office. We began counting assisted by our various staff, and except for a minor hitch when the ballot box from Southwest Bay was delayed, all went well. I had sent police to the other side to meet the box when it arrived but heavy rains had blocked the road and the police escort got lost on their return on foot. They still managed to return about daylight. For our district the results were four Vanuaku Party, and two MANH Party. Overall the Vanuaku Party supporters had an outright victory and their first policy announcement was that there would be independence in 1977.

On the station there were more staff changes. Dr Joeli replaced Dr Mills, Rod Jamieson became the British Works Foreman, and John Challis temporarily replaced Jerry Marston, who departed on leave asking to be returned for another tour to Lakatoro. This I was delighted about and secured exceptional approval for (the second tour of duty was normally required to be in Vila) because Jerry had been an incredibly helpful assistant.

BRC Mr Du Boulay departed on transfer to a London posting, much to some people's relief, and was replaced by a Colonial Service appointee John Champion, who had wide experience in West Africa.

There were more developments over the attempted poisoning of Oscar Newman by his most recent 'wife' Lily. The Criminal Investigation Department in Vila had procured sufficient evidence to prosecute, and Oscar was determined to support Lily with Sydney lawyers if necessary to defend her. We awaited further developments with great interest. The case against Lily for the thalidomide poisoning of Oscar had proceeded in Vila in the Court of First Instance. Despite a powerful legal team brought in from Australia and curiously paid for by Oscar, a conviction of three years imprisonment was ordered.

Oscar Newman's seventh de facto wife was a wonderful prisoner. I had had a prison gang build a separate thatch quarter for her and made her responsible for the upkeep of the two rest houses. There she did a very commendable job. It was a relief to Ida to know that when staying guests arrived they could be put into scrupulously clean quarters. Oscar, feeling very contrite but still suffering from the effects of the thalidomide poisoning, was a regular visitor every Sunday. After spending time with Lily in her quarters he would visit us, bringing welcome gifts of cream and the like,.

I was relieved when Jerry Marston's return to the station was approved. His replacement, John Challis, went off after the usual Metemet Club farewell party. My New Hebridean assistant Abel Kaloris and his wife Lepanga came to dinner with us before their departure. Abel too had proved himself very capable and I was sorry to see him go. Morrison Tangarisi who was New Hebrides' first university graduate with a degree from Cambridge replaced him. He was sent up to me from Vila with a report that said he was capable enough, but not interested in applying himself. If anything could be done with him I would be able to do it the report said. I was flattered but was unable to make very much use of him and he was shortly after called back to Vila and resigned the service to look for a life in other spheres.

We had a joint British/French medical dressers' course at Lakatoro with high-powered support from the World Health Organisation. It was conducted by Dr David McFadyen and Sister Bushra Jabney from Lebanon, the latter a charming lady whom we were to see more of in the year ahead. I took the opportunity to have my French colleague Mr Datchary to dinner with the WHO representatives, remembering that I had yet to be invited back by Mr Datchary, nonetheless it was a very pleasant evening. The next day, John Taffe the District Medical Officer, held a St Patrick's Day dinner at the club for the dressers attending the course and all those others involved. This went off very well but ended up a rather wild night.

Twenty-Four

1976 Lakatoro

Resident Commissioner's Visit

I had a busy week preparing tour plans, writing speeches and notes for the Resident Commissioner's visit (he was the second last British Resident Commissioner of the New Hebrides), and also, at last, getting the station spick and span. I always liked to see it looking nice, and this was an excuse to get all the prisoners on the job to create 'a treat for sore eyes'. The Poincianas were just coming out in all their glory and all grass edges were neat and tidy.

The Champions arrived at 11.30 with their son William (21), one of seven children. We gave them a cold lunch and settled them in. In the afternoon, we did the rounds of the station—Norsup, Tautu, and home for a late cup of tea. That night, William went off to join the VSOs for dinner at 'Home Sweet Home'. The four of us sat and talked until about ten Saturday evening.

Accompanied by Monsieur Bouvier, the public works engineer, I drove the Champions up north along the new road and we didn't get back until midday when 9 of us sat down for lunch, unusual for us to have all four children in the country at one time, We put the Champions in our guest wing and gave William the small rest house to himself. We had a lazy afternoon—not that the Champions believed in resting for long. They were very active, wanting to see things non-stop. In that way they were a bit exhausting but very nice people and very easy.

The Marstons had them for afternoon tea and then took them for a drive to Bushman's Bay. Simon went too and that left us free to prepare for the cocktail party of 60 at 6.30. We were well organised in plenty of time and I had asked the volunteers to act as drink waiters, which they did very well. That saved me a bit of worry and they seemed to enjoy doing it. The cocktail party was a success but as usual the French got into a huddle at one end of the verandah and didn't budge! They make no effort to mix. It was good that Mr Champion saw the way they behaved though as it was a constant problem. In fact, he was rather shattered at the behaviour of the Norsup crowd generally. And he asked me to fly to Vila next week for the undersecretary's first visit, and explain to Mr Stanley personally the difficulties we are having getting on with our colleagues—something that was evidently not appreciated in London where everyone thought it was one big happy 'entente cordiale'.

After the cocktail party, we went down to the club where Henry (wonderful, flamboyant, fijian friend) put on a sumptuous meal including stuffed pumpkin and curried chicken. There were about 30 of us and I got the girls to 'place name' people so that everyone mixed well. There was a little dance afterwards. I'm sure the Champions enjoyed it all.

On Sunday, we went to the service in our little bamboo open-air church, only spoilt by the aroma of a dead rat or something occasionally polluting the nice fresh breeze blowing. Then we went by speedboat (our new one) over to Suaru for a picnic. We grilled chops and had a lazy day swimming and talking. The Champions said they thoroughly enjoyed themselves; They seemed to enjoy the simple things. The next day we set off on tour on the 'Euphrosyne'—superb weather all the way and all went according to plan. Mr Champion said it had been "splendidly" planned.

We met up with Monsieur Datchary on the Monday and Wednesday for council openings, and anchored at Paama on the Monday night where Alison Todd joined us for dinner. The next morning we looked over the clinic and the school and had a meeting with the chiefs. Alison gave us a delicious morning tea before we sailed for South Malekula, calling in at Toman Island—a Nagriamel stronghold, which I wanted the British Resident Commissioner to visit unannounced, just to make the point we could and would when we wanted to do so. At South West Bay we were given a great welcome. We were greeted by Small Nambas armed to the teeth with bows and arrows, which they rather alarmingly pointed at us with bows strung. They then escorted us to the council chambers where after speeches and the official opening, there was some very spectacular dancing. When we finally waved the Champions off, stepping off the same plane were the Australian Aid people—so there was no respite for the wicked! I whisked them around—we wanted to impress because the aid was significant, over 1.5 million dollars per year. Ida gave them a spectacular lunch and then off they went. It was not until evening that we were able to relax, and we were in bed by 8 o'clock. It is amazing how tiring visitors are and of course one had to be constantly on the 'qui vive'.

OBE & Silver Jubilee Medals

It was traditional to announce Queen's Birthday honours at the Queen's Birthday celebrations. On this occasion, it was a very moving one for us personally because we had been informed that both Ida and I would be presented with the Silver Jubilee Medal. It had also been announced in Vila that I had been awarded the OBE, but I felt that it would be wrong for me to announce this at the Queen's Birthday. So that evening at the Queen's Birthday cocktail party, which was held at our residency, Jerry Marston, my number two, announced the award of the Order of the British Empire OBE to me, and the Silver Jubilee medal to both Ida and I. For Ida it was particularly pleasing because if anyone had worked all those years for both me and the district, it was Ida—very well deserved!

Jerry presented them to us. He did it so nicely with a little speech, first in English and then in French. The applause was tremendous, and we both felt very much flattered. Two thirds of the applause was for Ida, and a great number of New Hebrideans remarked how good it was to see her receive an award.

During April 1976, the political front continued to disintegrate. There were demonstrations by the Vanuaku Party in all headquarters, which proceeded peacefully except in Santo where the MANH Party and Tabwemasana conflicted with the demonstrators and about 30 people were hospitalised. The Tabwemasana was led mostly by French *"colons"* (plantation settlers) who quite rightly could see that their whole livelihood would be challenged with the overthrow of both governments and a takeover by the New Hebrideans. Nagriamel, the third main opposition group to the Vanuaku party, had in the past been financed mostly by a small group of very wealthy expatriate American undesirables—all with unsavoury records in other parts of the Pacific. It was finally agreed jointly that they would be expelled from the country, and this undermined the Nagriamel's financial resources. The Vanuaku Party was fast losing interest in unofficial British backing because we were clearly not standing up to our French colleagues, and they then turned to the United Nations, sending a deputation to New York to put their case forward.

Meanwhile, the Representative Assembly had met but was boycotted by the Vanuaku Party and only about 14 members attended, passing a resolution that two chiefs would represent the chiefs who were the stumbling block from each of the four districts. Datchary, in walking out of our meeting to elect the Central District chief representative, had set his foot amongst the pigeons (probably purposefully so). Chief Bongmatur from North Ambrym officially remained our representative, and was later to become chairman of the chief's council on independence. However because he was not recognised as a representative of the district by the French government, it was not possible for the representative council to proceed. We were at a stalemate again.

Santo Break

We enjoyed having a break in Santo—good to meet up with people there—however Santo was not a happy place. No one dared mention politics as everyone was against everyone else, especially, of course, the British who were a marked minority. It was good to see Dick Hutchinson and we had some long chats. He, like me, felt discouraged by the way things were going. We knew what we should be doing, but the French seemed to rule the roost and we had to do as we're told … London does as Paris dictates. I was afraid the New Hebridean leaders had lost all their faith in the British Administration.

This was all just stalling for time which suited the French who wanted to delay progress towards independence. What the National Party would do next I didn't know, but I could not see them sitting quietly for long, though they had been commendably restrained so far.

Janet and Horrie's Wedding

An example of Ida's involvement in the very close Lakatoro community follows, in her own words, in a letter to our children.

"Mary & Peter (my old friends) Darve and I decorated Darve's office and put in lots of flowers. Later we decorated the cakes which I had made previously, and Jerry Marston helped me make pillars to hold the top tier. All were ready for the wedding at 3.30 pm. Darve in the office, and Jerry drove Horrie in his car and John Bent drove Janet in our car—both open and decorated with ribbons. They looked very smart.

We had a nice little service with a choir to sing, we threw streamers and confetti and lots of photos were taken. Janet looked really nice in a fitted lace frock and veil and Horrie looked smart in Darve's suit. Afterwards, everyone came up to our house for afternoon tea, then we had to hurriedly dress and go down to the Metemet Club. Everything looked so nice down there with long tables set and filled to overflowing with food—*laplap*, pig, beef, and chicken. After eating, Darve made a very good speech, the couple cut the cake and asked me to cut it up—which I did and managed to divide the larger cake between 200 people! Janet and Horrie were very tickled to be able to take the top cake home with them. After the speeches, Henry danced his usual beautiful Hawaiian dance then the party started and everyone danced!

The only unfortunate incident was when Dresser James gave his wife a 'rabbit chop' to the back of her neck, pushed her down, and then dragged her out the door by one leg! It was awful! I wanted Darve to help but he really wasn't up to it after a lot of rum punch. However, the poor girl ran away next morning and James felt very sorry for himself the next day after spending the night in No 6 (the naughty person prison cell in Lakatoro gaol). Everyone sang, including Jerry, Henry, Morrison, Atis, and Avok with his usual number! There was a spirit of spontaneity and everyone enjoyed the evening immensely. Peter told me that all the men were finishing off the punch in Fanta cans! I guess he was right—it certainly had a kick!"

Twenty-Five

Vignette - General District Life in CD2

Here are a few reflections and observations on life and work in CD2 drawn from my experiences, particularly in 1972-1977.

Ida

Vanuatu was a very different kettle of fish, and so different to our balmy days in Tanganyika. I was far more involved in my work, with frequent touring. Although it was necessary to camp out on these tours—evidently not done by my predecessors—I realised that this was the only way I was going to familiarise myself with the local peoples' ways and, equally importantly, win some of their confidence in me. This meant that for the first time, Ida was frequently on her own for days on end, and in the long years ahead of us in Vanuatu, this became the norm. Ida found herself more often than not the sole white person living in a community of New Hebrideans. She accepted and adjusted to this way of life. A city girl born and bred, she had an admirable ability of getting along with people black, white, or brindle, and with her sense of humour and ready laugh, and her sympathetic ear for listening to those in trouble, she became loved very quickly. I look back now on those long and happy years in Vanuatu with admiration for the way she coped with all the trials and tribulations, and was always so understanding, with a warm and ready smile.

Lakatoro – A Garden of Eden

Whilst using my yam spade to transplant a small tree on my property at Bilambil Heights, Northern New South Wales, Australia, (also named Lakatoro), my thoughts went back to gardening in Lakatoro. This yam spade was purchased with British National Service funds for station maintenance in 1964. It was an especially good one, made in Sheffield with a narrower mouth than those subsequently manufactured. The narrow mouth facilitated the digging up of yams, some of which extended in length the height of an average man, straight down into the soil. It also made it easier to dig carefully around the yam without breaking the skin—once broken, a yam will begin to rot very quickly, whereas if there is no damage then it can be stored in a sheltered rack for many months.

But I have digressed. My great love during my leisure time (which was usually on a Sunday afternoon when I was not on tour), was to don my old clothes and my work boots, shoulder my precious yam spade, and go planting. I always came home from tour with cuttings of one sort or another, particularly an enormous variety of hibiscus. A couple of throws of the yam spade, which penetrated the extraordinarily deep topsoil very easily, loosened the soil. I would drive in a good stout cutting—maybe an inch thick—and press down, and within three months, I'd be guaranteed a new flowering shrub.

The New Hebridean to a man were extraordinarily good gardeners and always interested in ornamental plants. They would willingly give me as many cuttings as I wanted from any plant. As they grew to know my interest, they would take me out of their way to show me some unusual specimens.

I remember when Ida and I took the Small Nambas dance group to Fiji for the South Pacific Arts Festival, I was able to collect some very exotic plants, including a Hawaiian hibiscus with enormous dinner-plate-sized flowers. I planted this on the road which passed 100 metres below our house, and led from the District Office across the creek to the staff houses. I did this purposefully so I could keep an eye on it. It grew well, but never reached the height of more than about three feet, and this was because my prisoners could not resist taking a cutting for themselves when they were discharged. Over the years, an enormous range of hibiscus, crotons, frangipani, poinsettias, and garrya lined the corralled net of roads throughout the station. The creek banks were literally smothered with the lovely red rosella, and bougainvillea of every hue clambered over rocks and into trees.

Being a fanatical gardener, I realised as soon as I saw the land that became Lakatoro that it provided enormous potential, and my aim was to create around the station, its offices, quarters, and workshops, a parkland second to none. The fine existing trees, one as high as 100 feet, the service roads outlined in white limestone with a coral top dressing, the jungle-clad mountains rising precipitously immediately behind and to the west, all added to what was a picturesque village. As the years passed, even my French colleagues would bring their VIPs to Lakatoro to see its beauty.

I was fortunate in having the manpower in the form of prisoners to carry out my ideas. During my Sunday jaunts I would mark out new terraces—a bush clearing or a new path—ready for the Monday issue of orders, and on my return from tour, it would be all done.

I used to say to the local landowners—Sauli, Buomani, Simo, and the neigbouring villages at Senal, Tautu, Litzlitz, and Uripiv—Lakatoro would become the best District headquarters in the New Hebrides. This and the clearing pleased them very much, and they took pride in the station.

The good quality housing, particularly my own big dwelling, the water supply, the large new generators established in 1974, the electric bread oven, the Metemet Club with its enormous natora posts (which Atis with his usual tenacity and ingenuity procured from the hinterland with the aid of a tractor, trucks, and a big team of prisoners) were regularly shown off with pride by the locals to their visitors.

I was perhaps over fanatical about Lakatoro's appearance. I regularly did rounds (in good naval tradition) with my assistant (clerk, later ABDA) and OIC Police to see that rubbish was properly disposed of. The ubiquitous Foster's beer cans were my bête noire, but also any domestic rubbish, plastic bags, papers etc. My rounds, which usually took place on a Saturday morning, perhaps twice a month, also included an inspection of all the quarters, including police barracks, prison, workshops, and staff quarters. This gave me legal access to private homes (I suppose I was an intruder but people I think appreciated my interest and I gave them the opportunity to point out defects needing attention, and encouraged them to be tidy and to take pride in their homes).

I instituted an annual prize for the best house and garden and insisted that clothes lines be placed as inconspicuously as possible. I asked staff wives not to put out washing when we had VIPs visiting such as the Resident Commissioners, High Commissioners or other overseas government officials.

I looked on Lakatoro as my creation over the 13 years from its inception, and it was very heart wrenching to make my departure.

Queen's Birthday Celebrations

This was a British tradition throughout the New Hebrides, the French had their national Bastille Day celebration on July 14th, but never seemed to make as much of it as we did. At Lakatoro, in the early days the celebrations were minimal because there were insufficient personnel to do very much, however each year they became more and more important and more welcomed by the island population. By 1976 the celebrations had an attendance of 3000 people and I'd like to describe those celebrations as an example of Queen's Birthday Celebrations at their height.

First and foremost when the day began, was the 'raising of the colours'. The police detachment, in this case under the command of Sergeant Bambara, were well trained and rehearsed and accompanied by stirring broadcast military music. It was my duty to arrive formally in my Land Rover with Pennant flying, having literally been sewn into my traditional British uniform by Ida. Thankfully, I only had to wear it once a year. I would be bedecked in my traditional starched white Colonial Service uniform with Pith Helmet, high collar, brass tabs on the shoulders, and ceremonial sword. Upon arrival on the football field in front of the Metemet Club I would be met by the Sergeant of

Police who saluted and reported the guard ready for inspection. They would present arms while I inspected them, I would return to the Dais and the flag would then be hoisted by the marine officers, with the National Anthem booming out. This ended the formal part of the ceremony.

A procession of some ten floats circulated the field coming from north and south—some very spectacular and professional indeed. Custom dancing followed with different traditional dances from different villages. The education department with John Bent in charge of a team of willing teachers arranged the school sports which had always been an important feature of the celebrations. It was nice that we could overcome the seemingly insurmountable transport problems and bring in teams from all the outer islands, although this was not always possible.

At midday came the traditional feast, organised most years by Carpenter Atis Aviu and in an extremely efficient fashion including the cooking of a number of beasts both bullock and pigs. The 3000 villagers all were undoubtedly well fed. In the afternoon the presentation of prizes to the school children, custom dancers and the floats were presented by Ida, and at night came the traditional all night dance at the famous Metemet Club. For the dancing in the club and on the football field, music was provided by local and visiting bands, led by Sergeant Willie's police band. There was an enormous quantity of beer consumed, some 110 cartons I was told, and by the look of the 'sea' of empty cans on the football field the next day, I'd believe it. And thanks to the efficient organisation by the president of the Metemet Club, his committee and the police all of whom were on duty all night there were no untoward incidents to mar an altogether splendid evening.

My French Colleagues

Of my French colleagues I found Fabre the most cooperative to work with but perhaps a little lackadaisical. He was a very intelligent man and later went on to dizzy heights in the French Colonial Service based in Paris. Boileau his replacement however, was a different kettle of fish. He was younger than I with no children and threw himself into the job with great energy, determined to make inroads on my little empire. He was bumptious, but his English was better than my French, and unless he was very angry about something, when he lapsed into French, our discussions were normally in English. It was agreed that for District administration we would take turnabout monthly with court work and public works, one taking responsibility for Malekula the other the outer islands of Pentecost, Paama and Ambrym. I should record here that fairly early in the piece I had been able to persuade Vila that Epi should be reallocated to Vila because I had a far bigger area and population to deal with. The agreement with Boileau over work made a considerable difference to the workload and was a logical decision.

Volunteers

From the beginning I welcomed the VSO and other volunteers 'system' and they made considerable contribution to the District development, as well as the station life. Apart from their qualifications and experience and application of it to the jobs at hand, it was an opportunity for the local community and the areas where they worked to get to know young Europeans, and I am sure that the New Hebrideans benefited from it. The VSOs most certainly did. I think my first VSO officer was Roger, a school leaver who came to us at Lakatoro in 1966. He was a fitness fanatic who, when sitting on our verandah for afternoon tea, would be bouncing up and down on the balls of his feet or squeezing a ball to strengthen his wrists or his thigh muscles. I put him to work visiting the schools and taking PT classes. He did reasonably well considering his lack of experience and age. It would have been unreasonable to send him too far afield, so he worked on the eastern coast of Lakatoro returning to base at night. It was the qualified VSOs who were much more useful.

Before any qualified volunteers arrived, I had two further school leavers, one very difficult to utilise and the other very keen and willing to try his hand at anything, anywhere. He was based at Paama for a few months where the mission staff at Liro mothered him. He seemed to get on well with the Paamese and helped to build a school classroom there. When he returned to Lakatoro he had a shock of blond hair, which he asked Ida to cut. I can still see them on the verandah now with Ida hacking her way through the tangle of straw, which he reckoned had not seen soap and water for months.

By the early seventies I had as many as six volunteers at a time. I gather that most of my colleagues had no use for them so I always scored by taking on the unwanted ones. The latter were especially glad to get out of Vila, saying quite rightly that they had come to work with the local people and mix with them, not to work as glorified clerks in an urban society.

My innovative and ingenious carpenter, Atis Aviu, son of Chief Aviu, and magic man from Epi, was put to work building a VSOs quarter, which they quickly named "Home Sweet Home". It was constructed in local materials, plaited bamboo walls, and a thatched roof, (later we replaced this with galvanised iron). It had a cement floor, sewerage, hot and cold water, and was quite comfortable. As there was inevitably no funds to build this, the goat bag, together with written off furniture, did the job and had the auditors scratching their heads.

The agriculturally qualified volunteers worked closely with Barry Weightman, the New Hebrides' first genuine agricultural officer who contributed much to the development of agriculture in Vanuatu.

One of my engineering volunteers built the permanent cooperative store at Tautu. An architect built two dispensaries at Milip and Vunmavis. Tony the plumber erected water tanks with connecting supply to village centres on north-west Malekula, south-east Ambrym and Paama. With the best will in the world poor Tony was a constant headache, going off to isolated regions and forgetting to take the basic equipment, leaving a trail of hard won tools throughout the District which for a year after his departure we kept collecting.

Alan Hardiman, a builder, designed and built a fine European style house for our first permanent health sister, a New Zealander, Sister Ponninghouse. This we did have legal funds for.

Two volunteers, Colin Oram and Ian Hardy, worked hard to build the first clinic on Ahamb; Stuart Baldwin built a grand new classroom block at Tautu; and Peter Grealish, another builder, constructed the island's first abattoir at Loltong on North Pentecost. A string of volunteers including John Burdett and Roger Greenfield helped develop and oversee the burgeoning rural cooperative society network. Keith Farley Pettman, who had just begun as a banker with a London bank wasn't exactly practical, but he sang well, and organised concerts and the library in the Metemet Club.

The volunteers were a great crowd of young Englishmen, and we all enjoyed having them around. They would get fed up to the back teeth, sometimes living for months on end in isolated spots on the smell of an oily rag. Their allowance was pitifully small and they would be glad to get back to Home Sweet Home for a break and the local high life (the Metemet Club and small European community). But most of all they loved to sit on our verandah where my wife would serve them freshly baked banana cake with their tea and they would skylark with our kids, listen to their latest records and just relax.

When Ida and I went to England in 1990, Jerry Marston, my third and last ABDA, organised a reunion at Lydiard Millicent near Swindon, to which most of the Lakatoro volunteers came. Not one but all of them said in turn that it was the most wonderful two years of their lives and they would never forget it. Very rewarding.

Alan Hardiman from Bath subsequently asked us to dinner to see his home and meet the family. Alan's wife had baked a banana cake and brought a bottle of fresh milk. And therein lies a tale, because one of the first things I did when we settled in Lakatoro was to buy a cow and calf. Being a country lad by birth, fresh milk was not a luxury but a necessity. The next thing was to find someone to milk the cow, and I didn't think I could justify the time to teach someone to do it. Then right at our door step (I think it was Madeline Gidley at Bushman's Bay who told me) was Kilman. Madeline's father Mr Corlette had adopted him with a number of other New Hebridean children and he had taught him to milk. Kilman was a goldmine, a great and careful driver. He knew the island well and he became my henchman and stuck with me through thick and thin until my last days on Malekula. Kilman would never fail—rain, hail, hurricane or earthquake—to be there waiting for me with my Land Rover and a thermos of tea at the end of the road when I had struggled in, tired and dirty after a long walking tour. Well, Kilman milked my herd, and as the herd grew throughout our Lakatoro days, I would be very particular in making sure that a bottle of fresh milk was in the volunteers' fridge when they returned from tour. Unfortuately, we often had 'pink milk'! The cows loved consuming a vigorous weed with a bright red berry that grew in certain parts of the paddock and this gave the milk a revolting taste and turned it pink, much to the childrens' disgust!

The Big Nambas

When I took over Malekula in 1963 the majority of the Big Nambas tribe was renowned throughout the Pacific as cannibals and being warlike. People in villages still certainly remembered having eaten human flesh—typically the odd person picked off in war and carted away and divided amongst the men. It is very difficult to establish a date, but I think the last incidence of cannibalism would have been in or soon after the last war. Certainly there was some tribal fighting until much later, and in 1963, about the time I arrived, one of the plateau villagers had been picked off and shot. This was later amicably sorted out by an exchange of a girl in place of the man who was shot and payment of pigs in compensation.

The Big Nambas still wore the traditional dress. The term 'Big Nambas' is derived from the garment that they wear, a narrow strip of scarlet matting that is wound around the base of the penis and the fibre of this matting is not fully plaited. All the ends are left free to form a great plume of scarlet thread that is tucked up under a bark belt. Sometimes a number of bark belts may be worn. The belts, about eight inches thick, bulge out in an odd sort of way when a man walks or sits. Tom Harrison very aptly describes it as a "silent concertina". The garb exposes a man's testicles, again to quote Harrison, "left elegantly hanging and exposed". The men often wore trade beads, bracelets, armlets and a bone through the nose, and sometimes pig's hair earrings.

The majority had moved from the plateau on north-west Malekula, down to coastal villages. The villages were either Presbyterian, Catholic or, in the far north, Seventh Day Adventist. But the biggest village of all, Amok, was still inhabited by something like 200 Big Nambas, living in their primitive state with the paramount Chief Virhambath as their hereditary chief.

It goes without saying that the Big Nambas on the coast were Anglophone or Francophone according to the church that they had joined. The Francophone were Catholic, and Anglophone being Protestant, Presbyterian, or Seventh Day Adventist. The pagans up on the plateau resisted the proselytising of the various missions but because they were so well known throughout the group, they became the subject of much competition between my French colleague and I in our endeavours to 'win them over to our side', as it were. I had the advantage here because I don't think there was ever an occasion where my French colleagues, any of them, ever camped in the villages. This I always felt was one of the reasons I was able to obtain the confidence of so many of the people in the district.

I had in the first few months of my tenure on Malekula in 1963 concentrated on the villages scattered along the foreshores of this fertile, mountainous island, enriched from the volcanic ash showered upon it from the neighbouring island Ambrym. Scattered along the coast there were mission outposts and plantation owners, mostly French, who seemingly had little to do but shout at and complain about their Melanesian labourers and watch coconuts falling from geometric rows and rows of stately palms, onto the close-cropped lawns that were pastured by depressingly poor cattle.

It was now time to visit Chief Virhambath at Amok. I decided to go up to the plateau unescorted rather than with a posse of police as my predecessors had done, because of their renowned cannibal and warlike reputation. My intention was to endeavour to make a favourable impression on Virhambath without the obvious force of the law, with the long-term intention of establishing educational and medical facilities.

They were no longer cannibals and their internal wars were brought under control in the fifties. Kali the paramount chief who was feared by both missionaries and blackbirders alike was now dead, succeeded by his son Virhambath. Virhambath had resisted pressure from the missionaries to move down to the coast. He tenaciously clung to live with his 200 odd tribesmen in the way of life followed by his ancestors over the centuries. Sporadic fighting still occurred, with the rest of the Big Nambas ostensibly now living on the coast and converted to Christianity. These disputes were predominantly over the exchange of women, bride price and land. Fear of the law had certainly eradicated the practice of cannibalism.

I set out across the waist of the island with my essentials: toiletries, mosquito net, change of clothes, a billy can, tea, sugar and the luxury of a packet of Marie biscuits. I walked with a porter from Norsup to Brenwe; about three hours. The track through the heavy vegetation and rainforest was reasonably well defined and by afternoon, wet with sweat, I descended the escarpment to the western coast.

After a quick dip in the azure blue sea I trudged along the coral encrusted beaches to the Catholic village of Brenwe, then on to the Presbyterian village of Leviamp where I knew I would have a welcome from the government assessor and Elder, Paul.

Paul had abandoned his penis wrapper, donned shorts, and been converted to Presbyterianism ten years previously, and had settled on the coast. Paul showed me to my abode for the night, the PWMU (Presbyterian Women's Mothers Union) hut. His wife brought me a newly woven pandanus mat.

Paul helped me rig my mosquito net and showed me a superb freshwater pool by the beach where I bathed. Refreshed, I sat down on the beach and watched the sun sink down over the horizon, gently into the sea. Paul called me to *kaikai* and we sat cross-legged in his smoke-filled kitchen whilst his wife removed the oven stones with bamboo tongs and unfolded the *laplap* leaves encasing the evening meal. My heart sank when he revealed an entire flying fox with wings outspread encased in a pudding of grated yam and coconut milk. The odour was overpowering and though I knew that the French considered flying fox a luxury, I could not face it. In desperation and as diplomatically as possible I explained that eating such meat was contrary to my custom, but I would relish the pudding. With a ubiquitous bush knife he carved off a large hunk of pudding and I ate gingerly whilst they hoed into the dismembered flying fox. A hot tea followed and I then slept like the proverbial log.

After a breakfast of tea and cold, rather stodgy *laplap*, Paul said he would guide me up to the Big Nambas plateau. We set out through the flat, lightly timbered coastal fringe towards the hills. After an hour or so we began to climb and the undergrowth became denser. I was thankful for Paul in more ways than one. Like all Melanesians he wielded his bush knife with great skill and slowly we pushed our way through seemingly impenetrable entanglements of shrubs, vines and fallen trees bowled over by frequent hurricane winds. Another hour and we were climbing a much steeper escarpment, sometimes following a rocky stream, sometimes cutting our way through jungle. Sometimes Paul would call out "lukaot nangalat"—a most vicious stinging nettle.

By mid-afternoon, Paul and I had reached the plateau; the countryside levelling out into rolling hills, covered with wild cane and large spreading trees. Another hour and we began to see signs of cultivation, cleared land, yam gardens with their elaborate trellises of wild cane stem frond stalks, and the coloured leaves of the manioc plants and kava. There were more clearly defined narrow muddy tracks now leading in various directions, and again I was thankful of Paul's familiarity with the terrain.

Suddenly we came across a clearing with a thatched building with a beehive like façade and tiny entrance with a bamboo, waist high barricade. Five men, clay pipes in hand, came clumsily out over the barricade to look at us with astonishment. Paul evidently explained our presence, and one by one we shook hands. Each was dressed in the traditional garb.

A long conversation followed and they signalled for me to go into the *nakamal*. The entrance was only a tiny one, which you had to crawl through to get inside. It was as dark as pitch and it took some time for my eyes to adjust, when I saw a small, smouldering fire and a few coconut shells scattered around. We sat cross legged on some *laplap* leaves used as mats and when the fire was stoked a little, with a small glimmer of flame, I saw skulls against the back walls—victims or ancestors I did not enquire. Paul said that Virhambath was working in his garden with one of his seven wives. We waited; Paul and the others chattered away while I closed my eyes to rest them from the smoke and dozed off. Paul's voice "Virhambath" penetrated my brain and I woke to find Virhambath standing in front of me with his hand outstretched and a slight smile on his face.

He was an imposing figure, small in stature with thick broad shoulders and muscle-bound legs, and unlike the others was clean shaven, a stone and piglet tail tips in each ear and of course his nambas. We shook hands and he squatted beside me whilst we talked a little pidgin but mostly through Paul. I explained that I wanted to get to know him and his people and that this was a brief visit, but I hoped to come more regularly. Finally I asked if he could organise some water and a place to sleep. Paul who was more au fait with European ways, negotiated for an empty, and thankfully new, yam storage shed. After, there was another interestingly long conversation, and finally I thought I saw two men go off somewhat reluctantly to get my water.

At the time I was ignorant to the fact that the biggest problem here was the lack of water, because the Big Nambas only used water for mixing with kava. They never used it for washing, as washing was not part of their way of life. When I arrived and called for water, it was a major exercise to persuade anyone to go to get it. It meant walking for at least three or four miles to the nearest spring. (On subsequent visits I usually had to pay someone to collect water). The method of collecting it was with a length of bamboo. The various segments would be cut out and then the bamboo filled with water and the top plugged with a plug of leaves. A bamboo six feet long and probably the diameter of a billycan would carry a considerable amount of water. Probably at least three or four buckets and it would be quite heavy to carry. Virhambath and Paul chatted away and again I dozed off. An hour later when I was organising myself for the night in the yam shed, the young men returned with my length of bamboo full of water. It made a great water receptacle. Paul rigged it up on a forked stick and showed me that by tilting it forward on the fork, I had a great water supply for a shower bath.

As I was left alone for the night, I boiled my billy and had a delicious cup of tea, even down to a tube of condensed milk and sugar. I then stripped down, got out my soap and towel and began to relish a shower. It really was very welcome because it had been a hot long walk and I was very sticky and very tired. The water was cold and fresh. I soaped up well from head to foot, congratulating myself on this great life and enjoying the fresh cool night. I pulled the end of the bamboo forward again, uncorking the leaf plug. Suddenly the fork in the supporting stick broke, down came the bamboo, splitting its length and my beautiful water soaked rapidly into the dry ground. There was I, lathered in soap, with not a drop of water! I began scraping off some of the lather, cursing my luck. I suddenly had the inspiration about a solution and remembered that there was still a bit of tea left in my teapot. Teaspoon by teaspoon I frugally washed away the soap. When I got home two days later I still had tea leaves in my hair.

I was no sooner dry and dressed and smelling of tea, than Paul appeared and summoned me to the *nakamal*. There I found Virhambath and a dozen men squatting by a tiny fire, while three youths sat laboriously chewing kava root before spitting it out into a very chipped enamel hand basin, no doubt procured from a trader many years ago. From a small bamboo container a little water was added and the mixture stirred into a rich brown liquid. Virhambath took a coconut shell from the ground near him and scooped a generous portion, and ceremoniously presented it to me. My thoughts flashed back to the terribly poor teeth of the youths who had done the chewing, of tuberculosis and other terrible diseases. I thought, desperately searching for some custom taboo which might get me out of the fix, but nothing came to mind. There was no help at hand. I closed my eyes and drank it down, struggling not to gag, keeping my mind on other things. I sat back on my mat whilst Virhambath and others finished their draught in turn with much hawking and spitting.

I began to feel the effects at once on my lips, mouth and throat, numb, almost as though I had had an anaesthetic, and I felt lazily carefree. The youths were still chewing noisily and another batch was soon prepared. This time it was not quite such an effort. After all, the kava would kill off any germs, and, oh, what the hell. The second shell went down much more easily and I hawked and spat with the best of them. I made my way back to my mat somewhat unsteadily. My eyes were watering with all the smoke. Getting up for the third shell was much more difficult as my legs did not seem to want to function as they should, and one of my aides came to my rescue and brought my shell of kava back to me. I quaffed and lay back, my tealeaf-matted hair in the dust. Someone spat over the top of me and I felt a spray of saliva settle like a shower of rain upon me. I was too comfortable to move, my thoughts wafted like the breeze and I was pleasantly content.

I woke with a start to see a glimmer of light through the tiny opening of the *nakamal*—there were prostrate figures sleeping soundly all around me. Someone stirred, took a lump of wood and stoked the coals. A flame shot up and he lay back to sleep again. Still groggy, I crept to the entrance and with daylight I found my way back to my camp bed of leaves, praying for a little cold tea, but alas there was none. I crashed again.

Virhambath himself woke me up about nine with a great slab of yam and a coconut opened and ready to drink. It was more than welcome and the hangover I was dreading did not eventuate. We spent the morning visiting several *nakamals*, and with the aid of interpreters (quite a few of the men spoke pidgin), settled a dispute over bride price and issued several chiefs with gun licences. In the early days they had traded island produce for guns from traders.

The women stood aside as we passed by on narrow paths. They all wore low, over the hips scarlet grass skirts and an elaborate heavy plaited purple-red headdress the same colour as the men's nambas.

In the afternoon after learning that the descent to Brenwe was much closer than Leviamp, I set off with Paul. It was certainly a much easier walk down and we arrived at Brenwe at dusk. A Belgian missionary greeted me and insisted I stay the night. After an early breakfast of crusty bread and café au lait I set off for the east coast and home.

Over the years I was to get to know the Big Nambas very well. It was not long before I was able to arrange with Virhambath to have a small hut built as a rest house near the village of Amok. There I used to go and camp, sometimes taking a policeman and sometimes going by myself. There were always disputes to be settled, over land, bride price, and the exchange of women. Poor old Virhambath, he was pressurised from both sides; there was no doubt about that. Whenever he came down to the coast he was fêted and up in the hills he was offered everything from schools, dispensaries and roads and even showered with gifts, if not by government, then by the odd tourist who appeared. But I was never able to persuade them to accept a school or a dispensary.

With regard to 'tourists' to Big Nambas, I remember particularly a pseudo-anthropologist, an American, who had spent quite a bit of time amongst the pagan villages on south Pentecost and who came to Malekula and asked me if he could spend a few weeks or even months working with the Big Nambas at Amok. There was no reason I could object, provided he got a clearance from Virhambath himself. This he did, and I remember on one occasion going up to Amok to see how things were going, and there was Karl in the local regalia, a nambas with belt and all, and a very, very sunburnt white bottom!

Once I saw Virhambath at a cocktail party which the French District Agent was giving at Port Sandwich. Virhambath was standing there with his nambas on and his bark belt, quaffing a glass of champagne, and for the occasion, he had added a ladies 'bolero' a little short jacket without sleeves. He looked a real card with his woollen bright red bolero and his nambas—rather striking in amongst the European members of the congregation.

One school holidays I took the whole family up to Amok. We were able to boat to the other side of the island and walk from Brenwe up the mountainside to the village. I took the precaution of having the porters and a couple of sturdy policemen to help carry Peter, who was then only a boy of about five. He got very fed up with what was quite a hard walk. Although the police carried him the last few miles, he did very well. But he several times complained very angrily to me, saying, "Dad, why don't you do something about making these Nambas build a road?"

The family created quite a stir. We camped in my little hut and had two days walking around visiting people. The children especially fascinated the women folk. We went to see one of Virhambath's seven wives, who was squatting inside her own little house with the eaves built of thatch; natungura leaf right down to the ground with a tiny opening. The tiny openings, by the way, were attained from the days of warfare when it was easy to block the door and prevent raiders coming in. She sat at the entrance to this door, dark as pitch inside, and when I brought the family up, Peter peered in, naturally curious. Virhambath's wife was so thrilled that she grabbed him in both her rather smoky arms and pulled him inside. Peter turned quite pale. I think he thought his last day had come!

On tour around the Big Nambas coast, I passed through all the villages in turn, whether they were Catholic, Presbyterian, or Seventh Day Adventist, but for the most part I would camp in the Presbyterian villages. The village I liked particularly to camp in was Leviamp. Nearby to the village was a superb little stream with a great swimming pool and I used to enjoy my swim there in the evening before changing to get ready for the evening meetings. I didn't learn until years later that there were a couple of enormous eels living in that pool. Apparently one was about five feet long. Fortunately I never made contact with it. My great old friend there was Elder Paul. He was an elder in the Presbyterian Church at this stage and he used to enjoy looking after me when I arrived. I would usually sleep in the Presbyterian Mothers' Union building where mats would be spread out for me and I would set up my lilo (blow up mattress which I always carried) and my mosquito net. Then Paul would insist on personally cooking for me at night.

We would sit together in the kitchen, sitting on a mat, around the fire where the meal had been cooked. It would usually be rice, a bit of fish or a *laplap*, the local pudding. Afterwards we would have some great yarns. On one occasion, when I got to know him better, I asked him whether he had had any experience of cannibalism. He looked quite sheepish and smiled and said yes, he had tasted human flesh when he was a younger man. I then asked him what it tasted like and what was the most favoured part. He leant over and felt my forearm and smiled and said that was the bit he liked most and it tasted just like turtle.

Many years later (in 1988) I returned to Malekula and Amok with Simon, and lo and behold, we were able to drive by Land Rover across the island to the plateau. There was now a fine road over which the jungle was fast encroaching. Later this was to be called 'Wilkins Road'. Most of the houses were deserted, their inhabitants unable to resist the call of the coast and civilisation. There, sadly, was Virhambath with his seven wives and about four or five staunch supporters.

However it was Elder Paul whom I wanted to see on that last trip. The coastal road continued on to Leviamp and it was a great thrill to me to drive along it. A road which I had envisaged on the many times I had walked along the coast—crossing the very familiar creeks and skirting the little bays brought back many memories. We got to Leviamp village to find it half deserted. I asked for Elder Paul and was told that he had moved and his wife had died. They indicated a path to follow. I later got the story, which was a new church had quite recently taken over in Leviamp, 'Holiness Fellowship' it was called. Most of the villagers had been converted to this new following, but Elder Paul had stuck to his guns and because of this had been ostracised and forced out of the village. He had moved on to what was in fact his own land on the next peninsula, about two miles further on. So I walked on round the old path that I used to follow to his little hamlet.

When I got there, there was Paul pottering around just outside. He was bending over cutting coconuts with his bush knife. I called out and he stood up. "Olfalla mi come back now." He looked up. His eyes were not very good, his beard now white, and his once muscly legs now skinny. He peered at me. "Masta?" he said, and realising who I was, came forward and embraced me, kissed me on both cheeks and then he began to cry. I confess that I wept with him too. I left with him some clothing, including my father's old cardigan. At least it was warm. Poor recompense for his hospitality and friendship over so many years.

The Big Nambas reputedly had homosexual leanings, and it is said that the men took young boys and retained them as a sort of personal servant as well as lover until the year they were circumcised. I never saw any evidence of this myself and I think it was probably fairly unusual. It certainly is today very unusual generally with the Melanesian people in the New Hebrides. However it is certainly not unusual for example to see young men and adult men as well, holding hands. Physical contact I think in primitive peoples generally is much more prevalent and much more natural than it is in our own society.

There was one amusing incident in this regard. One day, Jerry Marston, my Assistant British District Agent and I, were visiting one of the Big Nambas villages, the village of Brenwe-Unmet, on the west coast. Jerry had not long arrived from England as a young English cadet. Virhambath and his eldest son, Nesai, who was later to succeed him as paramount chief, met us. Nesai was quite adult; I think he would have been into his thirties by that stage. I talked to them for a while and then Nesai signalled to me that he wanted to talk to me privately, and we walked down towards the beach. As we did so he moved across closer to me and took me by the hand and we walked hand in hand down to the beach and had a discussion. I think it was about a gun licence that he wanted, and then walked back again still hand in hand. When we got back, Jerry was looking at me goggle-eyed. Later he told me that he was rather taken aback until I was able to explain to him that it was quite acceptable to walk hand in hand with another man.

Over the years, there were terrible land problems on the north-west coast of Malekula where the Big Nambas had moved down from the plateau onto the coast. It was sad, because the land on the plateau was superb, wonderful for cattle grazing and it had tremendous potential. But people wanted to move onto the coast to have the advantages of ships calling, trading, co-operative stores, schools, and of course, above all, the missions. It was the missions who were instrumental in moving people. This was, in the long run, a mistake no doubt. It was understandable that people would want to come down to the coast. I have to admit that I never did win the battle for Amok ascendancy over Virhambath and his people and their support for the British side. Virhambath finally agreed to send his children to the French Catholic School at Unmet and his followers all joined the Catholic mission there. He himself was the last to live and die at Amok.

Pigs

Pigs were a vital part of traditional life. More so in Amok amongst the pagan people than elsewhere, but everywhere pigs were, and still are, vitally important. I once saw a baby pig being dealt with in order that it would grow the rounded, lower jaw tusks. In this case the operation was carried out by the pig owner, who seized the unfortunate little animal, it could not have been more than a couple of months old, and gouged out the two top teeth with a bush knife. It was a horrible sight and the unfortunate pig must have suffered terribly. They suffered for the rest of their lives because the tusks grew and rubbed against the upper jaw bones then turned back in a full circle, pushing back into the lower jaw and quite often pushing the lower molars out of the jaw as they turned. So the pig suffered a constant toothache. They were always sickly, the tusk pigs, and were tethered or kept in special pens with the fencing being padded with banana or *laplap* leaves so that when the pig rubbed his aching jaws against the post, the tusks were less likely to break.

Of course, the greater the number of turns the more valuable the pig and on Pentecost, for example, for the Queen's visit to New Hebrides in 1974, I was able to purchase a tusk from one of the local chiefs which had turned three complete circles. This was presented to the Queen in a very nicely made case made out of the local well-known hardwood, natora. She in turn presented it back to the cultural centre in Vila, and there it can still be seen. On north Ambrym, Chief Tienmal, whose son was Chief Tofor, was the most highly graded chief on north Ambrym and greatly feared. He ate at Tabu Fires, which meant that he alone could cook for himself. No one else was allowed to cook for him, or to eat with him, or come near him when he was eating. Tienmal wore something like 20 or 30 tusks on each arm for any ceremonial occasion, very imposing and a very dramatic sight.

Pigs of course posed a health problem. Every man owned pigs and marauding pigs were a constant problem. They ate into people's gardens and led to constant complaints, so that I always endeavoured to enforce the enclosure of pigs. This was not always welcomed, particularly by the pagan people. It was against their tradition and they felt that pigs should be given priority.

Travel and Toilet Facilities

On Vao Island, pigs roamed freely all over the island despite the fact that it was very heavily inhabited. There were no toilets and so people would defecate just beyond the precincts of their houses, leaving the pigs to clean up the mess. Inevitably, intestinal worms thrived. It never ceased to astonish me that on Vao where there was a very strong Catholic church with a number of medical sisters, no effort was made to encourage the construction of pit latrines. There was legislation under the Native Code to allow the District Agents to prosecute people who had not built and used pit latrines and I had no hesitation in using this legislation, when necessary. I kept up a constant barrage of propaganda about it and fell back on the legislation only as a last resort. On the other hand it was contrary to local tradition and was therefore very difficult for some people to accept, but you can imagine the health hazards that arose because of the lack of such hygiene. I had the support of one colleague in the latrine blitz and that was Boileau. He was as notorious as I for storming around the village and inspecting latrines. A dreadful job, but I gather that he would walk up to a latrine and if it wasn't properly built, he would give it a heave and push it over. This used to cause a great deal of merriment, but if no action was taken he would be hot on their tracks to prosecute the next time he came back. I did much the same thing and I think we got quite good results there.

Nonetheless, it was always a hazardous adventure having to use the local latrines when camping in the villages. One would be ceremonially escorted to what was considered to be the most up to date latrine in the village. That was always bad enough but I would hate to have had to use the worst ones.

People were incredibly kind and hospitable when I camped in the villages. They always seemed pleased and I would inevitably be given the best house in the village if I didn't have my own permanent rest house, which I did later organise in strategic spots. I would not only be given the best house but I would be given someone's mattress, someone else's clean bed sheets and so on. I could not have been made more welcome at any time. At night, I never asked for, but was always given a bucket of hot water, which was a luxury indeed, and a cup, and escorted to the side of a house or an empty shed or somewhere, for my bath. It is amazing what a good shower you can have with just one bucket of water and a cup.

Food

More often than not, I was brought the local traditional meal, which would be *laplap*, reasonably edible, sometimes terribly heavy. Banana *laplap* and taro *laplap* were extremely indigestible. On the other hand, yam was extremely good, provided it had a bit of salt. It was always cooked in the stones, root vegetable with coconut milk mixed into it, and more often than not, a tin of bully beef or some part of chicken cooked in with it. Quite often I would be given rice. In the villages rice was always expertly cooked and quite often I would be given curried chicken or curried tinned meat with it, and sometimes pork. I was not so enthusiastic about pork, because more often than not it was not properly cooked and I had visions of what it might have eaten and what vermin it carried. I always carried some food, but usually brought it back unused.

I certainly carried a tube of condensed milk and sugar because I could never survive without tea numerous times a day. I was well known for my tea drinking habits and used to get served up tea whenever I arrived in any village and it was always very welcome, despite the fact that it was often extremely weak. Leaf tea, it was called. All this was very much in contrast to the old days of the safaris in Africa where one carried everything but the kitchen sink, and had a meal served sitting up in state, served up by one's cook.

Marine Services

The arrival of the 'Euphrosyne' at Isangel on its maiden voyage commanded by Captain Harry Kirkwood, Marine Superintendent with the Resident Commissioner, John Rennie on board was a major triumph for the British National Service. Once again, it finally had a touring vessel for its officers. Amongst his newly recruited young crew was Leith Nassak of Tanna, who was later to command the 'Euphrosyne' himself, and after Independence became the Vila Harbour Master. Martin Ligo, who was captain of my vessel the 'Ida', also later captained the 'Euphrosyne'. In fact this initial crew formed the nucleus of a very fine batch of sailors who were to be responsible for our expanded Marine Service—'Mangaru', 'Keo', 'Lopevi' and the 'Ida'.

Harry Kirkwood was a typical R.N. Officer—a big man with a commanding presence. He called a spade a spade, and had no fear of telling anyone off, from the most junior officer to the Resident Commissioner himself. Harry made many tours for me and members of the Lakatoro staff; I found him most helpful and obliging. He accepted my rather erratic and unpunctual life style when touring, but nonetheless never hesitated to blast me off the decks when I was late or brought back prisoners to serve their term in Lakatoro prison. He hated to see anything come aboard which might have vermin or just dirt—his ship was always spotless in true Royal Navy tradition.

The 'Euphrosyne' was a great little ship, sturdy and quite luxurious by our standards at the time. I always enjoyed my tours in her, and always felt safe. This was more than I could say in the 'Ida', when with an inexperienced and young crew, we would be trapped in a poor anchorage or none at all with a hurricane blowing up.

I recall one occasion when Naika Samson of Uripiv was the captain of the 'Ida' and we were anchored off Nebul north Ambrym. Ashore I heard that a hurricane was on its way and I hurried back to the 'Ida'. Naika felt that we should run for Port Stanley and home, but my advice was to run for the nearest hurricane shelter where hopefully there was a lighthouse to guide us in. Darkness fell as we left the lee of Ambrym for the run across the channel to Port Sandwich—there was already a high wind on our starboard bow and a greasy high swell. I could see that Naika was worried—so of course, was I. I just prayed that the lighthouse on the southern Port Sandwich headland was operating. The seas built up rapidly and we rolled alarmingly. I was in a cold sweat until we caught sight of the beacon flashing and we steamed safely into calm waters. Port Sandwich offered one of the finest harbours in the group and we spent the next three long days sitting there waiting for the hurricane to pass over, hoping all was well at Lakatoro.

My constant cry at Lakatoro was for shipping, above all a vessel of my own. The dream came true with the arrival of the sister ship to the Lopevi allocated to the geological survey and cooperatives. Following the tradition of one of the early predecessors, Mr Adam, who called his little vessel the Honey after his daughter (whom I met on Norfolk Island in 1996), it was decided to name the new vessel after my wife 'Ida'—much to her consternation. The ship was 30 feet long and whilst not a luxury vessel, the cabin was taken up by a very large engine, which to my joy could move us along at up to nine knots and had seats running either side fore and aft. The interior cabin contained cooking facilities, a shower, toilet and bunks for the crew of two—skipper and engineer. Canvas blinds stopped most of the weather in normal times and when we dined together at anchorage—the skipper cooking the eternal rice and tinned meat, or occasionally tuna steaks if our drag line had been lucky—we used the engine top as a table.

From her arrival the 'Ida' was put to constant hard work and it was not long before Harry was on my back, saying the ship had to have time off for maintenance, and the crew compensating time off from work. It was Harry who had the wonderful proposal that I have two crews. After obtaining the necessary funds, I built a double Class 9 house down at the jetty where my crews were housed with the 'Ida' tied up some 50 yards distant. It was a great arrangement, apart from the regular trips to Vila for slipping, the little vessel was constantly at sea, having greater and greater demands as the station staff multiplied.

The wharf was constructed of rock and coral, extending about 40 yards into the channel. It was wide enough to allow a Land Rover to run its length which facilitated loading tremendously. After being partially damaged by hurricane, it was rebuilt with sophistications such as electric light, and running water piped down from the spring. A carpenter even built a comfortable bench seat at the end of the wharf where the station members would often sit and enjoy the lapping of the waves on the outer reefs. The initial construction was built from the ever-present goat bag (in this case unaccounted-for funds earned from copra and pig sales etc) but eventually when its importance was realised, I was able to fund it legitimately in my budget.

I make no bones about the fact that the 'Ida' was my pride and joy. It enabled efficient administration of the district. It gave me a tremendous edge over my colleague who was dependent on the occasional French vessels based in Vila and the two condominium vessels.

On returning alone from leave from Australia one time, ABDA Jerry Marston and education officer John Bent had played a practical joke on me. They had gathered sufficient wreckage, closely resembling the 'Ida', to a place on a small reef outcrop about 500 yards east of the Lakatoro passage. They knew full well that as I flew in down low over Port Stanley, making the run to land at Norsup I would be scrutinising the station and of course the passage. They hoped that I would pick up the wreckage, identifying to my horror that it was the 'Ida'. In the end the joke did not come off as I think the wreckage was washed away by the high tide before I arrived. It would certainly have hit home if it had come to pass.

The condominium vessels were the 'Don Quixote' (Captain Jack Barley) and the 'Rocinante' (Captain Guenet, and then Captain Bochenski). The Resident Commissioner's touring vessel 'Don Quixote' on which I rarely travelled, was not a very practical touring vessel, whereas the 'Rocinante' was a fine seaworthy vessel and ideal for district touring.

In the early days when shipping was a premium Duc Dufayard and I were able to procure the 'Rocinante' for a joint fortnight long tour, every three to five months. Occasionally we chartered the 'Trudy' run by the Paul brothers, again a good sea going vessel which was eventually lost in a hurricane with all hands.

Fabre and I used the 'Bonite' on a charter from time to time. She certainly tossed about in any sort of sea. Overall the Pacific Ocean was more often rough than calm and consequently touring was usually exceedingly uncomfortable. The 'Rocinante' and the 'Bonite' always smelt to high heaven and obviously needed a good spring clean. The 'Mangaru', on the other hand, like the 'Euphrosyne', was always spotless thanks to Captain Kirkwood's training.

Using vessels for touring was not without hazards—not including inclement weather and rough seas, crossing from South Pentecost to Ambrym was the biggest. It was a distance of about eight miles and if you broke down, there was nothing to stop you being carried by currents to the ice flows of Antarctica. I very soon decided it was foolish in the extreme and remembering I had a family at home, gave up the practice. This did not stop the growing practice of using unsuitable open speed boats to ply between Pentecost and Ambrym and Pentecost and Maewo. There were occasions where boats and passengers disappeared without a trace.

Speed boats along the coast to get from, say north Ambrym to the west, the two centres of population separated by a day's walking through unpopulated rugged country, were useful and one could always paddle ashore.

Newsletter and Clubs

There were two things I always had an ambition to start up in the District – the first a newsletter and the second a club.

The newsletter was not a success. I began it on Tanna with Richard Tarileo, my clerk. There were only copies run in English, which was a mistake anyway and news was hard to find. I wish I could remember how many copies we made and I wish I could find just one copy to refresh my mind on what we wrote, but anyway it was a failure and in due time died a natural death. The British Newsletter issued in Vila, quickly took its place anyhow and was welcomed throughout the villages.

I had thought a lot about a social club on Tanna but had neither the resources nor the confidence to try. The Tannese were somehow always suspicious, looking for a hidden motive perhaps and it would probably have never gotten off the ground.

Central district 2 however was quite different. There on Malekula people were glad to see me around, they welcomed the establishment of a British District agency at Lakatoro and there was obviously a need for a social get together at the right venue. It was important that we should make social contact with our neighbours, and that we should set a standard and pattern for similar village clubs. Initially we held occasional dances in Lakatoro's first bush classroom and everyone on the station and neighbouring villages turned up.

Early in the piece Tony Womer, the media representative in Vila, had sent up a 16 millimetres projector and some British Information films. One of my first requests to the Australian Consul in Noumea when he visited us was to procure more films and later refer us to a private commercial supplier of films. This was to be another function at the club.

The Metemet Club Updated

The Metemet Club was originally built in 1966 and used extensively by the station and its inhabitants. However, it really came into its own in the seventies when it was refurbished. With Atis and his team having access to substantial funds from my goat bag, we were able to refurbish and extend the original building. Atis and Wilben between them with a tractor and prisoners dragged new enormous natora logs (2 ft 6in in diameter) down from the mountain side to replace the now rotting originals. The roof was repaired from many thousands of leaf thatch that were ordered from throughout Malekula and Pentecost, and arrived on any vessel available over a long period of time. Simon helped build the club as an apprentice carpenter working with Atis. He was paid a princely sum of $10 a month for this privilege. I recall he also painted the front door sign "Metemet Club" in old fashioned gothic script which stood out somewhat against the bamboo and thatch. Everyone loved it though.

With a raised stage and a cement floor, it made a magnificent auditorium, opening out onto the playing field which had been cleared by winching out the necessary coconut trees (thus reducing my revenue for the 'goat bag').

Local bands were very easily procurable and vied for the honour of playing at a Saturday night dance which became a regular feature. Occasionally the odd young French official from Norsup would come along, but for the most part the European community was predominantly English speaking. The New Hebridean community came in great numbers. It was not unusual to have as many as 500 attend a Saturday night dance. Film nights were also a great success.

Best of all it was a wonderful venue for the Queen's Birthday celebrations, the biggest festival of the year where we would sometimes get as many as 2000 for the evening club celebrations. Lakatoro concerts became a feature, particularly with the innovative ideas initiated by Barry Weightman. The volunteers, New Hebridean and European staff all took part. Probably one of the best ever received acts was when Barry Weightman, George Hart and I were prisoners in a makeshift barred prison on the back of the station truck and George Hart endeavouring to escape got his head stuck in between the bars and had considerable difficulty in getting it free.

A committee had been formed to run the Club. Very early in the piece the question of an alcohol licence came up. New Hebrideans were permitted to access alcohol in the 1960s by John Rennie. I always sat in on club meetings as an ex officio member. I reluctantly agreed knowing that my colleague would also agree. In the event that there was excessive drinking at dances, there was always a policeman on duty, but there were rarely any serious difficulties.

The most difficult event was always the Queen's Birthday celebrations when alcohol flowed freely and there was always the odd skirmish, particularly as the night wore on towards dawn. It was not too often that things got too out of hand. The request from the club for a spirit licence I stalled for several years, agreeing in the mid-seventies, by which time the club had been extended again. There was very little abuse of the system and the bar meant that drinking in the home was reduced which I felt was a good thing.

With the extensions came a library, social room, another bar, and toilets with septic tank and running water. The installation of a chromed urinal which was ordered directly from Australia caused a stir among the men. It was a sign that Lakatoro was moving into the urbanised life style of Vila.

The Metemet Club ended up being the biggest local material building (except for the cement floor) in the district and created great interest throughout the islands. It stands much the same today and is the major meeting place for Malampa province. It is known as *Nimbaou* (meeting place)

Apprentices

It was the constant refrain of being asked to take an outboard motor back to base for repairs and seeing old Jeeps rusting away in the villages that made me think hard about giving some sort of mechanic training to some of the many uneducated youth in the villages. There were many abandoned vehicles on south east Ambrym in particular, which had a reasonable network of tracks and where ex US Army Jeeps had been brought in by the McCoys for their plantation and the many Tonkinese storekeepers.

The very limited opportunities in Vila were only open to youths who had at least got to one of the main high schools. In a very modest way I began an apprenticeship system at Lakatoro which served very well. For each of my trained or at least partly qualified staff, (mostly through experience rather than professional training), I would have one or two apprentices taken from chosen centres of population. Eventually I always had two apprentice mechanics, apprentice carpenters, electricians and even an apprentice painter. Without official funds to pay for them, their accommodation and rations, my goat bag would save the day. Apprentices would stay for about a year, or sometimes more, and then return to their villages where they could at least have a modicum of ability in fixing an outboard motor, cementing a floor, erecting a water tank etc. etc.

Tautu Land

It was not until 1975 on my return from leave, that I decided that this tour would be our final one and I began announcing this fact as I toured the District. One day after a meeting at Tautu, there seemed to be so many of them over the PRNH vs Tautu land matters and the airfield issues etc, Keneri pulled me aside. He said I should consider building a house on Malekula for our retirement. I laughed and said yes, there was nothing I would like to do better, but that I had commitments in Australia. We had made our minds up that we would return back to Dubbo to live, but I hoped to come back from time to time to retain our contacts with the islands.

Months later Keneri said to me that he had discussed the matter with Assessor and Chief David Apia and the village, and they had agreed that they would give me some land up in the valley behind Lakatoro where I should build myself a holiday house. The land would be for me and my children and their children. I was very taken aback and moved by this offer and said that I sincerely hoped that this might one day come to pass. It was not until 1980 when I returned for the Independence celebrations when I spent some time at Lakatoro, that Keneri offered to show me the site he proposed I should use. It was indeed a superb site on a small section of level land on the valley slopes facing north, with a magnificent enormous Banyan tree, a Natora and a black bean. It was evidently the site of a very old Nakamal. Even more enticing was a small stream which meandered down the slope from a source, a spring farther up. It was evidently a part of the same underground water supply that supplied Lakatoro and Litzlitz over the rise, a mile or so to the east.

The idea occupied my thoughts on many occasions after this and in 1987 when Simon and I visited Vanuatu, we walked over the site again and envisaged construction of a vehicular track and of a hurricane proof modest dwelling. In 1991 Peter and I did a foot tour together of south Malekula and again visited the site. Keneri again raised the matter, but over time I began to realise that despite the temptations it would not be practical because apart from the initial costs, there was the question of maintenance and access—not only from Australia but even within Vanuatu. The need to safeguard any investment with some sort of secure title was an action I was not prepared to even attempt. So the pipe dream was abandoned. I had however been tempted with investing in a property (as did my colleague Boileau) in Vila and continued to pursue this idea.

Masing Lauru

Early on in the development of the Lakatoro staff team, a young Ifira Islander Massing Lauru joined me as the junior administrative assistant, with responsibility for the communications across the district. He proved to be a valuable member of the team, and with my support, was able to pursue public administration training in the UK, and I was delighted that he went on to enjoy a successful career in the public service, including in the Electoral Office, Labour Department, and in Ifira Services. Massing and family also provided a very valuable community service to Peter, my youngest son, in the form of an endless supply of Milo. To this day they still refer to him as Milo. I was very happy to enjoy a lifelong friendship through to my return to Vanuatu in 2017.

Graham Talo

Setting up local councils in the islands I saw as really important and it was particularly challenging on the island of Ambrym. In South East Ambrym I found and worked with a young man, Graham Talo, to get the South East Ambrym going. I supported him to become the first council secretary and I and my assistant, Jerry, worked hard to enable him to progress things in a very difficult environment. Graham became a regular feature of my life joining me regularly at Dubbo after I retired and later in my Queensland property and was a regular visitor when I returned to Vanuatu in 2017. One of the highlights of my friendship with Graham were the regular late night phone calls, often getting me out of bed to discuss everything from the weather to planning new trips and visits. His family and ours became very close and our friendship has been one of the longest of my associations with Vanautu.

Twenty-Six

Vignette - Letters from Lakatoro

Below are extracts from a number of letters I wrote while at Lakatoro which I hope give the reader a sense of the people and the place.

Henry

Henry was the younger brother of Fijian Peter Wright, well known in the Norsup area. He was a flamboyant and talented character. I had just laid down for an afternoon siesta when the sergeant rang to say that he'd had a report that Henry had swallowed a lot of Nivaquine (anti-malarial medication) and very drunk, had run off into the bush. I went and lay down again thinking it was the usual nonsense then decided I'd better check up. I went down to Kilman's house where Henry lived and was told the report was true. Kilman and the children had been in the bush looking for him without success. Knowing how deadly poisonous Nivaquine is, I dashed back to Lakatoro and marshalled the police force and two football teams about to play a game and got them all out searching. We formed a long line and started walking up into the bush behind Kilman's house and sure enough, after ten minutes, he was found, sadly, already dead. He had been drinking all the previous night and had become depressed about his brother Peter's earlier car accident death, and announced to the Kilmans he was going to kill himself. He had left a note on his bed, such a tragedy.

Kilman

Today has been typical of the many problems faced with local staff. I was fast asleep and heard a knock at the door and a lot of shuffling, it was midnight. I staggered out with my heart thumping wondering what was wrong. Yesterday had been pay day and I knew there'd be grog flying. To my relief it was Kilman, my driver and he looked very forlorn with a bloody nose and face and was absolutely smashed. I took him in and sat him down, got some warm water and washed his face while he told me the story. Naughty Endelan had punched him and Edward and Stanley had also pushed him about because they said he didn't own the land where the condominium houses were. Of course he told them all about his father, Old Seouli leasing the land to the government. Basically, it was a land problem, Endelan's family also having claim to the land which I had purchased for the building of Lakatoro Station. Kilman was hurt in every way and just wanted someone to back him up. He said, "taem mi fall down, mi girup, mi talem se mbae Mr Wilkins hem i stretem samting ya". (Every time I fell down, I got back up and told them Mr Wilkins will settle this). He finally calmed down and I steered him outside and set him on his way home with my torch.

Chinchoo, Avok and Spooky

Later that morning, Chinchoo (wife of John Taffe, the Senior Health Officer) came to have a talk, and left her dog Spooky on the front verandah. Suddenly, Spooky barked loudly and there was a scuffle. As I glanced out the window I saw a figure flying up the verandah post, dashed out to find Avok, pale as a ghost, clinging to the post right up at the top like a monkey. We eventually persuaded him to slide down while Chinchoo held on to the dog. I had to smile, he looked so funny! The story was he had decided to put on a party that night for his friends to celebrate his wedding several weeks prior, and the recent arrival of his baby, (he thinks it's his baby!) also, he was being replaced and being just after pay day it seem like a good time to do it. He had a rifle with him, all the cartridges falling out of his pocket while he clung to the post. He had been trying to shoot a wild fowl for the celebrations without success and he wanted to buy one from us. I took him to the yard, gave him one of mine, and had to stop him shooting amongst the ducks and chooks. Leikari came and helped and between us we managed to secure the terrified chook. It really was terribly amusing. Harry came over that evening to borrow our coloured lights and later I heard drumming. I'm sure they had a good night.

Cyclone Elsa 1976

The next morning, there was another cyclone warning, ELSA. I packed the ship, (the 'Ida') off to shelter at Lamap and dug in at the Rest House at North Ambrym where I waited for strong winds and seas to abate. At least I had plenty of opportunity for discussions with the chiefs and elders over the forthcoming chiefs elections. Finally seas went down a little on Saturday morning so I contacted the 'Ida'—I had the use of a council radio nearby—and said to come over to pick me up. However by the time she arrived, the seas were rough again and the only way I managed to get aboard was by having villagers swim either side of the dinghy to keep it upright, but had to leave all my bags behind, including my glasses, alas! So we sheltered that night at Pentecost and returned the next morning when it was just possible to get the dinghy ashore and the baggage on board. We had a very rough eight hour trip home, arriving at five on Sunday morning, the first fine day in two weeks. I had been wet on and off for days, not that that worried me, in a warm climate one dries out quickly and as long as I had a dry bed, I was satisfied.

Chief Elections

There is still a diplomatic battle raging over the election of chiefs for the Assembly. We would have regular lengthy exchanges between our ambassador in Paris, and Steirn, the French Minister for overseas territories out here, with Miss Lestor from the British Government last year over the 'four to eight chiefs' issue. The French are all for eight chiefs thus assuring them or their sponsored Political Party, (UCNH), parity with the National Party in the Assembly while here, everyone on our side supports the initial legislation for four chiefs. The National Party are saying why change the legislation after the elections just to suit a noisy loquacious minority group and the French, but the problem is apparently, that both our powers that be, the Minister of State for The Foreign and Commonwealth Office is being very weak knee'd and just giving in to the French apparently because that can spill over into EEC matters and they don't want to rock the boat as say negotiations are critical over the EEC and all its complications. Isn't it disgusting? However, Keith Woodward is hopeful that we will finally win the day so we'll keep our fingers crossed. The problem now is that unless we get a decision by the 20th, The National Party will organise more demonstrations.

Political Situation in 1976

Politically, we are still at a standstill awaiting presumably a decision from London and Paris on the chiefs elections which in turn hold up the meeting of the new Assembly unless something is decided The political leaders, particularly the National Party, point out that it has taken the joint Administration months since the elections making promises to hold the first meeting of the Assembly and still no progress. That they say is a typical example of joint administration inefficiency so let's have a referendum and push one side out so that the others can get on with the task of reaching independence. There is also merit in that argument.

Meanwhile, Jimmy Stephens, heading the Nagriamel Movement is trying to rally the forces with his illicit radio station and adhere to his promise to evict both British and French Administrations from Santo on the first of April and declare independence for Santo island. It will be interesting to see what transpires from that exercise.

Jimmy Stephens Nagriamel

At Santo, there has been great tension last week with the Nagriamel ultimatum to both Governments to leave on the first of April and for Santo island to declare Independence. Extra police were flown in, all shipping and air services halted, but in the event, Jimmy Stevens did not appear. He sent a deputy of his henchmen saying they had postponed the announcement of Independence until August so he saved face, and many of his supporters failed to turn up and I think he lost some confidence. The French apparently were in a real panic as one would expect. The funny part was they gave great publicity to Jimmy's ultimatum when it was first announced that only the British Government would be got rid of on the first of April. However, but not a word when Jimmy about-faced again for the umpteenth time and said 'both' Governments were to leave. The French are of course very embarrassed. They made such a fuss of Jimmy, sending him to Paris, meeting with the President while envoys from Tahiti and New Caledonia were not even accorded an interview. Also, they poured money into schools, roads and medical dispensaries in Fanafo, Jimmy's headquarters, to win more favour. Whilst we were in Vila having drinks at the Champions, there was another telegram from Santo to the Resident Commissioners from The Tabwamasana Party, a small Roman Catholic pro-French group. They were viciously attacked by the National Party demonstrators the week prior and the telegram said that unless the Resident Commissioner deported Jimmy and his henchmen and removed his radio within three days, they would go in and burn out Jimmy and smash up his radio. So, you can imagine the negotiations and panic up at Santo now. The Americans who have given Jimmy all the support and cash in their own interests of course, because of their land development interests in Santo, have been declared illegal immigrants and removed. But that will not stop them sending money if they want to. Nonetheless I think Jimmy is becoming more and more isolated and it could be that his movement will collapse. I hope so. Regarding the opposition on Pentecost, when I was there recently, I sent a message to the Nagriamel villages saying that I would visit them on Sunday to meet their leaders. That Saturday night they sent a deputation to see me saying that I couldn't come without a written permit from Jimmy. I replied saying, "sorry" but as the District Agent I had no intention of asking anyone's permission and that of course I must come, explaining patiently that I was only coming to discuss things with them and hear their point of view. They went off most disgruntled. The next morning at daylight the deputation was there again at my doorstep, repeating that I was not to come and again I said, "Sorry but I am coming" and that I'd be there at 9am. At 8 I set off with a lad from the village who was inevitably very nervous. When we arrived at the village all was quiet but I could see a lookout posted who obviously called out the guard! Eight men came running out of what turned out to be the Nagriamel Office and, armed with wooden truncheons, lined up across the path. I was in a bit of a quandary as to what to do but decided I must press on. With some trepidation therefore I, only having an umbrella and my young aide to comfort me, who said "By Algeta I killim yumi na", (they're going to kill us now). I walked briskly up to the line of guards and said brightly, "good morning" and hurriedly put out my hand to shake hands. The leader, obviously taken aback, changed his truncheon, a sizeable piece of wood from the right to the left hand, to shake hands. I went briefly down the line following the same procedure and quickly sat down on the bench outside 'the office'. Obviously very annoyed and unsure what to do, they came and sat with me and we talked. Nonetheless they were very relieved but I doubt I could get away with that again.

Anyhow, for the moment we will just avoid conflict and see what happens. I wouldn't mind betting the outer island supporters will slowly give Jimmy away. On Ambrym, they've already done that, forming their own movement, very much in alliance with the British.

Jimmy Stephens is still in Paris and being 'well feted and wooed, I gather. Oscar (Newman) tells me he is dining with President Giscard D'Estaing which I could quite believe. They are certainly going all out to swing Nagriamel their way but I really don't think they'll have that much success eventually, and wouldn't be at all surprised if a lot of the New Hebridean members of the French orientated parties soon turn away from them.

House Inspections

I have had a week in the office. I did a housing inspection which took me the whole day with the works foreman and Station carpenter Atis. It is pleasing to see how much higher the standard of housing is these days compared to a few years ago. Generally speaking the houses are well cared for, flowers on the table, ornaments and pictures and a clean and tidy lot of rooms. We must have at least a million dollars' worth of housing on the Station at this stage.

Staff Meetings

Had my monthly staff meeting on Friday. I get the senior members of each department at a monthly round table conference in which each department recaps on its current activities and problems. This seems to work well. It is good practice for the New Hebrideans and helps coordinate efforts. As I said to them on Friday it is only a matter of a short time and come what may the New Hebrideans will be running their own country. I think this is something that a lot of people don't realise and of course basically the problem lies with the French Government which is doing its damndest to slow Independence whilst the British Government is determined to hand over as soon as possible.

Entertaining the French

We finally made the effort and had my colleague Monsieur Datchary to dinner on the Thursday night. We also had the new French-Mauritian doctor at Norsup who had a Belgian wife, together with Geoff and Helen Foggon, the Agricultural Officer and his wife. It was quite a successful dinner party and we did it in style with our best silver which I had cleaned especially for the occasion, looking very heart-warming by candlelight. Ida made a mayonnaise chicken, savoury rice and peas, all served on the silver venison dish which was so heavy, I had to carry it, followed by a chocolate fluff pudding. The doctor and his wife are bilingual so despite the handicap of Monsieur Datchary not speaking a word of English, it was quite a successful dinner party with lots of laughter, though a lot of effort for Ida.

Twenty-Seven

1977 Leaving Lakatoro

During the last few months of our final tour before leaving Vanuatu for Australia there were very many farewells, quite overwhelming, starting with Pentecost, north to south, south-west and north Ambrym, the island of Paama and central villages throughout Malekula. These visits were extremely moving because they were obviously genuine and everywhere there was a strong expression of regret that I was leaving. Their friendship, their appreciation of my work, was quite overwhelming.

North Ambrym was the first of many farewells we received prior to leaving the New Hebrides in 1977. The whole family travelled with me in the 'Mangaru'. We slept overnight in the rest house at Nebul and the next morning the celebrations began. We were met by Chief Tofor, the son of Chief Tienmal, who had been the most powerful and feared chief on Ambrym. Incidentally, I had imprisoned him for attempted murder and when he was taken to prison in Santo he was bedecked in a mass of fine pig tusks.

Tofor was at his peak, finely dressed in all his glamour, wearing his nambas, feathers, carrying his NullaNulla, pig's tusks on both arms, he really looked marvellous. Finally, we were all seated underneath a big shady tree and the farewell began. There was a song about me (Darvall), thanking me for my help and other songs, while Tofor danced to and fro, striding up and down, in and out, past us and back to the singers. He really would be wonderful on the stage. There were hundreds of people sitting about under the tree and on the hillside watching. It looked very attractive on the hillside, all so green and lush. Chief Willie Bongmatur was the MC for the event. He incidentally became a senior chief on the Assembly and was later to chair the chiefs' council Malfatumari which advised the assembly on traditional matters. After several more speeches by chiefs about myself and the family leaving the New Hebrides it was time for the feast.

We were seated on mats surrounding plates and leaves piled high with chicken, yam, and *laplap* which we thoroughly enjoyed; followed by fresh lime juice from a kettle. After we began eating the huge crowd was systematically fed. After eating we were seated on a line of chairs and the speeches and presentation began. We were each given gifts and fine, touching speeches were made. Finally, it was my turn to give my 'Last tok tok', and advice. Everyone said that "God willing, we would return".

Finally, every man, woman and child lined up to shake all our hands. I felt almost giddy at the endless stream of people passing by. I felt sad and touched by their warmth. It made me realise how hard it will be to say goodbye to all our friends on Malekula. We finally went back to our little rest house to admire all our lovely gifts and the next morning were waved off by hundreds as the 'Rocinante' raised her anchor and set sail for Malekula.

The Final Farewell

The last few weeks of our time at Lakatoro were tumultuous indeed. We were saying goodbye to a house that I had planned in detail, seen raised to roof level, swept to its very foundations by earthquake and then rebuilt. Leaving a house we as a family had grown to love over its 13 years of occupancy was heart rending. The packing of our goods and chattels was a slow process over some months. The preparation of detailed office handover notes also kept me busy as I was handing over the District to my successor Jerry Marston. Jerry had been my assistant for four years and had served me, and my District loyally.

Finally the day came. It was a warm sunny day and with all six of us in my faithful Land Rover, we drove up onto the airfield to find a massive crowd. The crowd lined both sides of the airfield and obviously expected us to say goodbye individually; this we did. My children and sometimes my wife were in tears as we shook hands with each and every one of them. There must have been a 1000 people on the airfield that day, and emotion overspilled as Chief Rion of Litzlitz decided to lead them in a poignant rendition of 'Now is the Hour'. As the Islander Aircraft taxied down bumpy Norsup runway with my family on board for the last time, we waved goodbye and wept.

We arrived in Vila and proceeded to the Rossi where we stayed overnight. The next morning when I woke, the 'Arcadia' had already berthed and as it were, was already waiting for us. I just couldn't believe that after 20 years it was really 'goodbye' to the New Hebrides. It left me with a very empty feeling indeed. I had become so involved and committed over the years and suddenly, after a few weeks of farewells, we were off! I was deeply moved by the depth and sincerity in the literally hundreds of speeches of tribute to my work. The letters from teachers, chiefs, dressers, young men and old, saying thank you. The ten dollar note pressed into my hand by a young sailor from the 'Euphrosyne' saying I had to have it because I had helped him get his job. He wanted me to send him a photo of the family, which I subsequently did. Waving from the 'Arcadia' decks as we steamed out was even more moving and we all felt quite relieved when darkness fell and we headed out to sea.

Twenty-Eight

1977 Retirement

By the end of September 1977, we were comfortably ensconced in my parents' old home in Dubbo, bequeathed to me when I had built two flats adjoining our property at the rear of the house, one of which my mother settled herself in very comfortably. Our home was one of Dubbo's oldest surviving homes, double brick with front and side verandahs, central hall with bedrooms leading off. Later I extended at the back where there was ample room, adding a master bedroom, en suite to the west, a central courtyard, and a music room on the eastern side.

Here I was, aged 55, with a comfortable home, a Rolls Royce, a Holden utility, and a British Government pension with nothing to do. Gardening had been my love from the time I was a toddler, following my grandfather as he pottered about his vegetable garden at Dulla. Perhaps I could get a job gardening to supplement my pension? I worked for a few weeks under the Dubbo Council's supervision (which was non-existent) cutting burrs on one of the council's 'parks' and that was enough for me.

By this time, my Rolls had arrived in Sydney and I hurried down to collect it and the hordes of luggage I had piled into the container beside it. Arriving at the designated wharf I was horrified to see my container with its flap down and my beautiful car pushed out onto the dusty track beside it. I envisaged damage but apart from curiosity and interest from the wharfies my precious car was as beautiful as ever, and I was able to drive her slowly home to Dubbo, crawling through the small country towns and getting plenty of waves.

The Rolls provided a minor source of income, being hired out for weddings. I soon became fed up with being a chauffeur, suitably clad most Saturday afternoons, and found a tenant in the second flat was happy to take on the job.

In early 1978, I thought I had decided on my post retirement career. I was able to buy a small 1920s cottage a block up from the principal shopping centre and opposite the RSL. There were minor alterations to be made—a wall removed between two small bedrooms and a door opened onto the side garden such as it was; a rock pool built into the front bay window with an electric pump to ensure the continuous spray of water from the pool centre. With the garden improved, and the interior suitably fitted with kitchen, tables and chairs, we purchased a savoury waffle machine in Sydney under our old friend Bud Brown's experienced eye (she ran a successful Tea Room in the new Centre Point, Sydney). My wonderful wife (poor Ida) agreed to the daily cooking of scones, cakes, hearty soups and tomato relish, Jasmine House Garden Shop and Tearooms was open for business!

We were certainly never overcrowded but the shop kept myself and Simon (who became the manager) reasonably busy. The months dragged on but our attendance never seemed to increase. "Nice", said some, "If only you were closer to the town centre". Ida toiled away at home on the delicious cakes and scones (I still believe she made the best scones ever). Then right next to the RSL and virtually opposite Jasmine House a cinema opened. I thought our fortune was made and waited for an influx of customers. I began opening Jasmine House in the evening for cinema goers to enjoy a cup of coffee after the show. Week after week I sat and waited… and waited. Very, very occasionally a customer might slip in but that was about it. We struggled on, Ida cooking and me waiting on tables. But customer attendance never seemed to increase. "Oh, it's a lovely spot and the food is delicious" they said, "but you're just too far away from the shopping centre". I thought surely a block away when you have a car is hardly inaccessible. But the customer is always right and by the end of 1982 we'd had enough. Jasmine House closed its doors and the building sold.

By now I was becoming more interested in antiques and old wares and began frequenting the garage sales, second hand shops and country clearing sales. I had also found two brothers in Mudgee, who had made some very attractive garden furniture using the natural shape to form garden chairs which they had tried unsuccessfully to sell locally. I was convinced that in Sydney they would sell. Thus began a small trade in garden furniture and old wares which monthly I trundled down to Sydney in my Holden van, trying different Sunday markets: Kirribilli, Crown St, Mosman etc. I would usually drive down on the Saturday, stay overnight at Ida's mother's unit, depart about 2 or 3am to choose my site, unload and display my goods, then drive back to Dubbo on the Monday. I also began attending a market which had been established at the Dubbo showground. Whilst I never made a fortune it was both enjoyable and challenging.

I had become heavily involved in the NSW National Trust which was then in the process of accepting from the Palmer family what was one of Australia's oldest farm cottages. It was on about 5 acres, close to the main road and fronting the Macquarie River, not more than 4 miles from the town centre. The already well established Dubbo Zoo, even closer on the same main road to Dubbo was less than mile distant from "Dundullimal". It therefore had the potential to become an impressive tourist attraction. An enthusiastic committee of volunteers was formed to support the project, of which I was elected chairman. This project demanded a lot of time with constant contact and negotiation with Trust headquarters in Sydney. The day came when Dundullimal was officially opened and slowly over the years it became a tourist attraction supporting Dubbo city. Later I gave up the chairmanship and began organising day and weekend bus tours for trust members to some of the long-established properties and homesteads within accessible distance. I was pleased to receive the National Trust medal for dedicated service.

Ida meanwhile had become heavily involved in many of the town's voluntary organisations, most notably the Red Cross from which she received an award for her years of service. By now we were both beginning to feel the urge to travel again and in September 1989 we flew to the UK and Europe, looking up old friends, hiring a car to travel around England, and then to hitch hike predominantly around Europe. Our return trip home was a six week voyage via the West Indies, Panama, San Francisco, Hawaii, New Zealand and then Sydney. The most upsetting event of this voyage in the West Indies, was when Ida and I were exploring a back street of the town and a local appeared from nowhere and snatched Ida's bag. I grabbed him, trying to retrieve the bag and we both crashed to the ground—a fight ensued and thankfully the assailant gave up and ran off. I was in something of a mess, covered in blood and missing bits of skin so we had to abandon our sightseeing and return to the ship where the ship's doctor patched me up. The wounds were superficial but I must have strained muscles in the lower thigh because I had much discomfort and difficulty walking for the remainder of the voyage.

The next few years passed pleasantly and quietly. I gave up my little trading exercises and concentrated more on my garden. Socially we saw more of our friends and of course the Martins at Dulla. Dulla remained and continued to remain very dear to my heart as my greatly loved home.

Then tragedy struck. With practically no warning Ida was taken ill and I rushed her to Sydney for specialist advice. She was diagnosed with a brain tumour. The next few weeks, based in our Mosman unit, saw Ida undergoing an operation and daily treatment. One terrible morning, of all days our wedding anniversary, I awoke and looked across to Ida. "It's our wedding anniversary" I said. She looked at me distantly and did not reply (it turned out the pressure on her brain affected her memory and emotions terribly). We were due early at the Royal Prince Alfred Hospital and I hurriedly helped her dress. She walked to the unit entrance and suddenly keeled over, unconscious. The ambulance was called and she was carried down into it. I stood at the open door, she raised her head, smiled and fell back on the pillow. The ambulance set off and I followed in the car, losing track of the ambulance with its siren sounding off and of course travelling much faster than I dared do.

When I finally got through the peak hour traffic to the hospital there was no sign of the ambulance. I dashed inside to enquire and was told the ambulance had diverted to the Royal North Shore Hospital because of the emergency. Then followed an agonising drive back through heavy traffic to Royal North Shore. Finally I found enquiries and after what seemed like ages was told where to go. I was met by Peter, poor lad, with a taut strained face just said "Dad, she's gone". I was taken to where Ida lay. There I said my goodbyes to my wonderful wife.

Ida and Darvall Vila 1996

Vanuatu Medal presentation with President Jean-Marie Leye in Port Vila

Darvall and Ida with their grandchildren

Darvall at Waratah before moving to Tweed Heads

Darvall getting ready to join the ANZAC march in Tweed Heads

Darvall Wilkins BDA and Jerry Marston ABDA, Lakatoro, Tweed Heads

Famly gathering, David, Meg, Billy, Buv and Darvall at Dulla

Darvall and the then Prime Minister, Sato Kilman

Sallie and Darvall in Vila harbour

Moving back to Vanuatu, Brisbane airport

Darvall and the President of Vanuatu, Tallis Obed Moses, Port Vila

Funeral procession at Lakatoro with custom dancers

Darvall's funeral service at Lakatoro

Simon Wilkins receiving the Honorary title Meltek Talinvanu
from the Hon Sato Kilman - Meltek Livtunvanu

Darvall and Ida's memorial headstone and plaque at Lakatoro

Darvall's Memorial at Lakatoro

Twenty-Nine

Vignette - Ida Mary Wilkins Obituary

Ida was born in Mosman where she was brought up with her elder sister Sheila and her cousin Charles Heard. She attended SCEGGS Redlands where she joined a children's support group for the Red Cross and won the Yvonne Harvey Memorial prize for Citizenship. After completing the leaving certificate she wanted to take up nursing, but because she was then rather frail her father would not agree and she turned to teaching, attending the Waverley kindergarten training college. After graduating she taught for the next seven years in various underprivileged areas, was the director of the Marrickville kindergarten and finally primary classes at SCEGGS Redlands. She had set her mind on travelling to Europe and with careful budgeting was able to travel first class on the P&O liner 'Himalaya' to London. In London she joined the staff of the fashionable Wetherby Primary school and taught there for the next two years. One of her pupils at Wetherby was a quaint little boy called Andrew Lloyd Webber. During the school holidays she hitchhiked around Europe. She attended a Buckingham Palace garden party where she was presented to Princess Margaret. Being a dedicated royalist this was to be the first of many thrilling occasions when she had the privilege of meeting and entertaining members of the royal family. She sat up all night in the Mall to secure a good view of the Coronation parade of Queen Elizabeth II. On board the 'Himalaya' on the way to London, she sat at dinner with a lady from Dubbo whose company she enjoyed—Lila Wilkins. On arrival at the London docks, Lila introduced her to her son Darvall, who was then studying at Cambridge University. Subsequently Darvall, with his mother and two college friends, invited Ida to join them in a tour of Ireland. At Blarney castle they all kissed the Blarney stone and perhaps this began a romance which was to develop into a lifelong partnership. At the end of 1952, Darvall, employed by the British Colonial Service, was appointed to the territory of Tanganyika in British East Africa. When Ida decided to return to Australia, Darvall wrote to her from Tanganyika suggesting she should make a detour through Tanganyika to see him. Darvall says with tongue in cheek Ida didn't take much persuading, but in fact, for an unaccompanied young lady in 1952 it was a rather hazardous journey. With her hard earned savings she disembarked at Aden, which was then in a state of emergency with a strict curfew. After almost a week there she sailed on down the coast of Africa to the Tanganyikan capital, Dar-Es-Salaam, and finally a three day journey by train where she was the only European passenger to Tabora, once the base camp for David Livingstone. Here she was met by Darvall, and not long after, under a starry African sky, he proposed and she accepted. Ida returned to Australia via Nairobi (where the MauMau rebellion was in full swing and she was given a revolver to keep in her purse during her stay), then to Khartoum, Aden again, and finally home.

Ida and Darvall were married in the Scots Kirk, Mosman on the 30th April 1955, one of the wettest days in Sydney's history. After a honeymoon in Surfers Paradise they returned to Tanganyika by sea via Bombay and Mombassa. Three carefree happy years followed in Dar-Es-Salaam where on weekends they went out into the open plains camping in their station wagon and photographing big game. A wonderful local leave was spent climbing Mt Kilimanjaro and travelling by paddle steamer on Lake Albert to the source of the Nile. It was whilst living in Dar-Es-Salaam that Ida's interest in the Red Cross revived and she worked with this association under Lady Twining, wife of the governor.

Their first child, Karen, was born at the Dar-Es-Salaam hospital on 2 April 1957. At the end of that year, Darvall was transferred to the Anglo-French condominium of the New Hebrides. With a six weeks old baby, they travelled by sea and train to Durban, Cape Town, then by the Dominion Monarch to Sydney where they were met by their respective parents. After leave in Australia they sailed to the New Hebrides, now Vanuatu.

Over the next 20 years in Vanuatu, Ida had to cope with many trials and tribulations, firstly on the small island of Tanna, en route to which in a 30 foot launch, they ran into the teeth of a hurricane. On Tanna, the only communication with the outside world was a six weekly visit by a small Burns Philp trading vessel and a pedal radio. Here her kitchen and kitchen table were used for an emergency appendix operation on a member of staff, because the house was the only one equipped with electric light; there were frequent earth tremors and the house was regularly coated with ash from a nearby active volcano. Simon was born at the mission station on the 1st of Aug 1958 and later, when an airstrip had been constructed, Ida was able fly to Vila for Sallie's birth on 24th Feb 1962 at the Paton Memorial Hospital.

Transferred to a much larger island, Malekula, Darvall established a new administrative centre there and a fine residence was built. Here they spent the next 16 years—extraordinarily happy ones despite Darvall's frequent absences as part of his duty touring the outer islands. Ida flew to Vila for Peter's 11th Dec 1966 birth and the return journey was something of a marathon. They landed on the south of the island because the airfield had been washed out by torrential rain. Darvall charted a copra vessel to take them on the next stage to the road terminus where Peter was fed in a copra shed. They proceeded home by Land Rover, arriving at dusk to find the children sitting on the steps to greet the new baby brother.

On Malekula Ida's life was frantically busy. She taught all four children by correspondence and with an inexperienced domestic staff, provided hospitality and frequently accommodation for an ever increasing stream of visitors, entertaining everyone from members of the royal family to French ministers of State and ex cannibal chiefs. Her home became the social centre for the station staff plantation and mission friends, regardless of race or colour. She was a mother figure to the many young Englishmen who came to work in this third world country as volunteers. When Ida and Darvall visited England in 1990, some 20 volunteers and their families gave them a surprise party and presented Ida with a banana cake as a reminder of the many she had made for them. Included in the apologies that day was one from David Attenborough who said he would never forget her hospitality.

Ida established the Red Cross branch on the island, encouraging the interest and support of the islanders. She also began a kindergarten for the children of Darvall's staff. She would regularly be found sitting cross legged on a pandanus mat at a Red Cross meeting or with the kindergarten group. She made wedding dresses and wedding cakes for station staff when they were married. When 20 years later the whole family returned to Vanuatu for a holiday Ida was greeted by the islanders with tremendous enthusiasm, affection and warmth. A memorial service is being held at the Paton Memorial Church in Vila this week for Ida, organised by her many Melanesian friends.

On Malekula too she had to cope with more tribulations; an earthquake which brought buildings crashing down and necessitated dragging children out of bed and into the open; hurricanes which forced open windows and doors and flooded the house with driving rain. Ida faced these trials with her usual calmness and courage.

Throughout her life she was a great and generous provider, always concerned that she had sufficient for her guests. The one time Darvall remembers her being exasperated over a guest was when at a luncheon reception for the British High Commissioner with some 80 guests, one of the island chiefs took a whole lemon meringue pie and handed it over the garden fence to his waiting children.

Returning to Dubbo on Darvall's retirement in 1977 she quickly made the old family home her own, and with her ready smile she soon made many friends. After 4 years cooking for Darvall's retirement enterprise, the Jasmine House garden shop and tea rooms, she became an active participant in many local charities, treasurer of the Dubbo Red Cross for 7 years, treasurer of the Embroiderers Guild, more recently a volunteer at the art gallery, and a member of the National Trust and a guide at Dundullimal. Only last Sunday she was to have been one of the guides commended by National Trust President Barry O'Keefe for 10 years of loyal guiding service.

It was babies and little children that gave Ida the greatest pleasure, above all of course her grandchildren. She kept a special drawer in which she had a stock of baby clothes on hand so that she was able to choose a suitable gift for the next baby of a relative or friend to arrive.

Ida was awarded the Queen Elizabeth Jubilee medal in 1977 and in 1996 the Australian Red Cross Long Service Medal.

With her caring attitude, her thoughtfulness, her love for others, her gentleness and her integrity she was loved and respected by all her family and her friends. Ida died peacefully after a suspected brain haemorrhage at the Royal North Shore hospital aged 73, on Thursday 30 April, the 43rd anniversary of her wedding.

Darvall Wilkins 2nd May 1998.

Thirty

1999 Tweed Heads

Back at Dubbo and an empty house. The days, weeks, months dragged on as I sat in the garden back yard and wept. I began to realise that I had to do something; reluctant as I was to leave the old house, I had to leave Dubbo and start again.

With Karen and the children for a base I began looking for a new home and was fortunate to find it very quickly. It was a home in Bilambil Heights in the hills above Tweed Heads that funnily enough Ida and I had looked at almost two years prior. The 'for sale' sign had gone but for some unknown reason I walked up the long drive and knocked at the door. Within a fortnight I had reached agreement with the owner who was confined to a wheelchair and desperate to sell, and within another month I was moving into the ground floor flat and Karen and family upstairs. It was the new and final "Lakatoro" with its four acres of bushland and ten minutes from town.

This was in 1999 and the succeeding years gave me great joy and pleasure. Enormous scope for a beautiful garden—some 50 cypress pines were removed (a task which took 2 years to complete). With the forest finally gone some fine native trees were planted and a swimming pool replaced a veritable forest of custard apple trees. The flowering trees and shrubs, paths winding through them, ponds with water lillies and fish. The pond and cast iron fountain I brought from the old family home, Waratah in Dubbo, gave me much pleasure. And above all, the birds! So many birds and I seemed to regularly discover new species singing to me from up in the trees.

During this period, I continued with my 'other profession' first established in Dubbo, of regularly attending clearing and garage sales to source items of interest to re-sell at local markets. This kept me extremely occupied and financially viable up until I retired (for the second time) in 2014, at the age of 92.

I loved the wheeling and dealing of the market life as you never knew just when the next bargain would turn up and realise a substantial profit. Attending the local sales became something of an addiction as a result of the excitement of the hunt. I had a well-established routine which was this: I would religiously set my alarm for around four on a Saturday morning, grab my local street directory, a thermos of coffee and head down to the local service station where

I would buy the local paper and, armed with a torch and magnifying glass, peruse all the advertised garage sales for potential bargains. Around five, I would set off on my route for the morning, stopping at the various sales to see what I could find. I must admit that on occasion I actually arrived before the advertised starting time, which didn't seem to worry anyone too much. Even at this time of the morning there were other regulars squabbling for the best purchases and specific items they invariably concentrated on. We became quite a connected group and were friendly to one another, but still guarded given the healthy competition. Once the morning was done, I would return home to unload my bargains for the next stage, the markets.

The markets were something I grew to love despite the long hours, hard work and often minimum returns. My habit was to pack my vehicle with a wide range of odds and sods the day before, then drive to the venue and sleep the night in my car before setting up early for the day ahead. Most stall owners did this as well so there were always others around doing the same thing. Once I had set up my stall, I would spend the day chatting to people and selling the odd piece. I never made enough to retire but it kept me occupied and engaged which was worth more than just monetary gain. In retrospect, it also kept me fit which in turn allowed me to concentrate on my gardening passion. All in all, a good arrangement.

Thirty-One

2017 Return to Vanuatu

As the years rolled by, there came a time when I found that I no longer had the fitness or the drive to maintain my business, and eventually my property. After many conversations with my children, we reached a conclusion on what my last adventure might look like.

In October 2017, I sold my property in Tweed Heads and returned to Vanuatu to live with my daughter Sallie and husband John and to see out my twilight years. I moved into a small bungalow on their property near the sea where I could sit and watch the ebb and flow of island life and listen to classical music.

I have had an extraordinary and charmed life, and as I approach the final curtain, I find myself extremely grateful that I am surrounded by family and friends and once again living in a tropical paradise.

Thirty-Two

Vignette – Dad (by Simon Wilkins)
The Last Journey

On the 14th July 2018, Dad passed away peacefully in his sleep in his own bed, with Sallie, John, and I nearby. Marie, his doting nurse, was with him at the time and so uneventful was his passing that she never noticed he was gone until Sallie came up to check on him a few minutes later. Sallie and I sat on the front verandah of the little cottage and talked about Dad until the sun came up. It was a sad time but curiously rewarding knowing we had both seen our father move into the next life so peacefully, without fuss or any pain, and after such a rewarding and full life.

In our many conversations Dad and I had chatted about dying and he always said the only thing he was ever worried about was feeling any pain. His local French doctors had always been amazed by both his health and resilience, so ill health was completely absent when he died. In the end it was just age that took him. If only we could all be that blessed.

Dad had always been clear about his funeral. He had already saved up and paid for a simple burial service to be held in Tweed Heads with only immediate family in attendance. He also knew once he moved back to Vanuatu all that would change. Sallie and he had spoken about burial options and the final decision was made that he would be buried in the local Pango Village cemetery overlooking the ocean. However, this was not to be.

Once local people were aware that Mista Wilkins was once again living in Vanuatu, he had a procession of both ordinary folk and Government leaders visiting him in his little cottage down by the sea. Some of these were old friends from the past, others were people who had heard about him and were keen to meet. The first President of Vanuatu, Ati George came to pay his respects as an old friend. The current President of Vanuatu, His Excellency Obed Moses, also arranged a state visit to do the same.

As a result of the attention, the Government decided that it was fitting that Dad should be given a State Funeral and be laid to rest on Lakatoro just below the old house we all had such happy memories of. Dad was rather tickled by this when we told him of the plans, and more than happy with the arrangements. I really don't think he had fully anticipated how much the nation of Vanuatu loved and respected him which is what we were to experience over the week that followed.

I have only recorded a summary here, which includes facts, anecdotal components and some more bizarre events that only made it all the more memorable. It would take too long to fully describe Dad's funeral and what occurred. Suffice to say it was an amazing experience and Dad would have been both honoured and slightly amused by it all.

Dad was embalmed by a local French practitioner who on completing his work invited me to view the results with an exclamation of "C'est magnifique!". Dad was dressed in smart casual clothes and looked like a happy relaxed version of himself, despite the fact that he was obviously gone.

As is the local custom in Vanuatu, a number of close friends came to say goodbye and leave flowers. For some unfathomable reason, ni-Vanuatu people had taken to bringing plastic flowers instead of readily available fresh flowers. We all knew Dad's abhorrence of plastic flowers, however given the circumstances there wasn't a whole lot we could do. I had planned to recycle them once he was placed in his coffin, however I didn't count on Sallie's staff's interest in the proceedings as the undertaker sealed the coffin. As a result, they carefully placed every plastic flower available in the cottage, into the coffin which was then firmly sealed. I must admit it amused me as I imagined Dad's reaction to be shuffled off into eternity surrounded by cheap plastic flowers. He would have seen the funny side and would have respected their commitment to him as well.

Dad was moved under a formal police guard of honour into Port Vila where he was laid in the main Presbyterian Church hall for a day to allow others to pay their respects. Hundreds of old friends came by to say goodbye and shake hands with the family who were all present. At the end of the day his coffin was moved into the PMH Church for a service that was to last three and half hours. I provided the eulogy translated in to bislama (local dialect) followed by tribute speeches from a number of ex-Prime Ministers, Government staff, family and friends. It was a moving service and all who spoke emphasised the positive influence Dad had had on their lives. Some of the speeches were extremely long, one in particular concluded after a full hour.

Following the conclusion of the service we shook hands with the congregation and returned home for a debrief and a short rest before moving onto the next part of the funeral plans.

We were all up bright and early the following day for the final journey, to Lakatoro. The police escort arrived slightly late, which was entirely in keeping with life in Vanuatu and welcomed by us all. They then transferred us and Dad to two waiting small aircraft for the short flight up to Lakatoro. Government dignitaries and VIPs went on the first flight so they could be there to greet the family and Dad, who were all on the second flight. It was a sombre flight for us and I think we all had thoughts of the finality of the last journey.

On arrival at Norsup airport, we disembarked to be met by another police escort and a troupe of custom dancers who were dressed in amazing traditional regalia. They shared the responsibility of escorting the coffin to a waiting funeral procession of 12 vehicles. The coffin was carefully placed on the back of a Toyota pickup truck, again very fitting, and we set off on a two and half hour funeral procession around the local towns and villages of the place we grew up and loved. Thousands of people lined the roads and would carefully throw flowers (both fresh and plastic) onto the coffin. Many of the older ones were family friends and acquaintances and their outpouring of grief was heartbreaking to us all. As we passed Lakatoro itself, we were greeted by the sight of thousands of school children lined up on the oval in front of Wilkins Stadium to say goodbye. None of these children would have known much about Dad or our family, however it was a mark of respect from the district that this had been organised and I know Dad would have been honoured by it.

We eventually ended up at the bottom of the road that led up to administrative headquarters of Lakatoro, Dad's old office. There another group of mourning custom dancers met us and slowly carried the coffin over a kilometre up to a waiting group of officials, friends and onlookers. As we got closer to the offices, another group of magnificently dressed custom dancers began beating slit gongs and playing booboos (conch trumpets) to signify the arrival of a chief's funeral procession.

The coffin was placed on the verandah of one of Dad's old offices where a large number of individuals and groups spoke and paid their respects. It was a very moving time and emotional for us all in such familiar surroundings and so surreal. Then something unexpected occurred which to this day amuses us all. A little man quietly snuck onto the verandah while a larger group with eyes closed were paying their solemn respects. He was dressed like a workman and carried a large tape measure. Bent over double he crept along the verandah until he reached the coffin and somewhat self-consciously measured the coffin. He then carefully made a note of the measurements on a piece of paper, measured it again, checked his notes and then carefully doubled up and snuck off again. Later on we found out what all this meant. He was actually part of the building team who having just completed Dad's tomb were doing some last minute alterations and were making sure the coffin would fit and that they could brick up the door!

It was at this point we realised that Dad wasn't to be buried, but placed in a substantial tomb built especially for him. We all knew he wouldn't have approved of this arrangement but again there was nothing we could say or do at this point. In fairness to the local organisers, this was the highest honour that could be afforded and nothing but respect was being offered. I'm confident that Dad would have been in agreement with the decision to let things progress.

With the farewells completed, the funeral procession then moved off to the little Church just below our old house, again led by the mourning dancers and chiefs. In the Church there were further eulogies and farewells including moving ones from His Excellency Obed Moses and ex Prime Minister Sato Kilman (son of Kilman mentioned previously in the narrative; a family friend and Dad's old communications operator on the station).

It was at this point that another bizarre thing happened. In the middle of a tribute from the officiating Pastor, Jerry Marston's plastic chair gave way, somewhat spectacularly. What made it all the more memorable, was that my cousin Ian Pettit had been sitting directly behind Jerry and was at this point happily dozing. When the chair let go, it did with a loud crack which woke Ian suddenly. He let out a loud cry which added to the moment and startled us all. I turned around to see Jerry lying on his back stuck to the remains of the plastic chair and waving his legs and arms around in a manner not dissimilar to an upended crab! Everyone seemed to take it in their stride though and once Jerry was moved to a sturdier chair, the Pastor continued unperturbed.

We then sang a hymn and the coffin was taken to the tomb and a number of farewell speeches made before being interred. As the coffin was placed there was a last minute surge of plastic flowers being piled up on the coffin before everything was firmly sealed behind a brick wall. I could only imagine Dad's face as his final look of Lakatoro as it were, was obscured by large wreaths made of plastic flowers. I know he would have been just as amused but accepting.

At this point in the proceedings I became the focus of attention as Sato and the local chiefs had explained that I would inherit Dad's chiefly title of Meltek Talinvanu as was the local custom when a chief dies. I was then armed with a serious looking club and told that I would now kill a pig to signify the exchange and to meet custom requirements as a newly named chief. I knew this would only be a ceremonial killing, however my wife and a number of our family group didn't know this and expected to see me actively fulfilling my chiefly duties, and as a result began to move away, at least out of direct line of sight and earshot. I had the opportunity to enlighten them much to their relief and when the time came I stood on the stone dais erected for the investiture, and touched the pig on the head ceremonially ever so lightly. Sato called out my title while tapping me on the shoulders with a custom plant and so I became Meltek Talinvanu.

It was at that moment that I began to understand what was in front of me in terms of my responsibility in taking over Dad's work. I hadn't earnt the title, and there was still work to be done. So under this new mantle of Dad and Mum's legacy, the Wilkins Family Foundation was born. More on that later.

Following a short reception and something to eat we made our way back to the airport and flew back to Vila, exhausted. On the way back in the plane I felt quite sad at leaving Dad behind at Lakatoro, thoughts I think we all experienced. That concluded the formal state funeral.

There is so much that happened over the week of Dad's death which I vividly recall, however there are too many thoughts to record here. Suffice to say, Dad's final journey was a memorable one and richly deserved. I suspect he would have been quite embarrassed by the attention, but also quite chuffed.

In the months that followed, the family held a memorial service for Dad in the Royal Botanical Gardens in Sydney Australia. It gave all those who couldn't make the trip over to Vanuatu for his actual funeral an opportunity to say goodbye. On a blustery spring day, a crowd gathered around the old slit gong which Dad had officiated over and had used for many meetings of the now defunct Friends of Vanuatu organisation. A number of people spoke including some moving eulogies from family. Kirk Huffman played a recording of slit gong drums which he had personally taped of another great chief's funeral signifying the esteem Dad was held in by the ni-Vanautu. We then all walked down to the harbour where we threw flowers into the water as a final goodbye while his grandchildren sang 'What a Wonderful World' by Louis Armstrong, Dad's favourite, and a song he had asked me to play at his funeral. After a light afternoon tea, a great number of people adjourned to Coogee for a family dinner and we had a wonderful time of reminiscing. All in all a fitting final farewell.

Thirty-Three

The Wilkins Family Foundation is Formed

After things had settled, I started following up on the idea of a family-based foundation to continue Dad and Mum's work in Vanuatu. Jerry Marston was my main ally in the initial planning, and between us with input from all our family, the Wilkins Family Foundation was born.

Within a month, we had registered the Foundation as a Not for Profit organisation based in Australia, opened a business account and started to accrue initial donations from family and friends.

With this modest amount we were able to make a start. We drafted our statement of intent and our vision, and Sallie (with John's support) agreed to become the Country Manager. We formed a board and we held our first meeting—we were well and truly underway.

I have included the following overview:

Wilkins Family Foundation

"developing future leaders through education"

Our Purpose

Our primary purpose is to empower future generations by raising up leaders who will inspire, develop and guide their nation into the future.

The Foundation will use education and learning as the basis for achieving our purpose. We will initially assist marginalised and disadvantaged girls to gain a complete education, from high school through to higher level learning programmes – such as university degrees and technical apprenticeships. This will be expanded in the future to include boys. The likelihood is that the majority of participants benefitting from our proposed programmes will be from the outer islands and rural areas, with diminished resources and less access to opportunities.

Our Core Values

The Foundation's core values are underpinned by Christian principles, and reflect those Darvall and Ida espoused and practised in their lives. They emphasise:

- Championing tolerance, respect and integrity
- Addressing disadvantage
- Promoting excellence in all spheres of life
- Building lasting friendships
- Advocating listening as a way of learning.

Subsequently, a number of the board flew to Vanuatu to meet with Government and Educational representatives, and as a result of a lot of discussion, work began in earnest.

In summary, we interviewed and selected the first four recipients to receive our ongoing scholarships which are designed to carry the individual through to their chosen career, be it higher education, trades or any other future. Our intent is to build leaders in every sphere of life. The Foundation has now sponsored additional girls and from this modest start, we expect great things to follow. The reader can find out a great deal more by locating the Foundation website online at

www.wilkinsfamilyfoundation.com.au

Conclusions - A Life Well Lived

In conclusion to my father's memoirs, I would like to highlight a number of areas that should be mentioned.

My father had countless close friends in a number of countries, and it would have been impossible to mention you all in the body of this book. A case in point is my own dear wife who both my parents loved dearly. Suffice to say, some names are mentioned, others aren't. You know who you all are and I'm confident you are in no doubt in regard to the esteem and love Dad had for you.

As this book was finalised and published post my Father's death, it is a given that it was a collegiate effort from family and friends to complete the work. I therefore would like to name those who assisted in the order they were cajoled into helping. Firstly Sallie (daughter) and John Latella (son in law) for the mammoth effort in painstakingly transcribing Dad's letters into the draft components of the book, myself for what felt like days, weeks and months for work to assemble the documents into an appropriate timeline, Ros Wilkins (my wife) for the first edit, Jerry Marston for ongoing edits, Anna Bishop (granddaughter) Mary Bishop, and Stan Combs for follow up edits, Peter and Cherie Wilkins (son and daughter in law), and Karen Hare (daughter) for input, advice and assistance. Suffice to say, without their involvement, this book wouldn't have made it to publication.

Most of all, thanks Dad for a life well lived.

Closing Thoughts

It would be remiss of me not to add in my own thoughts at this point in time which I will do. My father was an amazing man.

He had a blessed and fortunate life, achieved great things, was loved, admired and respected by many, many people, was a kind, caring, loving, considerate and protective father, a doting son, grandfather and great grandfather. He taught us the meaning of respect for all, regardless of race, colour or religion. He taught us about honesty, integrity and forgiveness, and demonstrated grace through his life.

He was an amazing man.

www.ingramcontent.com/pod-product-compliance
Lightning Source LLC
Chambersburg PA
CBHW061752290426
44108CB00029B/2973